Archaeoastronomy and the Maya

edited by

*Gerardo Aldana y Villalobos
and Edwin L. Barnhart*

Oxbow Books
Oxford & Philadelphia

Published in the United Kingdom in 2014 by
OXBOW BOOKS
10 Hythe Bridge Street, Oxford OX1 2EW

and in the United States by
OXBOW BOOKS
908 Darby Road, Havertown, PA 19083

Paperback Edition: ISBN 978-1-78297-643-1
Digital Edition: ISBN 978-1-78297-644-8

A CIP record for this book is available from the British Library

Library of Congress Cataloging-in-Publication Data

Archaeoastronomy and the Maya / edited by Gerardo Aldana y Villalobos and Edwin L. Barnhart. -- Paperback edition.
     pages cm
  Includes bibliographical references.
  ISBN 978-1-78297-643-1
 1. Maya astronomy. 2. Archaeoastronomy--Central America. 3. Archaeoastronomy--Mexico. I. Aldana y Villalobos, Gerardo, editor, author. II. Barnhart, Edwin Lawrence, editor.
  F1435.3.C14A73 2014
  972.81'016--dc23
                        2014019098

Printed in the United Kingdom by Berforts Information Press Ltd, Eynsham, Oxfordshire

For a complete list of Oxbow titles, please contact:

UNITED KINGDOM
Oxbow Books
Telephone (01865) 241249, Fax (01865) 794449
Email: oxbow@oxbowbooks.com
www.oxbowbooks.com

UNITED STATES OF AMERICA
Oxbow Books
Telephone (800) 791-9354, Fax (610) 853-9146
Email: queries@casemateacademic.com
www.casemateacademic.com/oxbow

Oxbow Books is part of the Casemate Group

Cover image: Photographs of Palenque architecture by Alonso Mendez

CONTENTS

CONTRIBUTORS

GERARDO ALDANA
Departments of Anthropology and Chicana/o Studies, University of California, Santa Barbara CA 93106

EDWIN L. BARNHART
Maya Exploration Center, 3267 Bee Caves Road, Suite 107–161, Austin, TX78746

HAROLD H.GREEN
Independent Scholar, 17705 Westside Hwy SW, Vashon, WA 98070

MICHAEL GROFE
Department of Anthropology, American River College, Sacramento CA 95841

CAROL KARASIK
Maya Exploration Center, San Cristóbal de las Casas, Chiapas, México

ALONSO MENDEZ
Independent Scholar, San Cristóbal de las Casas, Chiapas, México

SUSAN MILBRATH
Florida Museum of Natural History, 110 Dickinson Hall, Museum Road & Newell Drive, Gainesville, FL 32611

CHRISTOPHER POWELL
Maya Exploration Center, 3267 Bee Caves Road, Suite 107–161, Austin, TX78746

IVAN ŠPRAJC
Scientific Research Center of the Slovenian Academy of Sciences and Arts, Novi trg 2, 1000 Ljubljana, Slovenia

FOREWORD
The long and winding road to publication

Edwin Barnhart

This volume was born out of a Maya Archaeo-astronomy Symposium at the 2007 Society of American Archaeologists (SAA) meetings in Austin, Texas. Though its publication is now seven years later, I'm pleased to see that the contributions are still relevant and have stood the test of time as important studies (at least so far). It was in the fall of 2006 that my friend and colleague Hal Green called me and said, "Ed, I think the SAA's are ready for another Maya Archaeoastronomy symposium and I think you should organize it." I had met Hal at the Texas Maya Meetings, where we had shared our ideas and became supporters of one another's research. I had been making observations at Palenque along with my colleagues Christopher Powell, Alonso Mendez, and Carol Karasik for five years at that point and we were ready to share the results. Hal had been making observations of his own along the horizon at Chocolá and he too was keen to share. We had a core group together, but we would need more presenters to make an entire symposium. Who would we reach out to? Hal agreed to help me brainstorm and get the invitations out.

I proposed that we make it a meeting of newly contributing scholars and seasoned veterans in the field of archaeoastronomy. My initial thoughts for upcoming scholars fell to Michael Grofe and Ignacio Cases, both of whom were making some interesting breakthroughs in our understanding of the

Maya Lunar Series. It was Hal who suggested the co-editor of this volume Gerardo Aldana. Hal had read Aldana's work on the origins of the Haab calendar in the inscriptions of Takalik Abaj and was duly impressed. For the more established scholars of our group, we reached out to Susan Milbrath, author of "Star Gods of the Maya," linguistic and epigraphic experts Martha Macri and John Justeson, Maya mathematics expert Stan Iwaniszewski, and veteran archaeoastronomer and archaeologist Ivan Sprajc. To our delight, each of them accepted the invitation and submitted papers. Finally, like the icing on the cake, acknowledged father of Mesoamerican archaeoastronomy Anthony Aveni agreed to be the symposium's discussant.

The day of the symposium was April 27, 2007 and it was a well-received success. The lecture hall was full (which rarely happens at archaeological conferences) and many of our respected colleagues sat in. Aveni's final comments were full of praise for how far the field had advanced since the 1970s. In the months before the meeting, we members of the symposium agreed that the SAA's 15 minute per presenter time limit was insufficient and that we should plan a follow up meeting that evening. Maya Exploration Center sponsored that meeting in a conference room at the downtown Austin *Radisson*. Each member in turn had a chance to elaborate on their research and receive helpful feedback. Ignacio Cases, who preferred to be called by his nickname "Nacho," explained his hypothesis that our trouble in linking the Maya Lunar Series with actual moon cycles may lie in the fact that the Maya were not counting the days of the moon's disappearance during new moon as part of the cycle. Christopher Powell spoke about possible building alignments towards lunar maximums and minimums. Aveni objected to Powell's idea, but Powell countered with a challenge to Aveni to list the number of Venus alignments we can actually prove (Aveni has supported the idea of Venus alignments in multiple publications). As each of them could only come up with two examples, it was a draw. The last person to speak at the extended session was Michael Grofe, who explained his new ideas about evidence that the Maya were tracking sidereal periods of planets and how it could have led them to an ability to calculate precession of the equinoxes. Grofe's ideas were offhandedly dismissed by Aveni and Justeson, but members like Carol Karasik and myself were more convinced. That was 2007, and in 2012 Grofe's ideas in this regard reached such wide acceptance that even Aveni publicly retracted his criticism (which he had voiced again in his own 2012 book) and congratulated Grofe on his groundbreaking discoveries.

Encouraged by Hal and Gerardo, I sought a contract to publish the symposium's papers into a single edited volume. After about eight months, I had a contract in hand and brought it to the other members. Most were happy to contribute, though a few like Justeson and Macri had already found other publication opportunities for their papers. The omission of Cases's paper is the one I personally regret the most, but family illnesses followed by his own protracted illness prevented him from contributing. The few papers that dropped out triggered a new round of contract revisions and a few more months. Then collecting the papers took a few more months. Then "life happened" and yet more months went by. Finally, about three years after the symposium's conclusion, Gerardo contacted me and generously offered to help me get the volume back on track. So in 2010, he and I became co-editors and things got rolling again.

Largely through the Gerardo's efforts, the papers were compiled into a coherent volume and sent to the publisher for peer review. Perhaps due to the still relatively esoteric nature of archaeoastronomy studies, qualified reviewers were difficult to find. Through a very long process of review and revision, though, the volume has found a happy home through the tireless efforts of Julie Gardiner and Julie Blackmore at Oxbow Books. So now, seven years later, our long road comes to an end and the volume is finally out. I hope it serves a foundation stone on the path to better understanding ancient Maya astronomy and an inspiration to the next generation of archaeoastronomers.

GLOSSARY

260-Day Count: Calendric count unique to Mesoamerica made up of 13 coefficients and 20 Day Signs. Referred to by modern K'iche' *ajqiij* ("daykeepers") as the *ch'ol qiij* or 'the order of days.' In this book, the Yucatec names for the Day Signs are used such that a sequence of dates would be: *1 Imix, 2 Ik', 3 Ak'bal, 4 K'an, 5 Chikchan, 6 Kimi, 7 Manik, 8 Lamat, 9 Muluk, 10 Ok, 11 Chuwen, 12 Eb, 13 Ben, 1 Ix, 2 Men, 3 Kib, 4 Kaban, 5 Etz'nab, 6 Kawak, 7 Ajaw, 8 Imix, 9 Ik'…*

365-Day Count: Calendric count approximating the tropical year. Each month was initiated by its "seating," followed by a count through coefficients of 1 through 19. This is often rendered 0–19 for the 20 days of each month: *Pohp, Wo, Sip, Sotz', Tzek, Xul, Yaxk'in, Mol, Ch'en, Yax, Sak, Keh, Mak, K'ank'in, Muwan, Pax, K'ayab, Kumk'u.* The final five days ("seating" through 4) were contained in the period of *Wayeb.* The 365 Day Count did not incorporate a leap day; it therefore slipped through the seasons during the Classic Maya period.

Ajk'in: Yucatec Mayan phrase linguistically rendered as the agentive prefixed to 'time,' and so often translated as 'daykeeper.' In K'iche' Mayan, the cognate term is *ajqiij.*

Calendar Correlation: Because the Long Count is a strict count of days, it is mathematically equivalent to the Julian Day Number. Dates can therefore be converted between the two systems by adding an integer constant. The most commonly accepted Calendar Correlation Constant is the GMT of 584,283 days such that a Long Count date can be converted to a Gregorian date using: LC + 584,283 = JD. Recently, however, the GMT has come under concerted critique, and so may not accurately translate between the two calendars.

Celestial Equator: One tradition for mapping the celestial realm is based on defining positions relative to the observed axis of rotation of the celestial sphere. The Earth's equator is projected onto the rotation such that the Celestial Equator has a declination of 0°,

the North Celestial Pole is 90° and the South Celestial Pole is -90°.

Declination: Relative to the celestial equator, defined as the angle along an hour circle either north (+) or south (-).

Draconic Month: The number of days it takes for the Moon to return to the same node in its orbit, where a node is the point of intersection between the Moon's orbit and the Ecliptic. Eclipses will only occur when the Moon is at a node.

E-Group complexes: Architectural groups first found in the Middle Preclassic comprising a long platform stretching north-south to the east of a plaza. In the middle of the plaza, a viewing pyramid was situated so that the summer solstice sunrise could be viewed behind a structure at the north extreme of the platform, the winter solstice sunrise behind the southern structure, and the equinoxes behind the central structure. The first of these identified archaeologically was at Uaxactun, the map designation of which inspired the name "E-Group."

Equinox: Observationally, the days on which the Sun rises due East, which correspond approximately to March 21 (as the Vernal Equinox) and September 22 (the Autumnal Equinox).

Gregorian Calendar: Currently used system, resulting from the revision to the Julian Calendar used by the Catholic Church until 1582. Where the Julian Calendar only used 1 leap day every four years, thus setting a period of 365. 25 days per year, the Gregorian year incorporates accommodations at the level of centuries to more closely approximate the tropical year with a period of 365. 2425 days.

Initial Series: Often the lead hieroglyphs of a carved inscription. The first element is a standardized symbol known as the Initial Series Introductory Glyph (ISIG) and includes a variable element connected to the current 365 Day Count month. The Long Count, 260 Day Count, 365 Day Count and Supplementary Series make up the rest of the Initial Series.

Julian Day Number: A linear count of days set to zero on January 1, 4713 BC. Astronomers adopted the system in the late 19th century to avoid cumbersome calculations based on Gregorian years with leap days. Julian Day Numbers represent pure intervals of time and should not be confused with Julian Calendar dates.

Long Count: A modified vigesimal (base 20) system of numeration. A transcribed Long Count date might be *bolon pih bolon winikhaab' ka haab' kan winik waxak k'in*, which is then translated in the academic literature as 9 pih, 9 winikhaab', 2 haab', 4 winik, 8 k'in, or 9 bak'tun, 9 k'atun, 2 tun, 4 winal, 8 k'in and rendered 9.9.2.4.8. In decimal notation, 9.9.2.4.8 equals $9 \times 144000 + 9 \times 7200 + 2 \times 360 + 4 \times 20 + 8 = 1,361,608$ and corresponds to the number of days elapsed from the Long Count "zero" date.

K'in: Base period of the Long Count, equivalent to 1 day. In hieroglyphic texts it can also refer explicitly to the Sun, or more abstractly to time.

Winal: Period of 20 k'in. The glyphic referent is now read as *winik*.

Tun: Period of 360 days. Intermediate period within the Long Count, incorporating the modification from a strict vigesimal numeration. One tun is eighteen winal. The glyphic referent is now read as *haab'*.

K'atun: Period of 7,200 days. Intermediate period within the Long Count; one k'atun is 20 tun. The glyphic referent is now read as *winikhaab'*.

Bak'tun: Period of 144,000 days. Most commonly the largest period of the Long Count, equivalent to 20 k'atun. (Occasionally, larger periods were used for numerological and/or mythological purposes.) The glyphic referent is now read as *pih*.

Lunar Series: Subset of the Supplementary Series used to place the Moon Age into a numerological context. Glyph A gives the period of the current lunar synodic period, either 29 or 30 days. Glyph X gives the hieroglyphic name of the current lunar synodic period. Glyph B is a hieroglyphic phrase reading: *u ch'ok k'aaba* or 'the sprouting name of' (referring to the name of the Moon at its first visibility for that period). Glyph C contains the numerological construct, assigning any given synodic month to one of 6 possible periods associated with 3 different deities. The overall construct places any given lunar month within a cycle of 18 unique lunar periods, but the hieroglyphic record makes clear that the overall length was sometimes modified from 18. Glyph D is made up of a coefficient term (between 1 and 20) and a hieroglyphic phrase reading: *huliiy* or 'since it arrived,' so that together they give the Moon Age as the number of days since the newly sprouted Moon arrived. Glyph E provides the glyph for '20' to be used when the Moon Age is greater than 19.

Moon Age: Number of days elapsed relative to the defined start of a lunar synodic period. For a tradition initiating months by conjunction of the Moon with the Sun, the Moon Age is approximately 7 days at first quarter (when it is half-moon waxing), 15 days at full moon, and 22 days at third quarter (when it is half-moon waning). The length of the current month is recorded in the Supplementary Series as Glyph A, alternating as 29 or 30 days in long-term approximation to the Moon's synodic period of 29. 53 days.

Nadir: Defined as the opposite of zenith.

Period Ending Dates: Completions of the tun period within the Long Count all may be considered period-ending dates, though the officially commemorated ones are those of bak'tuns, k'atuns, and 5-tun, 10-tun, 15-tun and 13-tun dates, e.g. 9.0.0.0.0, 9.16.0.0.0, 9.16.15.0.0.

Solstice: Observationally, the days of the extreme northerly or southerly rises (and sets) of the Sun, corresponding to approximately June 21 (Summer Solstice) and December 21 (Winter Solstice).

Supplementary Series: Hieroglyphic text often included with a Long Count date, frequently placed as a clause between the 260 Day Count and the 365 Day Count dates. Because the latter portions of this text were the most frequently represented among the inscriptions considered by Sylvanus Morley, he gave the glyphs within the Supplementary Series letter designations, starting from the end, so that a full date could be transcribed as: Coeff. Bak'tun, Coeff. K'atun, Coeff. Tun, Coeff. Winal, Coeff. K'in. 260DC date G F E D C B X A 365 DC date. Glyphs A, X, B, C, D, and E have been determined to represent a complete description of a Moon Age within the numerological context of the Lunar Series. Glyphs F and G have been understood to represent parallels to the Aztec Yohualteuctin ('Lords of the Night') and so were used for counting the hours of the night and for generating astrological omens. Their further investigation is the subject of Chapter 7 of this volume.

Synodic Period: The number of days it takes for a celestial body to return to a defined position relative to the Sun. For the planets, the synodic period is an average from which any given observable period may deviate by multiple days.

Sidereal Period: The number of days it takes for a celestial body to return to a defined position relative to another star (i.e. not our Sun).

Tropical Year: Actual number of days it takes for the Earth to orbit the Sun, or 365.2422.

Zenith: Defined relative to an observer as a distant point directly above her/him (i.e. along the normal vector to the earth's tangent plane at the position of the observer).

Introduction:
Towards an archaeoastronomy 2.0?

Gerardo Aldana y Villalobos

The study of Mesoamerican astronomy through the archaeological record has a long history. Half a century before "archaeoastronomy" was officially conceptualized, an interest in astronomy shaped the earliest years of research into ancient Mayan civilization. The trajectory travelled by astronomy within Mayan studies reaches back before scientific expeditions were marshaled, and passes through unstable times, including close encounters with science fiction and popular culture. A brief review of this historical trajectory provides a useful context for its state today and, in turn, the contributions making up the chapters of this book.

Spurred by the work of a German librarian puzzling over a bark-paper manuscript filled with hieroglyphic words, numbers, and calendric records, an interpretation of Mayan culture based on impressive Mayan astronomical accomplishments began to take shape by the end of the nineteenth century. Training his attention on the Dresden Codex, Ernst Förstemann first deciphered the base-twenty numerical system represented on nearly every page (1894; Coe 1999: 108). He then used this to reveal provocative astronomical patterns. Making use of some of the basic glyphs interpreted (the decipherment was still almost a century away) by other Mayanists,

Förstemann contributed the first major insight into ancient Mayan scientific activity. On 14 of the 78 pages of the manuscript, he found tables capturing the cyclical visibilities of Venus and lunar cycles behind eclipses (1894; 1895). At the turn of the century within a small and relatively new field, Förstemann had laid the groundwork to establish the astronomy in the Dresden Codex as an important anchor to the interpretation of ancient Mayan cultures.

Förstemann's work didn't just impact the field on interpretive levels. The early twentieth-century Mayanist (and U.S. spy in Central America) Sylvanus Morley tailored his investigations to incorporate Förstemann's insights (Coe 1999: 129). Morley eventually became director of the Carnegie Institute's archaeological operations, setting up a large-scale excavation at Chich'en Itza, which in turn produced two of the best known Mayan archaeologists of the twentieth century: Tatiana Proskouriakoff and Eric Thompson. But Morley started his archaeological intervention into the Maya area years before working at Chich'en Itza at the region's southern boundary. Beginning with sponsorship by the School of American Archaeology (Santa Fe), Morley traveled to Copan, Honduras in 1910. He returned six times over the next nine years

(Fash 1991: 53), halfway through picking up the backing of the Carnegie Institution of Washington (Morley 1920: 27).

Throughout this early research, Morley was steadfast in his motivation and objective:

> limited to a consideration of the chronological data found in the Copan inscriptions. In the present state of knowledge it has appeared inadvisable to extend the research beyond this point into the realm of the undeciphered glyphs, since too little is yet known about them even to approximate their meanings. (Morley 1920: 33)

At first blush, Morley's appears to be a rational, if conservative, approach to work in the field. The basics of the calendar had been worked out, so he focused on recovering more calendric data. But there is more underlying his meaning of "inadvisable," which we find in his further discussion of the content of the inscriptional material.

> Unlike the inscriptions of every other people of antiquity, the Maya records on stone do not appear to have been concerned – at least primarily – with the exploits of man, such as the achievements of rulers, priests, or warriors – in short, with the purely personal phenomena of life; on the contrary, *time in its many manifestations was their chief content.* (Morley 1920: 33; emphasis added)

Förstemann's impressive astronomical records had been appropriated into a growing model of Mayan civilization as being centered on astronomy.

Granted, Morley did find this anomalous, and he even provided contradictory material from Aztec records, which did explicitly record historical events. He therefore conceded that it was reasonable to suspect that some "residuum" of historical data might be found within Mayan inscriptions (Morley 1920: 45). Nevertheless, he was confident in his approach.

> The record of these three [calendric] counts, the Initial, Supplementary, and Secondary Series, the first and third solar, the second lunar, comprises approximately one-half of the Maya inscriptions, and enough has already been said concerning them to show their intimate connection with, and dependence upon, the counting of time. To the ultimate solution of these and other related problems, therefore, not only in this archaeological area, but also in the much broader field of contemporary ancient America, an accurate knowledge of Maya chronology is indispensable; and in the present volume this particular phase of the inscriptions at one of the largest Maya cities has been exhaustively reviewed. (Morley 1920: 46)

Morley's approach, therefore, was not simply intellectually conservative; it represented a clear conviction that the only material in the inscriptions worthy of scholarly attention was that related to chronology (*cf.* Fash 1991: 54; Coe 1999: 132).

In his history of the decipherment of Mayan hieroglyphs, *Breaking the Maya Code*, Michael Coe (1999) notes a specific impact of Morley's astronomical focus on his final reports on Copan and his subsequent forays into the Peten. In some cases Morley photographed hieroglyphic texts (albeit with low quality); in other cases he provided only sub-standard line drawings (Coe 1999: 129). Rather than include complete records of the inscriptions he recovered, that is – in the style of Alfred Maudslay or Teobert Maler – Morley preserved only the portions of the inscriptions that contained dates (Coe 1999: 129). The point is that instead of providing a robust set of archaeological records, Morley prioritized the recovery of just enough data to further the astronomical hypothesis.

During the first half of the twentieth century, astronomers, engineers, and enthusiasts joined forces to comb through the dates that Morley accumulated along with the growing corpus of hieroglyphic inscriptions, finding within them what looked like even more celestial information. In the 1920s and 1930s John Teeple, a chemical engineer, tinkered with the inscriptions at Morley's urging (Coe 1999: 130). Teeple was able to make a name for himself as a Mayanist relatively quickly by deciphering the Lunar Series (1925) within what Morley had dubbed the "Supplementary Series" (1916). For his *magnum opus* in 1931, Teeple went so far as to find a solar purpose for those dates that were not Period Ending dates. Teeple proposed that these were attempts at accurately measuring the length of the solar year in what he called his "Determinant Theory."

The results of Teeple's Determinant Theory still show up in modern discussions of Mayan astronomy (popular and some scholarly) as a demonstration of their acumen. It is often suggested, for example, that the Mayan calendar is "more accurate" than the Julian or even the Gregorian year. This comes directly from Teeple's 1931 monograph in which he includes the following table (1931: 74):

Present year length	365.2422	days
Length 600 AD	365.2423	
Julian year	365.2500	
Gregorian year	365.2425	
Copan Maya year	365.2420	

Since his "Copan Maya year" differed from his "present year" by only 0.0002 days (or 17 seconds), and the Gregorian by 0.0003 days (or 26 seconds), Teeple concluded that ancient Maya astronomers were more accurate in computing the length of the tropical year.

The complication, of course, is that Teeple derived this result following Morley's position that virtually all dates were astronomically inspired; Teeple claimed accordingly that different cities "emphasized" certain dates to facilitate solar computations. For Copan, an "emphasized date" during the Late Classic was 9.16.12.5.17 6 Kaban 10 Mol. Teeple suggested that this 6 Kaban 10 Mol date served as a shorthand for tropical year calculations:

> The priests selected a time 3876 years after 4 Ahau 8 Cumhu to make the computation, this being exactly 204 × 19 years, or 47940 moons. According to Copan 47940 moons = 9.16.12-7-18. So 9.16.12-7-18, 8 Eznab 11 Yax was the anniversary of 4 Ahau 8 Cumhu and the year had traveled twice through the vague year plus the distance from 8 Cumhu to 11 Yax = 208 days. So in this thirteenth year of Katun 17, 18 Cumhu, which was to end Katun 17, was the anniversary of a day 10 Mol in the calendar 3876 years before; 18 Cumhu – 208 days = 10 Mol. The vague year anniversary of this same date was 9.16.12-5-17, 6 Caban 10 Mol. (Teeple 1931: 72)

In other words, "emphasized dates" provided anchors in historical times for the discord that had accumulated between the 365-Day Count and the tropical year. "Priests" could then use these anchors to reconstruct the contemporary position of the tropical year events recorded in mythical times.

Teeple, however, was unable to find the same computation at other sites. He did find what he considered to be a similar, less accurate, computation at Palenque, but was forced to concede that there were so many dates available, it might not constitute confirmation for his Determinant Theory (Teeple 1931: 76). In fact, the Determinant Theory never did pan out. Michael Coe said of it 60 years later: "A little over thirty years were to elapse before the Determinant Theory went the way of the inter-galactic aether, and disappeared forever: Teeple had wasted his time" (Coe 1999: 135).

For some 30–40 years, though, Teeple had provided a visual symbol to go along with his interpretation. He argued that it would have taken considerable computational effort for Mayan astronomers to produce the Determinant (or "emphasized date") – an undertaking that would have been required every 50–75 years (1931: 80). With so many hands involved, he found both an accounting of the error creeping into the records that didn't accord very well with his theory and a cause for celebration (1931: 80).

> That such a determination was not a one man job is shown by the group photograph of the Copan Academy of Sciences taken just after the sessions in which they decided that 6 Caban 10 Mol was the determinant for Katun 17. (1931: 80)

For Teeple, the figures carved around the perimeter of Copan Altar Q were members of an astronomical congress commemorated in stone for their Determinant Theory accomplishments.

Even though it did not pass the test of time, the results of his Determinant Theory and Teeple's reputation in the field pushed even further Morley's contention that the inscriptions were predominantly concerned with astronomy and calendrics. Not all such interpretations, however, fared so well.

In the early 1930s, for instance, the German astrophysicist, Hans Ludendorff, pooled together Long Count dates from several sites in a now common approach to seeking astronomical patterns. He went on to find that within fourteen dates at Copan, eight corresponded to significant positions of Saturn and/or Jupiter in the night sky according to his use of the Spinden correlation (Thompson 1935: 84). Eric Thompson noted that these findings "appear[ed] very convincing" as support for the Spinden correlation (1935: 83). This represented something of a problem, however, since Thompson was interested in replacing that correlation with his own correlation between Christian and Mayan calendars – what would become known as the GMT. So Thompson went back through Ludendorff's dates to find that several of the inscriptions in Ludendorff's study had been misread. Thompson's reanalysis showed that seven of Ludendorff's reconstructions were in error, and that out of these seven, six corresponded to Ludendorff's planetary events. With the correct dates, the planetary patterns went away, showing "that the dates that are wrong have a higher percentage of the astronomical phenomena than the dates that are correctly read" (Thompson 1935: 83–85).

Thompson didn't stop there, though; he also issued a larger caveat to studies based solely on numerical patterns.

> It would seem, then, that Ludendorff has not established the correctness of the Spinden correlation, but, unwittingly, has shown that astronomical phenomena are worthless as proofs of correlations unless accompanied by glyphs indicating the nature of the phenomenon. Even with this last safeguard, the evidence is not certain, for, as has been pointed out on page 78, the Venus glyphs attached to dates can be used as supporting evidence for more than one correlation. (Thompson 1975: 89)

While Ludendorff's and other interpretations were thus discredited in the academic literature, by the latter half of the twentieth century the overall impression on the field was one of impressive Mayan astronomical acumen. At some level, this was enabled by two factors aside from pattern-seeking investigations in the fashion of Teeple or Ludendorff. For one, the Venus Table in the Dresden Codex remained a solid interpretation, and further scholarship on it only became more sophisticated as the century wore on (Thompson 1972; Lounsbury 1983; 1992a; 1992b; *cf.* Bricker and Bricker 2007). For the second, Morley and his associates working for the Carnegie Institution of Washington augmented their inscriptional studies with another form of data to strengthen the case.

Alongside the compilation of hieroglyphic dates in his *Inscriptions of Copan*, Morley took up a different kind of astronomical investigation. Two of the inscriptions that he recovered and mapped were carved into stelae that were raised on small cobblestone platforms in the foothills bordering the Copan Valley (Morley 1920: 133, 143). Painted red and raised on hills of approximately the same height above the valley floor, Morley thought to explore the possibility that these suburban stelae might have held some important alignment relative to each other. Using the coordinates he himself mapped, Morley turned to his colleague of the "Harvard Astronomical Department," Robert Willson, who wrote:

> [T]he sun, as seen from Stela 12, would set behind Stela 10, 20.3 days after the vernal equinox and 20.6 days before the autumnal equinox (i.e., April 9 and September 10 of the present year, 1916 (Gregorian Calendar)). (Letter from Willson to Morley dated November 29, 1916, quoted in Morley 1920: 133)

While April 9 did not stand out immediately as an important date in the solar year, Morley did find that local practice was to begin burning the fields in early April. That is, in the swidden agriculture Morley witnessed in the region during the early twentieth century, agricultural fields were burned just prior to the rainy season to prepare them for planting. He suggested that the alignment might have been used as a signal for the beginning of the agricultural cycle during Classic times (Aveni 1980: 240; Baudez 1987: 65; Morley 1925).

There was, however, one key complication to his hypothesis, as he quickly found out firsthand. The smoke from the burning of the fields (already begun before April 9) made it impossible for him to visually verify the sunset alignment.

> [A]fter burning had once been started, no sunset observation on Stela 10 would have been possible from Stela 12. Such was the hazy smoke-laden condition of the atmosphere from April 9 to 14 of the present year at Copan, that even with a high-powered telescope it was impossible to see Stela 10 from Stela 12 at sunset…. (Aveni 1980: 240–241).

While the lack of observed verification complicated his hypothesis, with this investigation, Morley's work on the Valley Stelae took Mayan astronomy out of "pure science" and/ or "chronology"; Morley was now contributing a mundane purpose for astronomy during the Classic period. Moreover, he was using the inscriptions to find astronomical patterns as we saw above, but he was also looking to archaeological sites themselves to find evidence of astronomical interest. Anachronistically, then – given the scope of his work – we might be inclined to consider Morley the 'father of Mesoamerican archaeoastronomy.'

Perhaps as important, Morley impacted the field via an extensive network of associates from which he was able to recruit researchers for Carnegie once he took on the directorship. Frans Blom, for example, had been working for an oil company in Chiapas and Tabasco (Mexico), where he found the opportunity "to visit ruins" (Byers 1966: 406). According to Douglas Byers, Blom sent a drawing (with notes) of El Tortuguero Stela 1 to Morley, who was so impressed, he brought him into the field (1966: 406). Oliver Ricketson – who travelled with Blom to Uaxactun under the direction of Harvard University professor Alfred Tozzer – followed up on Blom's earlier work, in part to pursue the growing hypothesis of astronomical representation. Blom and Ricketson noticed that the equinoxes and solstices were captured by a pair of architectural features.

To the east of the "Group E" plaza at Uaxactun, Blom and Ricketson revealed a long, low platform supporting three structures ("Pyramids I, II, and III") equally spaced along its length. Opposite this platform (to the west), a symmetrical pyramid (Pyramid VII) served as a viewing station. In Blom's interpretation, an observer would sit on the steps of the symmetrical structure and watch the sunrise over the course of the year.

> Frans Blom, who visited Uaxactun for the Carnegie Institution in 1924, noted that certain lines of sight from Pyramid VII to Pyramids I, II and III, respectively, corresponded very closely to the amplitudes of the sun at the solstices and the equinoxes. (Ricketson 1933: 77)

On the equinoxes, that is, the Sun would appear to rise out of the center of Pyramid II, whereas on the solstices, it would appear to rise off the extreme edges of Pyramids I and III. Ricketson called this the "Group of the Solar Observatory," but the identification of similar "observatories" at other sites resulted in them all being named after the Uaxactun 'prototype' as "E-Group complexes" (Aveni and Hartung 1989; Rice and Aimers 2006). With it, Ricketson, Blom, and Morley bolstered interpretations of Mayan interests in astronomy.

Ricketson's 1926 work at Uaxactun was not his first in the field or his first investigation into Mayan astronomy. Having been initially discouraged by his travel across the Yucatan Peninsula with Morley in 1921, Ricketson found new inspiration in 1924, going straight from Uaxactun with Blom to Baking Pot in British Honduras (to conduct his own excavation), and then to work with Morley at Chich'en Itza (Lothrop 1953: 70). Together Ricketson and Morley trained their attention on the structure referred to as the Caracol or "the Observatory." Unfortunately for their interests, much of the upper levels of the structure had already crumbled by the time they began work there. Nevertheless, Ricketson took compass data on the windows that were still intact, complaining that his efforts to use

a theodolite were foiled by the cramped space (1928: 442). Noting that he was "without even a rudimentary knowledge of astronomy," he sent his compass readings to Louis Bauer, director of the Carnegie Department of Terrestrial Magnetism. Bauer's computations confirmed Ricketson's 1924 direct observation of the vernal equinox sunset sighted along the "*right inner* jamb to *left outer* jamb" of Window 1 (1928: 442–443). Likewise, the "*right inner* jamb to *left outer* jamb" of Window 3 pointed due South (1928: 443). Bauer also informed Ricketson that two sightlines from the windows marked the extreme declinations of the Moon, leaving him, Ricketson, to conclude that:

> [t]hese two discoveries are of importance in that they have opened a new and more practical field for the study of Maya astronomy. It is sincerely to be hoped that ... all investigators ... will take accurate and copious bearings whenever the opportunity offers or the faintest suspicion arises that the arrangement of buildings or structural features may have been designed in accordance with astronomical directions. (Ricketson 1928: 444)

Between 1925 and 1931, then, Teeple was pulling the Lunar Series from the Supplementary Series and pushing the comprehension of the Dresden Codex Venus Table. Meanwhile, from 1920 to 1933, Ricketson, Blom, and Morley were finding complements in the architecture. The results presented a coherent image of Classic Mayan urban planning and intellectual culture as very concerned with astronomy. The discrediting of Ludendorff, for example, or the questioning of other specific interpretations did not come together to form a fundamental challenge to this standard interpretation of Maya culture. The coherence of this representation along with its championing by Eric Thompson is what made it possible to ward off attempts at deciphering the hieroglyphic script well into the twentieth century (*cf.* Coe 1999: 143).

Given this backdrop, one might suspect that the overturning of Thompson's perspective and the decipherment of the hieroglyphic script – beginning concertedly in the 1970s – might have derailed the importance of astronomy within the basic interpretation of Mayan civilization. Indeed, Tatiana Proskouriakoff had shown in 1960 that the very tools utilized to propose astronomical knowledge were much more convincing in demonstrating that the content of the inscriptions were historical, not purely astronomical or calendrical. That is, Proskouriakoff started with a set of inscriptions sharing iconographic similarities at Piedras Negras, and looked through the dates within them for patterns among the intervals (1960: 455). She found that they easily fell into a sequence of important events in the lives of hypothetical historical rulers. She went on to find that certain glyphs anchored the dates corresponding to "birth" and "accession," and that the accession events fit well with presumed lifespans for previous rulers (Proskouriakoff 1960: 460). Proskouriakoff's hypothesis was accepted universally – even Thompson conceded immediately after reading the paper (Coe 1999: 176). The decipherment proper blossomed through a combination of her work with the linguistic hypotheses of Yuri Knorosov and Heinrich Berlin (Coe 1999: 176–184).

This 'linguistic turn,' however, did not prove fatal to investigations of Mayan astronomy – even though some work certainly did suffer directly. Teeple's interpretation of Copan Altar Q, for example, was questioned by John Carlson at the dawn of the decipherment (1977). Carlson showed that the source of Teeple's "astronomical congress" could be found in Herbert Spinden's efforts to establish a calendar correlation, which in turn was built on Morley's work. That the image on Copan Altar Q (as well as a similar one on the bench in Structure 10L-11) represented "more or less formalized pictures of an astronomical congress held in 503 AD." (Spinden 1924: 140, quoted in Carlson 1977: 107) supported Spinden's correlation, which relied principally on Teeple's Determinant Theory and a "constellation" of astronomical evidence (Carlson 1977: 107). Carlson sided with the mounting support for Thompson's correlation against Spinden's and so he challenged the evidence behind the astronomical interpretation of Copan Altar Q (1977: 107). His results were ambiguous. While he refused to deny the possibility of astronomy somewhere on the monument, Carlson also recorded David Kelley's rejection of Teeple's Determinant Theory by the late 1970s (1977: 107).

Regardless, over the next two decades, the astronomical interpretation of Altar Q fell completely to Joyce Marcus, Berthold Riese, and David Stuart's demonstration that the figures around the perimeter of the monument were seated upon hieroglyphic representations of their own names (Coe 1999: 253; Fash 1991: 26). The figures represented the 16 members of the Copan dynasty, from the founder, Yax K'uk' Mo', to the sixteenth, Yax Pahsaj Chan Yopat – the patron of the inscription that Teeple misunderstood to have borne the Determinant discussed above.

So some astronomical interpretation did suffer, but there would have been implicit bounds on the potential impact of the hieroglyphic decipherment; it would not have been able to undo all astronomical interpretation. The Supplementary Series, for example, would still be understood as centered on the Lunar Series, and the Eclipse and Venus Tables in the Dresden Codex would not be challenged. Yet astronomy remained a prominent component of interpretation of Maya culture through the 1970s, '80s, and '90s (Aveni and Hotaling 1994; Dutting 1985; Closs 1994; Kelley 1980; Bricker *et al.* 2001; Tate 1985; Sprajc 1996) – even while the texts were deciphered as recording other matters entirely. This preservation, it appears, was made possible by an independent intellectual development, transpiring across the Atlantic.

During the 1960s, the astrophysicist Gerald Hawkins took an interest in the great monolithic ruins of Stonehenge in England. The idea of exploring astronomical knowledge encoded within ancient architecture was not new within European scholarship; Stonehenge itself had been considered astronomically relevant since the Middle Ages, and was periodically re-assessed as such into the twentieth century (Fernie 1990: 103). When Hawkins took it up, proposals had already been debated concerning its use as a calendar and its alignment to solar phenomena (Fernie 1990: 104; Hawkins 1964). What Hawkins introduced, though, through his training as an astrophysicist was the exhaustive computational power of an IBM computer. Hawkins employed this computational power to check every possible architectural alignment against as many rising and setting positions of the Sun, Moon, planets, and bright stars as possible. The result was a proposal that Stonehenge encoded more than just solar alignments; it also encoded the motion of the Moon (Hawkins 1964; Aveni 2003: 150–151)

Hawkins's finds did not escape critique – scholars challenged his statistical analysis as well as his apparent disregard for archaeological context (Fernie 1990: 104). But the work came at an auspicious time, bringing together "two magically appealing subjects at least one of which [the editors of *Scientific American*] invariably tried to include in every issue: archaeology and astronomy. The romance of space and the mystery of the past!" (Gingerich 1980: ix). Part of the appeal to Hawkins's work, then, may well have been its resonance within Euro-American popular culture(s).

The Space Age was launched with Sputnik on October 4, 1957. The orbiting of the Earth by John Glenn in 1962, and the technological race culminating in Neil Anderson's steps on the Moon on July 20, 1969 filled the media in various forms. Very quickly, astronomy and "outer space" became ubiquitous in American popular culture. In the thick of it, Walter Wingo of the "Science News-Letter" referred to NASA's establishment of "a public relations program unrivaled in the history of the U.S. Government [intended] to sell the people on the benefits of the space program" (1963: 341). Alton Frye of the Harvard University Center for International Affairs described the "American public" as potentially "saturated into apathy by news media seeking to keep up with the most visibly exciting area of technology…" (1966: 103).

The public interest in space, of course, was not restricted to matters of international politics; "by the 1970s, science fiction had become an established part of popular culture" (Consolmagno 1996: 129). Science fiction titles, mixing fantasy and outer space, made it onto national bestseller lists (*ibid.*). This intriguing interplay between astronomy, the Space Race, science fiction, and ancient history was in part captured by Michael Coe's overview of *Native American Astronomy* in 1977:

> [t]he public on both sides of the Atlantic has been led to believe in the existence of voyagers from outer space, in sunken continents, in white 'culture gods,' and in heaven knows what else, a state of affairs heavily exploited by book publishers and television producers. (1977: ix)

And that the interest made it into academic circles was anecdotally attested by John Eddy in his 1977 review for the *Journal for the History of Astronomy*:

> This volume [*Archaeoastronomy in Pre-Columbian America*] compiles 18 of the 26 papers presented at a joint Mexican-U.S. meeting on pre-Columbian archaeoastronomy held in Mexico City in June 1973.

> I am a little surprised at what a popular book it has proven to be. Both of the copies in the University of Colorado libraries seem perennially checked out, I see a number of private copies around, and somebody is always borrowing mine. (1977: 497)

It may well be that this public interest is what helped archaeoastronomy survive the onslaught of an advancing hieroglyphic decipherment. Years later, Anthony Aveni implied as much, referring to the public's role in the development of the field in the 1960s and '70s:

> the flood of trade and popular works on archaeoastronomy, though useful in bringing new ideas to a wider audience, did little to contribute to its professional status. Although archaeoastronomy has shed much of the burden of the sensationalist baggage it once acquired in the aftermath of the Stonehenge controversy, popular works that advocate an extraordinary and oft-difficult-to-document role for astronomy in shaping human culture still reach the level of trade text publications (e.g., Bauval, 1995; Sullivan, 1996; Ulansey, 1989). Many of these works exhibit both millenarian and deterministic qualities in which seminal cosmic events drive the course of civilization. (Aveni 2003: 151)

Its popular aspect also may underlie Horst Hartung's introductory remarks in 1975:

> Contrary to the reluctance characteristic of the forties, fifties, and sixties, in the seventies scholars of Mesoamerican cultures generally accept the idea that there existed a consideration of astronomical events in pre-Columbian architecture and planning. (1975: 111)

Hartung, it turns out, was to play an important role in the preservation of astronomical interpretation within Mesoamerican cultures into the 1970s and beyond.

Hartung was born in Germany, immigrating to Mexico at the age of 32 to form part of the new faculty of architecture at the University of Guadalajara. Salvador Díaz-García states that while he did design some important buildings in Jalisco, his greater contribution grew out of an interest in ancient Mesoamerican architecture (2006). Hartung's first publication on the subject, *Die Zeremonialzentren der Maya* (1971), took an architect's consideration of urban design back to Chich'en Itza, adding to it investigations into the urban centers of Piedras Negras, Yaxchilan and Uxmal. In his work, Hartung looked for celestial orientations defined by the alignment of architectural features to other monuments – very much in the spirit of Ricketson and Blom's interpretation of Group E at Uaxactun, or Morley's Valley Stelae at Copan.

Katherine Haramundanis, of the Smithsonian Astrophysical Observatory and a specialist in scientific measurement, however, responded to Hartung's book immediately and without much sympathy. She found his results unconvincing primarily because he worked from maps that Haramundanis considered to be "of insufficient accuracy for drawing conclusions concerning astronomical orientations" (1973: 202). This concern was, in fact, the same one raised more generally by Jonathan Reyman (1973), echoed in his review of the re-nascent field (1975: 210).

Haramundanis's critique would not be sustainable for long. In 1969, Michael Coe connected Hartung to a recently minted PhD in Astronomy, Anthony Aveni (Aveni, personal communication, 2013). Aveni's early work, in fact, had not escaped critique either. Anthropologist John Reyman wrote:

[t]he search for alignments, at times, seems to reflect a haphazard, almost random 'groping,' and the accompanying explanations have tended to be after-the-fact (see Aveni and Linsley 1972). In short, archaeoastronomers have all too rarely used anything approaching the scientific method. (1975: 208)

The new partnership turned out to be valuable in addressing both critiques.

Four years after they first met, Hartung and Aveni collaborated on two fronts. For one, their task, sponsored by both the American Association for the Advancement of Science and the Consejo Nacional de Ciencia y Tecnologia, consisted of the "first organized gathering of archaeoastronomers" to consider Western Hemisphere astronomies (Aveni 1977: xii). They thus explicitly brought the project inspired by Hawkins across the Atlantic for the (re)new(ed) interest in Mesoamerican astronomy. Aveni makes this explicit, writing of his new NSF sponsored project that "[i]n all cases the guidelines set up by Hawkins (1962) and Reyman (1973) have been followed …" (1975: 163). Aveni also found his second calling here, editing the conference proceedings, and initiating a publishing trajectory from the center of the field, which coalesced in the follow-up meeting, two years later at Colgate in 1975.

The second collaboration spoke directly to Haramundis and Reyman's concerns. In her review of Hartung's work, Haramundanis had thrown down a clear challenge:

It is unfortunate that to this date, although an enormous amount of work has been done and a vast literature has grown up around the Maya, there exists no definitive work that can answer the question of whether Maya buildings had astronomical orientations or even if the Maya themselves made astronomical observations. (1973: 202)

During the winters of 1973 and 1974, Hartung and Aveni worked with Historian of Science Sharon Gibbs – a researcher at Colgate where Aveni was teaching – to revisit the measurements of the Caracol at Chich'en Itza (1975: 977). Aveni seemed to be responding directly to Haramundanis, describing his research as an "organized study of the possible extent of astronomical orientations throughout ancient Mesoamerica," involving

direct measurement with a transit instrument of particular alignments at the archaeological sites and their subsequent matching with local astronomical rise-set phenomena utilizing a set of computerized tables (Aveni 1972) (Aveni 1975: 163).

The challenge had been accepted.

Through their work at Chich'en Itza, Aveni, Gibbs and Hartung showed that the Caracol was measurably skewed relative to other buildings at the site and it was this deviation that pointed to the alignments with planetary phenomena. Going beyond Ricketson's results, Aveni *et al.* also found a much more compelling celestial referent in Venus, which seems to have been behind Haramundanis's closing remarks.

A recent analysis of the Dresden Codex (by J. Eric Thompson) suggests that it contains a Venus table in addition to its astrological texts; and accurate site surveys which can determine if reasonable orientations exist to astronomical objects are only now being made. (Haramundanis 1973: 202)

The results of Aveni *et al.*'s "accurate site surveys" were that:

[t]he provisions for correction of the formal Venus tables in the Dresden Codex suggest that observations of Venus were indeed made. We may suppose that the Caracol windows were placed to aid such observations and specifically to preserve the direction of the most predictable disappearances of Venus before heliacal rise. (1975: 983–984)

Aveni, Hartung, and Gibbs had reached all the way back to Förstemann's original insights to combine them with the archaeological investigations of Morley and Ricketson, and re-vivify them with Hawkins's computational methods.

Hartung and Aveni's efforts thus rescued

the study of astronomy from obsolescence building on the foundation laid by Morley, Ricketson, Teeple, Thompson, and others. As Coe put it in his introduction to the collection of essays produced for the Colgate sponsored symposium on "Native American Astronomy" in 1975:

> [t]hey have revived a forgotten tradition of scholarship, for in the last century some outstanding Americanists like Daniel G. Brinton and Zelia Nuttall were interested in like matters. (1977: ix)

Their skills took them far and wide, with Aveni carrying the torch when Hartung's age got the better of him. With the close of the decade, Aveni firmly established himself as the authority in the field through a monograph synthesizing his own work with a review of much of the material in his two edited volumes, combined with an extensive primer on naked-eye astronomy. The volume synthesizing it all: *Skywatchers of Ancient Mexico* provided a legitimacy to astronomical investigations (and acknowledged its popular appeal), coming from the pen of a trained astrophysicist, and striving to:

> introduce all readers to the basic components of the interdisciplinary field of archaeoastronomy. It is offered as a bridge connecting the established disciplines of astronomy, archaeology, culture history, and the history of astronomy and is intended to serve as a platform for the exchange of ideas among students of these seemingly disparate fields. Since the synthesis is presented at an elementary level, the text should benefit the interested lay person as well as the informed visitor to the ruins. (Aveni 1980: 7)

But the movement did not go uncontested. In 1992, Keith Kintigh, an archaeologist digging in the Southwestern U.S., penned the provocatively titled: "I wasn't going to say anything, but since you asked: Archaeoastronomy and Archaeology" for the Quarterly Bulletin of the Center for Archaeoastronomy. Kintigh "shoots from the hip" (1992: 1), provoking that by the early 1990s, much archaeoastronomy "remains high-tech celestial butterfly collecting" (1992: 4). Acknowledging that there is a well-defined and rigorous method behind the pursuit, Kintigh suggests that butterfly collecting is an end in itself. He levels precisely this aspect of the metaphor against archaeoastronomy saying that in it and rock art, "both research domains seem largely self-contained. The practitioners propose and answer their own questions and communicate largely

with one another" (1992: 1). Kintigh extends this metaphor to argue that archaeoastronomers should not imitate butterfly collectors. "[T]he generation of facts," he writes

> astronomical observation and identification of alignments – is easy (analogous to excavation, classification and dating). However, it is my suspicion that it will be difficult to make *rigorous and testable* arguments linking archaeoastronomical observations with serious anthropological questions. (1992: 4)

Kintigh suggests that archaeoastronomy would do better to see itself as a toolkit that should be applied within anthropology. It should be brought in to perform the task of generating facts, but the generation should be motivated by archaeological investigation. To extend the analogy, all of the tools of lepidoptery could be brought into ecological studies to take specimens, but their larger value would be to include them in a census, which might contribute to a study of environmental change within a region.

Aveni wasted no time in responding. Kintigh's comments came out in the Autumnal Equinox bulletin; Aveni responded in the Winter Solstice edition of the same year. For the most part, however, Aveni agreed with his antagonist, writing that "Kintigh is right," and

> [a]rchaeologist Jim Judge once remarked that a lot of archaeoastronomy is concerned with the Anglo population's rediscovery of how the sky works. Likewise, many amateur Mayanists are enthralled by their revelations about planetary conjunctions acquired with their PCs. (1992: 4)

Aveni was careful, though, to point out that Kintigh may have been too influenced by archaeoastronomy of the Southwest, and that a broader view of the Americas would turn up some work in various areas that did engage research questions relevant to "archaeology, anthropology, art history, ethnohistory, etc." (1992: 1). He therefore intends to distinguish quality archaeoastronomy from: "the all too proliferous reportage of what lines up with what or whether this or that standstill was being observed" (1992: 4).

Aveni's conclusion, however, appears internally conflicted. He writes that

> Kintigh and his colleagues in all the disciplines that border on archaeoastronomy must, therefore, allow the validity of contributions to archaeoastronomy to be decided by the quality of work that appears in refereed publications, especially those in the standard disciplines. (1992: 4)

This sentence begins by putting archaeo-astronomy at the center – noting that these other "standard disciplines" "border" it, and so seeming to give it a degree of intellectual autonomy. But then the sentence ends by deferring the field's legitimacy to acceptance by "standard disciplines." So is archaeoastronomy a specialized set of tools to be brought into established/standard fields and used therein – as Kintigh would recommend? Or is it an "interdiscipline" requiring not just data from different fields, but attendant epistemological accommodations, as Aveni hints? The latter would suggest that not only does archaeoastronomy have to become more anthropological, but also that anthropology must make some space for "science" and especially "science" in "Other cultures" (*cf.* Aldana 2007: 197–198).

Twenty years later, archaeoastronomy still cannot be said to have settled these questions. The debacle of 2012 demonstrates at least a guilt by association that facilitates the marginalization of the field. But the success of *Skywatchers*, and its revision in 2002 speak to the endurance of the sub-discipline, encompassing a wide range of study reaching back to Förstemann, passing through archaeoastronomy proper, and including geographers and historians. The chapters in this book speak to the consolidation and acceptance hard won by Aveni and the archaeoastronomers of the late twentieth century. Appealing to the work of Aveni, Hartung, Floyd Lounsbury, Victoria and Harvey Bricker, and David Kelley, these chapters also reach out in new directions, seeking innovation that might lead to new coherence and productivity.

In Chapter 1 Harold Green turns to Guatemala's southern coast to take up (Geographer) Vincent Malmström's hypothesis concerning the origin of the 260-Day Count at the Preclassic site of Izapa (Guatemala). During the 1980s, Malmström pursued the notion, which was first proposed by Zelia Nuttall in 1928, that the 260-Day Count had been invented in order to capture a celestial phenomenon occurring only in a very specific region of southern Mesoamerica (1997: 4). Along the latitude of 14.8 degrees north of the equator – a geographic line that passes through Copan, Honduras, and Izapa, Guatemala – the zenith passage of the Sun calendrically divides the year into two parts. Zenith passage on August 13 through winter solstice and back to zenith passage on April 29 at the site of Izapa takes a total of 260 days. Malmström suggested that the 260-Day Count was invented to capture this observed interval at Izapa (1997). Since other cities throughout Preclassic and early Classic Mesoamerica also seemed to possess architectural alignments to the 13 August sunrise, including Teotihuacan, Malmström argued that they were all commemorating the birth of the 260-Day Count (1997: 9).

In his study, Green considers Malmström's hypothesis through Izapa's neighbor and contemporary, Chocolá, located to the east along the Pacific Coast piedmont. In line with Aveni and Hartung's response to Haramundians's critique, Green goes beyond Malmström's investigation; uncontent with measurements derived from maps of various sites, Green observes and photographs the horizon phenomena from Chocolá itself. In so doing, he finds that there is much to be interpreted from these sunrise observations. For example, Green brings new data to bear on the question of the 360-day *haab'* relative to the 365-day solar year. He finds that at the site of Chocolá, there is a calendrical symmetry between zenith and nadir passages of the Sun. As at Izapa, the interval of time from zenith through winter solstice and back through zenith produces an interval of 260 days; Green notes further that nadir through summer solstice, through nadir generates an interval of 265 days. Except for five days, the celestial symmetry between zenith and nadir would be visible on the Chocolá eastern horizon. Green suggests that this observation was probably not lost on observers at Chocolá, and that it may have provided the impetus for creating a calendric symmetry symbolized by the 360-day *haab'* – the 365-day tropical year minus the unsymmetrical five days – Green's Chapter 1 thus suggests a new hypothesis for the basis of the Long Count.

An observational device of the same 'family' is taken up by Ivan Sprajc in Chapter 2. Sprajc's work is made possible by a large-scale archaeological survey of southeastern Campeche. Through an examination of 23 structures at 11 sites, all with Preclassic occupations, Sprajc comes across a pattern within the layout of the largest structures. He finds, for example, that at Yaxnohcah (20 km southeast of Calakmul) Structures C-1 and E-1 are aligned such that the Sun appears to rise out of Structure E-1 viewed from Structure C-1: on February 12 and October 30. These two dates, he notes, partition the year into intervals of 260 days (from 2/12 to 10/30) and 105 days (from 10/31 to 2/11). Resonant with Green's work at Chocolá, then, Sprajc reaches back into the Preclassic to look for the origins of Mesoamerican calendrics and observable horizon phenomena.

In his chapter, Sprajc identifies the same alignment at several sites in the region. In each case, it is built to inscribe sunrise phenomena, and in each case it involves two of the largest structures at the site – two structures that are intervisible above the floral canopy (*cf.* Aldana 2005). Sprajc makes particular note of cross-site imitation in order to suggest that his results call into question contemporary consensus regarding the direction of the cultural influence these alignments represent. Namely, the generally held opinion is that this family of orientations was developed in central Mexico, and introduced later in the Mayan region. Sprajc, however, shows that the constructs in southeastern Campeche are earlier than those in central Mexico, and may tie to even earlier versions at Kohunlich and El Mirador. While Sprajc's methods are perfectly in line with Aveni and Hartung's, his application of them to a concentrated region and time period provides new interpretations.

In Chapter 3, Mendez, Barnhart, Powell, and Karasik, study an architectural instrument that is a distant descendent of the devices investigated by Green and Sprajc. Mendez *et al.* explore the relationships between astronomical events and their observable effects in the Cross Group at Palenque – a set of three structures patronized by the eleventh ruler of the dynasty, Kan B'ahlam during the Late Classic – some 6–700 years after the horizon calendars of Chocolá and Yaxnohcah.

The astronomical device taken up by Mendez *et al.* is generated by a complex interaction of architectural walls, rays of the sun, and human observation. They reflect on the symmetry, for one, within the floor plan of the Temple of the Sun, and its similarity in design to the other two temples of the Cross Group – the Temple of the Cross, and the Temple of the Foliated Cross. But they go on to demonstrate that the walls of the Temple of the Sun were intentionally modified to

break symmetry – and that this violation of symmetry is precisely what creates the astronomical effect of interest. Namely, on the summer solstice, a ray of light enters the building at sunrise. With the movement of the Sun over the course of the morning, this ray of light reaches toward the back of the temple, shaped by the walls to form a thin dagger.[1] Mendez *et al.* interpret this as a "hierophany" resonating with the recognized importance of astronomy in the construction of the Cross Group (Aldana 2007; Anderson *et al.* 1981; Carlson 1976).

While their work represents an important revision to earlier interpretations of astronomically oriented architecture at Palenque – principally that of John Carlson and Linda Schele – as well as an expansion of more recent interpretations (Aldana 2007; Stuart 2005), this chapter goes further in reconstructing the Palenque astronomer's work. The authors go beyond the argument for the recognition of an astronomical instrument. Mendez *et al.* show that the construction of these temples requires more than just the knowledge of how to physically assemble building materials in a structurally sound fashion. There is a geometry underlying the wall positions that is critical to the final structure as instrument. This geometry they suggest, is not accidental, but can be derived from techniques available to the ancient architect. For this, Mendez *et al.* nucleate their efforts with ethnographically described methods for constructing houses. Drawing cords and planting stakes provide the base method of design, and turn out to be sufficient to generate useful geometric configurations. They then fill out the construction methods with astronomical observations and site locations available to the elite. In the end, they provide a convincing argument for the work done by historical actors in the physical construction of the Temple of the Sun as an architectural instrument.

In a similar spirit of attempting to access the astronomer's daily work, Chapter 4 on the Dresden Codex Venus Table moves upstream from the final product – the table of dates itself – to contextualize it within other known Mayan calendric practices. This chapter directly addresses one of Aveni's principle caveats over the years, which concerns the influence of how modern scholars conceptualize "science" on the astronomy they recover from ancient cultures

(1980: 3). If we take for granted, for example, that they were most interested in the accuracy of their geometric predictions, then that conditions the types of methods (mathematical and observational) that we expect they would have used, and the resulting picture begins to look very much like a proto-Western science.

Chapter 4 starts by recognizing that while the Venus Table has long been interpreted as an ephemeris for the planet (Aveni 1980; Bricker and Bricker 2007; Lounsbury 1983; 1992a; 1992b; Thompson 1972), the rest of the document is predominantly concerned with omens. Furthermore, these omens are intimately dependent on the functioning of the 260-Day Count and Mayan calendrics generally. Moreover, we have an extremely well documented example of the use of Mayan calendrics for the generation of omens in Barbara Tedlock's ethnographic study of K'iche' daykeepers. Chapter 4, therefore, finds a new coherence to the work of the ancient astronomer/daykeeper by placing the operation of the Venus Table within a context of the intellectual labor reflected in the rest of the manuscript. In so doing, it turns to the need to culturally translate intellectual labor, and so constructs the conception of an oracle within modern culture. This allows us to reconsider the oracular context of the astronomer's work, and so place it in dialogue with the ontology of the indigenous Mayan cosmos. By finally focusing on the linguistic analysis of the titles taken by astronomers and rulers, an intellectual context is developed for the arena in which omens, economics, and politics (for example) would be mediated by the ruler of a given city. In other words, this reconstruction of the astronomer's labor makes possible a recognition of the interactions astronomy may have had with other realms of knowledge without implicitly invoking a romanticized image of Galileo confronting the Church (or some antithesis).

In Chapter 5, Mendez and Karasik follow directly upon the investigation of Mendez *et al.* in Chapter 3 to suggest that various forms of astronomy have been woven together within the temples of the Cross Group at Palenque. As with the following two chapters, Mendez and Karasik follow a practice within archaeoastronomy initiated in the 1980s with the increased application of personal computers to academic work. All three chapters take up the approach popularized by Linda Schele and David Freidel (1993), taking artistic images and hieroglyphic texts as maps of celestial events. The upshot is that by invoking a calendar correlation, Mayan dates can be converted into Julian dates, which can in turn be "looked up" in planetarium software.[2] If the correct calendar correlation is utilized and if Schele and Freidel's hypothesis[3] is invoked, then this type of investigation allows for the recovery of a very rich astronomical dataset.[4] Not only are astronomical events recorded directly, but the artistic context provides layers of further information on the nesting of astronomical knowledge into other elite intellectual activities. This might provide one form of access into the types of sociological, political, and/or religious pressures impinging on astronomical investigation and inscription.

Mendez and Karasik use this method to explore zenith and nadir passages of the Sun within the artistic and architectural patronage of Kan B'ahlam at Palenque. They begin with the mythistory detailed in the Temple of the Cross at Palenque, reading the events transpiring in the narrative relative to events observable in the night sky. As the Palenque patron deity dedicates a house in the North, Mendez and Karasik find that the event occurs on a nadir passage of the Sun at Palenque. Through a metaphoric link between the North and nadir passage, they argue that the mythology becomes a record of astronomical events.

The authors move on to the orientations of the temples to argue that zenith and nadir passages of the Sun are attested: zenith passage (May 7 and August 5 at Palenque) is marked by sunrise out of the center of the Temple of the Cross roof comb from the central doorway of the Temple of the Sun, and by sunset behind the Temple of Inscriptions from the Temple of the Cross. Nadir passage (January 29 and November 9 at Palenque) is marked by sunset behind the Temple of the Sun viewed from the Temple of the Cross and sunrise behind the Temple of the Cross, viewed from the Temple of Inscriptions. Mendez and Karasik turn to dynastic history records along with the geometry of Janaab' Pakal's sarcophagus lid to argue for a coherent message constructed out of mythology, history, geometry, artistic imagery, and astronomy – a dense astronomical inscription in the "service of religion" (King 1993).

In Chapter 6, Susan Milbrath takes a broad

look at the "Venus Almanac" in various forms of representation throughout Mesoamerica. The key to Milbrath's argument is the proposal that the 584-day synodic period of Venus was recognized early in Mesoamerican history, and then was iconologized via the "Mexican year sign," as well as the iconographic quincunx pattern. The link between Venus and the Year Sign provokes a reconsideration of a specific almanac within the Madrid Codex, on Pages 12 through 18, which iconographically represents Chaak (the "Rain God"), rain, and serpents. Milbrath turns to the GMT to provide her with specific historical dates against which she tests her hypothesis that the pattern of 260-Day Count dates refer to an agricultural application of Venus observations.

The recognition of a Venus inscription within the Madrid Codex inspires Milbrath to look for similar constructs in other Mayan as well as Central Mexican venues. Chapter 6 goes on to unpack Venus applications in the almanacs of pages 46–50 in the Dresden Codex as well as Pages 27–28 and 29–46 in the Codex Borgia. In turn, these inspire the reconsideration of possible Venus representations at Bilbao, Chich'en Itza, and Mayapan from the Classic well into the Late Postclassic.

Finally, in Chapter 7, Michael Grofe reconsiders Glyphs F and G of the Supplementary Series. Not unlike the first two chapters of this book, Grofe returns to a question of origins in order to investigate the meaning of the introductory portion of the Supplementary Series. Glyphs G and F (constituting a hieroglyphic phrase) have long been understood in operation, though their intent has eluded elaboration. Grofe follows up a lead provided by Martha Macri that they may maintain a lunar function. Similar to a hypothesis proffered by David Kelley (1980) on the identities of the visible planets within Mayan calendrics, Grofe finds eclipse patterns in an originary sequence of G1 through G9.

Specifically, Grofe builds from Teeple's recognition that each subsequent repetition of a 260-Day Count date corresponds to a backwards sequence through the Glyphs G1 through G9. He suggests that a skywatcher keeping track of this pattern would be able to correlate it with the fact that three draconic periods are (very nearly) equivalent to two 260-Day rounds ($3 \times 173.31 = 519.93 \sim 2 \times 260 =$ 520). Finding that any eclipse event will occur within four days of a Glyph G9, Grofe suggests that the reading of G9 as *yih k'in nal*, which he translates as 'the place of the old sun,' points to the origin of the cycle in eclipse tracking. Here again, we confront a sophisticated application of computer software to verify the association, but also an intriguing argument for an astronomical inscription (eclipse records) within a ubiquitous calendric device (the "cycle of nine"). In the end, Grofe is suggesting that the immediate hieroglyphic context of what has been considered a rather opaque calendric component may illuminate the astronomical origins buried within the utility of the nine-day cycle.

These essays are not the final product establishing a new field – that is, they do not represent an Archaeoastronomy 2.0. Rather, they represent an array of the work currently being conducted in the field. Any one of these chapters may establish the agenda for the future, or it may be a combination of them drawn together, which establishes a new coherence. The final chapter attempts to provide one possibility – one theoretical paradigm for movement toward an established coherence, but it is a first draft of one, and certainly does not enjoy the complete support of everyone contributing to this volume, let alone the field as a whole. Nonetheless, it is intended to spur the conversation and provide further incentive for archaeoastronomers to find allies in related fields in order to push the collective work into a new space of relevance. Such alliances can only help to strengthen the resulting interpretations and value to Maya Studies more broadly.

Notes

1   The resulting effect is strongly reminiscent of the solar calendars found within rock formations in Baja California, and the much later solar ray effects within (currently United States Southwest) Pueblo cultures. At some level, this pattern begs for historical study to address the role that Mayan astronomy may have played in the diffusion of culture throughout the Western Hemisphere.

2   Two notes of caution are worth mentioning here. The first is that we have to recall that any such reconstruction was only hypothetically visible; even the most provocative celestial events can be rendered inaccessible by cloud cover, or fog, or even smoke. Second, I note

the "deep historical past" since even the most
sophisticated planetary models contain some
error, which propagates the farther one departs
from present observable data. These errors were
even greater during the 1980s and 1990s when
less accurate algorithms were used to project
into the past for the sake of computational
efficiency. The increased speed of more recent
machines has allowed for the incorporation of
greater accuracy even into free, open-source
planetaria software.

3   Schele and Freidel (1990: 87) in turn base their
interpretations on assumptions similar to those
behind Von Dechend's *Hamlet's Mill*.

4   Two notes are warranted regarding the accuracy of the calendar correlation. The first
is simply that the GMT family represents
three calendar correlation constants spanning
three days. While insignificant for many
astronomical events, a three-day tolerance can
prove significant for certain cases. Second, new
evidence has arisen recently that challenges the
accuracy of the GMT. If the GMT is incorrect
by more than a few days, then any work
dependent on it will be called into question.

References

Aimers, James J. and Prudence M. Rice, 2006.
Astronomy, Ritual, and the Interpretation of Maya
'E-Group' Architectural Assemblages. *Ancient
Mesoamerica* 17, 79–96.

Aldana, Gerardo, 2007. *The Apotheosis of Janaab' Pakal:
Science, History, and Religion at Classic Maya Palenque.*
University Press of Colorado, Boulder.

Anderson, Neal, Alfonso Morales and Moises Morales,
1981. A Solar Alignment of the Palace Tower at
Palenque. *Archaeoastronomy: the Bulletin of the Center
for Archaeoastronomy*, IV(3), 34–36.

Aveni, Anthony, 1975. *Possible Astronomical Orientations
in Ancient Mesoamerica. Archaeoastronomy in Pre-
Columbian America*. University of Texas Press, Austin,
163–190.

Aveni, Anthony, 1977. Concepts of positional astronomy
employed in ancient Mesoamerican architecture.
Native American Astronomy. University of Texas Press,
Austin, 3–19.

Aveni, Anthony, 1980. *Skywatchers of Ancient Mexico*.
University of Texas Press, Austin.

Aveni, Anthony, 1992. Moon and the Venus table: an
example of commensuration in the Maya calendar.
The Sky in Mayan Literature. Oxford University Press,
New York, 87–101.

Aveni, Anthony, 1992. Nobody Asked, but I Couldn't
Resist: a Response to Keith Kintigh on Archaeo-
astronomy and Archaeology. *Archaeoastronomy and
Ethnoastronomy News* 6, pp. 1, 4.

Aveni, Anthony, 2003. Archaeoastronomy in the Ancient
Americas. *Journal of Archaeological Research* 11(2)
June, 149–191.

Aveni, Anthony, Anne S. Dowd and Benjamin Vining,
2003. Maya Calendar Reform? Evidence from

Orientations of Specialized Architectural Assemblages.
Latin American Antiquity 14(2) June, 159–178

Aveni, Anthony and Horst Hartung, 1989. Uaxactun,
Guatemala, Group E and similar assemblages: An
archaeoastronomical reconsideration. In *World
Archaeoastronomy*, ed. A. Aveni. Cambridge University
Press, Cambridge. 441–460.

Aveni, Anthony and Lorren Hotaling 1994. Monumental
Inscriptions and the Observational Basis of Maya
Planetary Astronomy. *Archaeoastronomy* 19/*JHA* 25,
S21–S54.

Aveni, Anthony, Sharon Gibbs and Horst Hartung,
1975. The Caracol tower at Chichen Itza. an Ancient
Astronomical Observatory? *Science* 188, 977–985.

Baudez, Claude, 1987. Archaeoastronomy at Copan: an
Appraisal. *Indiana* 11, 63–71.

Bricker, Harvey, Anthony Aveni and Victoria Bricker
2001. Ancient Maya Documents Concerning the
Movements of Mars. *Proceedings of the National
Academy of Sciences* 98:4, 2107–2110.

Bricker, Harvey and Victoria Bricker, 2007. When was
the Dresden Codex Efficaceous? In *Skywatching in the
Ancient World: New Perspectives in Cultural Astronomy
Studies in Honor of Anthony F. Aveni* (C. Ruggles and G.
Urton, eds). University of Texas Press, Austin, 95–120.

Byers, Douglas, 1966. Frans Blom, 1893–1963. *American
Antiquity*, 31.3(1) January, 406–407.

Carlson, John, 1976. Astronomical Investigations
and Site Orientation Influences at Palenque. *Art,
Iconography and Dynastic History of Palenque Part 3.*
Pre-Columbian Art Research Institute, Pebble Beach,
CA, 107–122.

Carlson, John B., 1977. Copan Altar Q: the Maya
Astronomical Congress of A.D. 763? *Native American
Astronomy*. University of Texas Press, Austin, 100–109.

Closs, Michael, 1994. "Glyph for Venus as Evening Star."
Seventh Palenque Round Table, 1989, edited by Virginia
M. Fields. Pre-Columbian Art Research Institute, San
Francisco, 229–236.

Closs, Michael, Anthony Aveni and Bruce Crowley, 1984.
The Planet Venus and Temple 22 at Copán. *Indiana*
9, 221–247.

Coe, Michael D., 1975. "Native astronomy in Mesoamerica." *Archaeoastronomy in Pre-Columbian America.*
A. F. Aveni, editor. Austin: University of Texas Press,
pp. 3–31.

Coe, Michael D. 1999. "Foreward" *Native American
Astronomy*. (A. Aveni ed.). University of Texas Press,
Austin, p. ix.

Coe, Michael, 1999. *Breaking the Maya Code*. Thames &
Hudson, London.

Consolmagno, Guy J., 1966. Astronomy, Science Fiction
and Popular Culture: 1277 to 2001 (and Beyond).
Leonardo 29(2), 127–132.

Díaz-García, Salvador, 2006. *Monografías de Arquitectos
Siglo XX, Horst G. Hartung Franz*, Secretaría de Cultura
del Gobierno de Jalisco.

Dutting, Dieter, 1985. Lunar Periods and the Quest
for Rebirth in the Mayan Hieroglyphic Inscriptions.
Estudios de Cultura Maya 16, 113–147.

Eddy, John, 1977. Review of Archaeoastronomy in Pre-
Columbian America. *American Anthropologist* 79,
497–498.

Fash, William L., 1991. *Scribes, Warriors and Kings.*
Thames & Hudson, London.

Fernie, J. Donald, 1990. Marginalia: Stonehenge and the Archaeoastronomers. *American Scientist* 78(2) March–April, 103–105.

Freidel, David, Linda Schele and Joy Parker, 1993. *Maya Cosmos: Three Thousand Years on the Shaman's Path.* William Morrow and Co., New York.

Frye, Alton, 1966. Politics – The First Dimension of Space a review of Pride and Power: The Rationale of the Space Program by Vernon Van Dyke; Space and Society by Howard J. Taubenfeld; The Moon-Doggle: Domestic and International Implications of the Space Race by Amitai Etzioni. *Journal of Conflict Resolution* 10(1) March, 103–112.

Förstemann, Ernst, 1894. Zur Entzifferiing der Mayahandschriften, IV, Blatt 24 der Dresdener Mayahandschrift. So, 17. Dresden. English translation in *Bureau of Ethnology Bulletin* 28, 1904, Washington, 431–443.

Förstemann, Ernst, 1895. Entzifferung der Mayahand-schriften, V, Zu Ilresd. 71–73 und 51–58. 8, 12, Dresden. English translation in *Bureau of Ethnology Bulletin 2Q, 1904,* Washington, 445–453.

Gingerich, Owen, 1980. Forward. *Skywatchers of Ancient Mexico.* University of Texas Press, Austin.

Hartung, Horst, 1971. *Die Zeremonialzentren der Maya.* Akademische Druck und Verlagsanstalt, Graz.

Hartung, Horst, 1975. A Scheme of Probable Astronomical Projections in Mesoamerican Architecture. In *Archaeoastronomy in Pre-Columbian America.* (A. Aveni ed.). University of Texas Press, Austin, pp. 191–204.

Haramundanis, Katherine, 1973. Mayan Astro-archaeology: Review of *Die Zeremonialzentren der Maya. Journal for the History of Astronomy* 4, 201–202

Hawkins, Gerald S., 1965. *Stonehenge Decoded.* Doubleday, Garden City, N.Y.

Kelley, David H., 1980. Astronomical Identities of Mesoamerican Gods. *Journal for the History of Astronomy* 11 (*Archaeoastronomy Supplement (2)*), S1–S54.

King, David A., 1993. Science in the Service of Religion: The Case of Islam. In *Astronomy in the Service of Islam* (D.A. King ed.). Varorium Collected Studies, Ashgate, Aldershot.

Kintigh, Keith, 1992. I Wasn't Going to Say Anything but Since You Asked; Archaeoastronomy and Archaeology. *Archaeoastronomy and Ethnoastronomy News* 5(**1**), pp. 1, 4.

Lothrop, S. K., 1953. Oliver Garrison Ricketson, Jr. 1894–1952. *American Antiquity* 19(1) July, 69–72.

Lounsbury, Floyd, 1983. The Base of the Venus Table of the Dresden Codex, and its Significance for the Calendar–Correlation Problem. In *Calendars in Mesoamerica and Peru: Native American Computations of Time* (A. F. Aveni and G. Brotherston eds). BAR International Series 174, Archaeopress, Oxford, 1–26.

Lounsbury, Floyd, 1992a. Derivation of the Mayan-to-Julian Calendar Correlation from the Dresden Codex Venus Chronology. In *The Sky in Mayan Literature* (A. Aveni ed.). Oxford University Press, New York, 184–206.

Lounsbury, Floyd, 1992b. A Solution for the Number 1.5.5.0 of the Mayan Venus Table. In *The Sky in Mayan Literature* (A. F. Aveni ed.). Oxford University Press, New York, 207–215.

Malmström, Vincent, 1997. *Cycles of the Sun, Mysteries of the Moon: the Calendar in Mesoamerican Civilization.* University of Texas Press, Austin.

Morley, Sylvanus Griswold, 1916. The Supplementary Series in the Maya Inscriptions. *Holmes Anniversary Volume.* Carnegie Institution of Washington, 366–396.

Morley, Sylvanus Griswold, 1920. *The Inscriptions at Copan.* Carnegie Institution of Washington.

Morley, Sylvanus, 1925. The Copan expedition. *Carnegie Institution of Washington Yearbook 25,* 277–286.

Proskouriakoff, Tatiana, 1960. Historical Implications of a Pattern of Dates at Piedras Negras, Guatemala. *American Antiquity* XXV, No. 4, pp. 454–475.

Reyman, Jonathan, 1975. The nature and nurture of archaeoastronomical studies. *Archaeoastronomy in Pre-Columbian America* (A. Aveni ed.). University of Texas Press, Austin, 205–215.

Ricketson, Oliver, 1928. Notes on Two Maya Astronomic Observatories. *American Anthropologist* New Series 30(3) July–September, 434–444.

Ricketson, Oliver G., 1933. Excavations at Uaxactun. *Scientific Monthly* 37(1) July, 72–86.

Schele, Linda and David Freidel, 1990. *A Forest of Kings: the Untold Story of the Ancient Maya.* William and Morrow, New York.

Spinden, Herbert J., 1924. The Reduction of Maya Dates. *Papers of Peabody Museum Archaeology and Ethnology* VI(4), Cambridge, MA, Peabody Museum.

Sprajc, Ivan, 1996. *Venus, lluvia y maíz: Simbolismo y astronomía en la cosmovisión mesoamericana.* Colección Científica 318. Instituto Nacional de Antropología e Historia, México.

Stuart, David, 2005. *The Inscriptions from Temple XIX at Palenque.* Pre-Columbian Art Research Institute, San Francisco.

Tate, Carolyn, 1985. Summer Solstice Ceremonies Performed by Bird Jaguar III of Yaxchilan, Chiapas, Mexico. *Estudios de Cultura Maya* 16, 85–112.

Teeple, John E., 1925. Maya Inscriptions: Glyphs C, D, and E of the Supplementary Series. *American Anthropologist* New Series 27, 108–115.

Teeple, John E. 1931. Maya Astronomy. *Carnegie Institution of Washington Contributions to American Archaeology* 1(2), Publication 403.

Thompson, J. Eric., 1935. Maya Chronology: the Correlation Question. *Carnegie Institution of Washington Contributions to American Archaeology* 14

Thompson, J. Eric S., 1972. *A Commentary on the Dresden Codex.* American Philosophical Society, Philadelphia.

Thompson, J. Eric S., 1975. *Maya Hieroglyphic Writing: An Introduction.* University of Oklahoma Press, Norman.

Santillana, George and Hertha Von Dechend, 1969. *Hamlet's Mill.* Gambit, Boston.

Wingo, Walter, 1963. The Scramble into Space. *Science News-Letter* 84(22) November, 341–343.

1

Cosmic order at Chocolá: implications of solar observations of the eastern horizon at Chocolá, Suchitepéquez, Guatemala

Harold H. Green

Introduction

The eastern horizon at Chocolá, a Preclassic site on the Pacific piedmont of Guatemala at 14.6° N latitude, provides a physical template for the derivation of the pan-Mesoamerican 260-day "sacred" count and the 360-day count that is the chronological unit of the Maya Long Count.

Viewed from the site, peaks on the eastern horizon (and one prominent gap between peaks) delimit 20-day periods as they mark sunrises on days of zenith and nadir passage as well as the chronological midpoints between zenith passage and equinox and between equinox and nadir passage.[1] The long interval between the two zenith passages is 260 days, the time that the sun, tracked at the horizon, spends south of the zenith passage marker. The August 13 endpoint of this cycle also recalls the solar zenith passage at the Chocolá latitude that marked completion of the previous Maya era on 13.0.0.0.0 4 Ajaw 8 Kumk'u, August 13, 3114 BC. While other sites have been proposed as the place of origin of the 260-day count – notably Izapa and Copán – only at Chocolá has a horizon been identified with solar markers from which that count could have been readily derived. That the 260-day "sacred"

cycle may trace its origin to this zenith passage interval at Chocolá[2] is supported by the many alignments throughout Mesoamerica, from Teotihuacan to Copán, and from the Preclassic to the Postclassic, to sunrise or sunset on the dates that mark its endpoints at the Chocolá latitude, August 13 and April 30.

While the sun's journey along the horizon from zenith to winter solstice and back takes 260 days, that from the nadir passage marker to summer solstice and back requires 265 days. This 5-day asymmetry may provide an astronomical explanation for the five "uncounted," "unnamed" days of the *way haab* period that follows each 360-day *haab*. But for these five "extra" days in the north, the solar cycle would be 360-days and would pivot symmetrically about each of the principal solar event axes (solstices, equinoxes, and zenith and nadir passages). Just as the 260-day sacred count may have been derived from observing the sun's path along the horizon between the two zenith passages at this latitude, the 360-day count that is the chronological unit of the Long Count underlying the Classic Maya practice of marking period endings (multiples of 360-

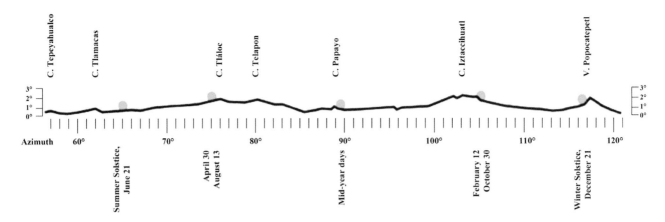

Fig. 1.1. The eastern horizon seen from Cuicuilco (after Broda 1993: 279–280, fig. 9.11 and table 9.1)

day periods) with "great stones," may have its origin in this idealized 360-day solar cycle observable at the Chocolá horizon.

The horizon evidence to be presented in this chapter supports the conclusion that Chocolá was sited where it is at least in part because the natural markers on the site's eastern horizon readily enabled derivation of the 260-day and 360-day counts fundamental to calendrical development.

Solar horizon markers in Mesoamerica

Both in method and motivation, research at Chocolá has found inspiration in previous reporting related to ancient solar horizon observations in Mesoamerica. Alignment studies by Aveni and Hartung document "a scheme for counting the days derived by following the annual course of the sun on the horizon" (Aveni and Hartung 1986: 1–2, 1991: 86). Barbara Tedlock has described how both the ancient and contemporary Maya have marked the sun at the horizon:

> The sun is the ruler of the cosmos for ancient as well as contemporary Maya peoples, and his two annual passages across the zenith were, and still are, used to fix dates in the agricultural calendar. Today, as in the past, the eastern and western directions are established through the observation of the intersection of the daily path of the sun with the horizon, and time is marked by the sun's progress along the horizon. (B. Tedlock 1992: 19)

At Waxactun, the Late Preclassic prototype E-group marks the northern and southern extremes (the solstices) and the approximate midpoint (the equinoxes) of the annual solar journey (Aveni and Hartung 1989), and, as

will be demonstrated later in this chapter, likely zenith and nadir passages as well.

Johanna Broda (1993) has described ancient solar horizon observations in the central Mexican highlands, especially at the eastern horizon of Cuicuilco, situated approximately 2 km southeast of Cerro Zacatepetl in southwestern Mexico City. Viewing this horizon from the great Preclassic pyramid at the site, the summer solstice sunrise "occurs close to Cerro Tlamacas;" the "mid-year days" (as distinct from the equinoxes)[3] are "marked by the conspicuous horizon elevation of Cerro Papayo"; and the winter solstice sun rises "behind the northern slope of Popocatepetl" (Broda 1993: 277–280). Broda describes "another remarkable property" of the Cuicuilco horizon: two other peaks (Tlaloc and Iztaccihuatl) are located such that they approximately mark sunrises that correspond to the dates of April 30, August 13, October 30, and February 12. The first two dates are "symmetrically placed about the June solstice" and the latter two dates are "symmetrically placed about the December solstice," such that "the four dates … delimit two fixed calendar cycles of 260 days within each solar year …"[4] (Broda 1993: 280, 261) (See Fig. 1.1). Broda concludes that the Cuicuilco site was consciously selected for the purpose of making these observations, and that it

> was related to the very origins of calendrical practice and the construction of the Mesoamerican calendrical and geometrical system during the first millennium BC. The great volcanoes were used, in this case, as natural markers on the horizon. (Broda 1993: 283)[5]

Iwaniszewski has documented a "solar horizon calendar" on the eastern horizon

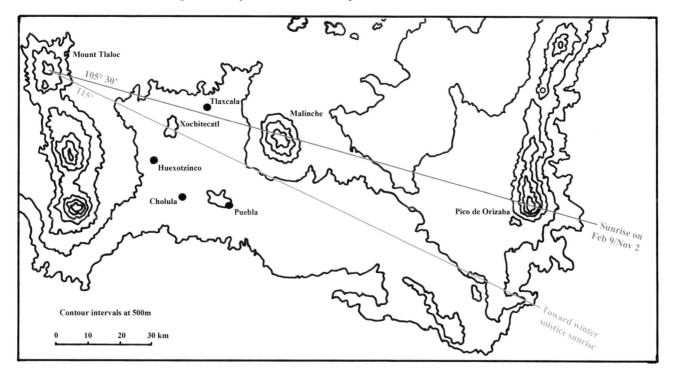

viewed from an ancient rectangular double-walled stone enclosure atop Mount Tlaloc (4150 m), the highest peak in the Sierra del Frio located approximately 51 km northeast (14° north of east) of the Cuicuilco pyramid (Iwaniszewski 1994; Broda 1993: 280, table 9.1).[6] From this viewpoint, alignments to peaks on the eastern horizon or of walls of the enclosure delimit 20-day periods as they mark sunrises on February 9–10, March 1, and the vernal equinox (March 21), as well as sunrises on the autumnal equinox (September 22), October 13, and November 1–2. The sun rises over La Malinche and Pico de Orizaba, the first peak aligned in front of the second, on February 9 and 10, and again on November 1 and 2 (see Fig. 1.2). The southern walls of the stone structure are aligned to sunrise on March 1 and October 13, 20 days later/earlier than the La Malinche/Pico de Orizaba dates. The northern interior wall is aligned very close to the equinox sunrise, leading Iwaniszewski to conclude that, as documented by Aveni and colleagues at the Templo Mayor in Tenochtitlan (Aveni *et al.* 1988), "the equinoxes were pivotal points in the horizon calendar" (Iwaniszewski 1994: 167). Iwaniszeski further concluded that the Mount Tlaloc evidence was consistent with ideas of Tichy and Aveni that ancient Mesoamericans

had used a "horizon-orientation calendar" based upon 20-day markers at the skyline (Iwaniszewski 1994: 173; see also Tichy 1981; 1990; Aveni *et al.* 1988).

The Ch'orti' Maya of southern Guatemala also derived calendric periods from solar markers at the horizon:

> … [T]he Chorti astronomer-elders observe the celestial phenomena on the visible horizon from the temple, placed in the center of the earth. In this way they trace sacred time upon astronomical time and their calendric periods upon the solar cycles. …

> From the temple balcony, each astronomer-elder observes the progressive movement of the sun, from the winter solstice to the summer solstice. In this regard they have points of reference on the visible horizon which serve them as geographic index markers: high hills, topographic irregularities or monuments (crosses), both in the east and in the west … These are the 'landmarks' corresponding to the 'junctions' (literal) of the sun which mark the angles of the world. (Girard 1995: 69, 56)

Most recently, Alonso Mendez and colleagues have described solar horizon markers at Palenque. As viewed from the Temple of the Sun in the Cross Group, markers on the eastern horizon demarcate the solstices, equinoxes, and zenith and nadir passages (Mendez *et al.* 2005). The summer solstice sunrise appears where the base of the Temple of the Cross meets the horizon; the zenith passages are marked by the

Fig. 1.2. Sunrises at the peaks of La Malinche and Pico de Orizaba, as viewed from Mount Tlaloc (Iwaniszewski 1994: 171, fig. 10, by permission of Stanislaw Iwaniszewski and the Society for American Archaeology)

center of the roof comb of the Temple of the Cross; the equinoxes by a gap in the horizon at the base of the Mirador; the nadir passages by a point on the north slope of the Mirador; and the winter solstice by the peak of the Mirador. Each of these solar events has a counterpart marker within the architecture of the Temple of the Sun itself: shafts of light, narrowed by that architecture, culminate at distinct points within the structure on each of the solar events.

Despite clear indications of the importance of the solar zenith and nadir passages at Palenque, questions remain concerning the antiquity of marking important solar events either at the horizon as at Cuicuilco or using manmade constructions as was done at Waxactun and, in part, at Palenque. This chapter addresses questions of where the practice of tracking the sun at the horizon may have originated and the purposes for which this tracking may have been intended. While the Late Preclassic Waxactun E-group marked the solstices and equinoxes with manmade structures, this complex likely had predecessors that used only the natural landscape. If so, where were they located? As the horizon at Palenque and the architecture of the Temple of the Sun were used to mark zenith and nadir passages as well as the solstices and the equinoxes, where and when did this broader tradition of marking the sun's journey along the horizon originate? To what extent did such a tradition contribute to the derivation of fundamental elements of cosmology and calendrics?

Sunrise observations at Chocolá's eastern horizon

The Chocolá archaeological site is located on the Pacific piedmont of Guatemala (latitude 14° 36.6' N, longitude 91° 25.7' W) at an elevation of 500–1000 m HAE, midway between Izapa and Kaminaljuyú, and close to Tak'alik Ab'aj and El Baúl, sites with some of the earliest hieroglyphic texts. For three seasons commencing in 2003 the Proyecto Arqueológico Chocolá (PACH), under the direction of Jonathan Kaplan, investigated the site. Reconnaissance and mapping resulted in the identification of more than 80 mounds, together with substantial remains of architecture and monuments, within an area of approximately 5.5 × 2 km along the terraced

ridge between the Rio Chocolá and the Rio Chichoy where the town of Chocolá is situated today (Kaplan and Valdés 2004; Kaplan 2008). Initial identification of elite residences in the North Group and an administrative/ceremonial center in the Central Group was confirmed during the 2004 field season (Kaplan *et al.* 2006: 56). Ceramics evidence indicates that the major developmental emphasis occurred at Chocolá between 900 and 100 BC, with occupation conceivably dating from as early as 1200 BC (Kaplan and Valdés 2004: 82–83; Kaplan 2008: 403).

The top of Mound 1 in the Central Group was selected for all horizon observations because it is one of the taller mounds identified to date, and it has an unparalleled view of the eastern horizon (Fig. 1.3).[7] Observations were made and documented of sunrises on or near the solstices, equinoxes, zenith and nadir passages, and the chronological midpoints between equinox and zenith passage and between equinox and nadir passage.

As a check on the accuracy of the observed horizon data, the positions (by azimuth and altitude) of the horizon markers were calculated from topographical maps and compared to solar positions (azimuths and altitudes) derived from U.S. Naval Observatory tables as well as Starry Night Pro software (Anderson *et al.* 1999).

Solstices and equinoxes

On June 21, 2003, PACH archaeologists observed the summer solstice sunrise at a "natural rest" on the northern slope of Cerro 2665[8] (Valdés *et al.* 2003: 452).

On March 21, 2006, sunrise occurred on the southern slope of Cerro Paquisís (Fig. 1.4a); the sun had passed the bottom of the prominent gap between Volcán Atitlán and Cerro Paquisís by sunrise on March 16, 2006. While there is no visible horizon feature on this slope of Cerro Paquisís to mark the equinox sunrise, there is a "virtual marker" that may have significance. Although it does not appear to be visible from Mound 1, Volcán Toliman (3158 m) is situated directly behind Cerro Paquisís, as illustrated in the Google Earth image (Fig. 1.5), and its south summit appears to coincide with, or very nearly approximate, the location of the "first gleam" of sunrise on March 21 (Fig. 1.6). This may, of course, be only coincidence, but its possible significance should be considered and explored further, given that Volcán Toliman is one of the three great volcanoes in the vicinity of Lake Atitlán, the others being Volcán Atitlán and Volcán San Pedro. If ancient Chocolenses were aware of the location of the Toliman summit in relation to Chocolá's eastern horizon as viewed from Mound 1, they would have known that this peak marked sunrise on the equinoxes.

On December 20, 2005,[9] the sun rose at an azimuth of approximately 114°, where the south slope of Volcán Atitlán merges into the horizon that slopes to the Pacific Ocean (Fig. 1.4b). Sunrises on the solstices are not associated with distinct natural markers at the Chocolá horizon.

Zenith and nadir passages

Sunrise observation on the solstices and the equinoxes has long been documented as a function of Lowland E-groups (Ricketson and Ricketson 1937; Aveni and Hartung 1989), and many Preclassic centers on the Pacific Coast were oriented to sunrise or sunset on the solstices (Malmström 1978; Aveni and Hartung 2000), including Izapa, Chiapa de Corzo, Kaminaljuyu, and Tak'alik Ab'aj.[10] However, according to Aveni, the principal reference points in the astronomy of ancient tropical civilizations were the solar zenith and nadir, marked at the horizon:

> [B]ecause of the remarkable differences in the arrangement and motion of celestial bodies as viewed from the tropical and temperate zones, we may expect that different systems of astronomy might develop in these zones … [N]early all tropical cultures that developed indigenous astronomical systems, regardless of whether the motive was largely practical or religious, gravitated toward a reference system consisting of zenith and nadir as poles and the horizon as a fundamental reference circle. Such an arrangement stands in remarkable contrast to the celestial pole-equator (or ecliptic) systems developed by ancient civilizations of the temperate zone. (Aveni 1981: 161)

At dawn on the day of northern zenith passage, April 30, 2006, the sun rose in the gap between Cerro 2665 and Cerro Paquisís (Fig. 1.7a). Sunrise on August 13 also occurs in this gap. The significance of this horizon marker for zenith passage derives at least in part from the fact that August 13 marks completion of the 13th baktun of the previous era, 13.0.0.0.0 4 Ajaw 8 Kumk'u (August 13, 3114 BC), also a zenith passage date at Chocolá.[11]

Far down on the south slope of Atitlán, Volcán Fuego can be seen on a clear morning from Mound 1 at an azimuth of approximately 105° (see Fig. 1.3), close to the azimuth of nadir passage sunrise.[12] On February 9, 2006, the sun rose at approximately 3 solar diameters to the right of the summit of Volcán Fuego (Fig. 1.7b), within parameters noted by Aveni and Hartung for evaluating solar orientations at Preclassic sites on the Pacific coast (Aveni and Hartung 2000: 64).[13] This orientation is similar to that documented by Iwaniszewski at Mount Tlaloc, from which the distant peaks of La Malinche and Pico de Orizaba mark sunrises on February 9–10 and November 1–2 and "[t]his orientation pattern appears in a great number of Mexican highland sites …" (Iwaniszewski 1994: 166–167, fig. 7 171, figure 10).

Solar markers between zenith passage and equinox, and between equinox and nadir passage

At the latitude of Chocolá and Copán, the interval between equinox and zenith passage is 40 days (2 *winal*), as is the interval between equinox and nadir passage. At Copán the approximate chronological midpoint between equinox and zenith passage, dividing the 40 days into two 20-day (1 *winal*) periods, is marked by the Stela 12-10 baseline (Aveni 2001: 252–255; Merrill 1945).[14] At the Chocolá horizon, Cerro Paquisís and Volcán Atitlán play an important role in the interpretation of solar events there because they mark sunrises that divide the 40–day periods between the equinox and zenith passage, and between the equinox and nadir passage, into approximately equal 20-day (*winal*) periods. In this way, they are analogous to the much later Stela 12-10 baseline at Copán (Aveni 2001: 251–255; Aldana 2002).[15]

On April 9, 2006,[16] the sun rose close to the summit of Cerro Paquisís (Fig. 1.8a). The chronological midpoints between zenith passage and equinox occur at Chocolá on April 10 and September 2. On March 3, 2006, the sun rose behind Volcán Atitlán (Fig. 1.8b). The chronological midpoints between equinox and nadir passage are March 1 and October 12. These sunrises occurred approximately 1–3 solar diameters to the right of each summit, within the 4–6 solar diameter parameter used by Aveni and Hartung in evaluating Preclassic solar orientations (Aveni and Hartung 2000:

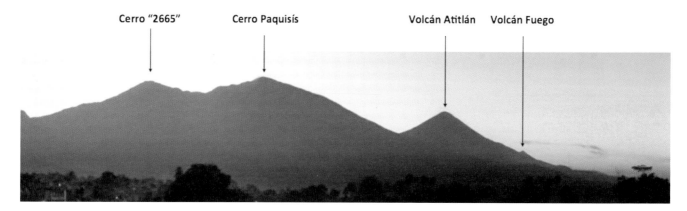

Fig. 1.3. (above) Panorama of the eastern horizon as seen from Mound 1 (photo by the author)

Fig. 1.4. Sunrises on (a) March 21, 2006 (photo by the author), and (b) (at the top of the opposite page) December 20, 2005 (photo by Molly Green)

64), and not significantly different from results that Aveni has reported for the Stela 12-10 baseline at Copán (Aveni 2001: 254). The existence of a natural horizon marker dividing the period between equinox and nadir passage into two 20-day *winal* periods has not previously been suggested in the literature or documented as such in the Mesoamerican landscape.[17]

Trecena marker

One other marker observed at Chocolá's eastern horizon may have been noted by ancient astronomers. The time for the sun to

move between the summit of Cerro 2665 and the zenith passage marker at the bottom of the gap between Cerro Paquisís and Cerro 2665 is 13 days (April 30 to May 13 and July 31 to August 13) (see Fig. 1.9).[18] This solar marker may have served as a 13-day alert for the onset of the rainy season during the sun's northern journey along the horizon. Perhaps more significantly, on the sun's southern journey this marker would have served as a 13-day alert for sunrise on southern zenith passage (August 13), the day that commemorates the completion of the previous era on 13.0.0.0.0 4 Ajaw 8 Kumk'u. It also signals the start of a new 260-day (13 *winal*) interval between solar zenith

Chocolá Mound 1

Fig. 1.5. Google Earth image illustrating the position of the south summit of Volcán Toliman in relation to Mound 1 at Chocolá

passages. This marker of the 13 days leading up to the commemoration of the 13 baktun cycle and to the beginning of a new 13 *winal* cycle may have marked what Eliade calls the "regeneration of time," a periodic repetition of or reference to cosmogonic events (Eliade 1954: 72; see Stuart 1996).

Summary of horizon data

The Chocolá sunrise data are set forth in Table 1.1, and are illustrated in Figure 1.10, showing the demarcation of the sun's path along that horizon by markers for zenith and nadir passages, and the chronological midpoints between zenith and equinox and equinox and nadir.

A measure of the accuracy of the observed horizon data can be obtained by calculating the azimuths of the horizon markers from topographical maps and comparing that data to solar positions derived from U.S. Naval Observatory tables as well as Starry Night Pro software (Anderson *et al.* 1999). The results are shown in Table 1.2. The positional difference for each solar horizon marker is less than the 2° parameter noted by Aveni and Hartung (Aveni and Hartung 2000: 64; see Note 13).

Aveni has presented the Copán data relating to the significance of the Stela 12-10 baseline by means of a time diagram "showing the hypothetical segmentation of the year into uinals based on sunsets observed along the Stela 12-10 baseline on the days of equinox, solstice, and solar zenith passage" (Aveni 2001: 254, fig. 90). However, if applied to Chocolá, such a time diagram would not illustrate important implications derived from the horizon itself, since the time diagram presents the solar cycle as pivoted about the equinoxes, emphasizing the asymmetrical division of the year by that axis into 180 and 185 days, rather than pivoted about zenith passage in "convenient 20-day blocks" (Aveni 2001: 254, and fig. 90). The implications of Chocolá's solar horizon markers can best be understood by avoiding assumptions based upon temperate zone astronomy (see Aveni 1981: 161), and by examining the sun's journey along the horizon, as illustrated in the Chocolá horizon diagram (Fig. 1.11).

Discussion: implications of the Chocolá horizon observations

One of the enduring questions about ancient Mesoamerica relates to when and where the 260-day count originated. The 260-day count does not have a clear or readily apparent justification, and a convincing rationale for its origin has long eluded researchers. The evidence from solar observations at Chocolá's eastern horizon affords a more precise explanation of the origin of the 260-day count than has been previously offered, and one that is also consistent with earlier ideas of Thompson, Malmström, and Aveni.

The Chocolá horizon data (see Fig. 1.11) also highlight the asymmetry between the sun's path along the horizon south of zenith passage to winter solstice and back (260 days), and its path north of nadir passage to summer solstice and back (265 days). What disturbs the symmetry are the five "extra" days of the sun's journey north of zenith passage — the days regarded throughout Mesoamerica as "uncounted," "nameless," and "leftover" (Thompson 1950: 106, 117–118; León-Portilla 1988: 47, 145). This 5-day asymmetry of the sun's path about the zenith and nadir reference markers appears to offer a heretofore unrecognized astronomical explanation for the "uncounted" and "nameless" characterization attributed to the five extra days. If it were not for these "leftover" days, the sun's annual cycle would be 360 days and would appear fully symmetrical about each of the solar axes (the solstices, equinoxes, and zenith and nadir passages). The ancient Maya have left substantial evidence that they understood the cosmic order represented by the symmetry of this 360-day count.

260-day cycle

Nuttall was the first to see a possible connection between the 260-day cycle and the 260-day interval between solar zenith passages in the narrow latitudinal band just south of 15° N (where Izapa, Tak'alik Ab'aj, Chocolá, and Copán are located) (Nuttall 1928). Ola Apenes and Helga Larsen both suggested that Copán might be the site where the 260-day count originated (Apenes 1936; Larsen 1936). Robert Merrill reached a similar conclusion, and speculated further that "the Maya calendar began with the zenith passage at Copán on August 14" in "about 40 BC" (Merrill 1945:

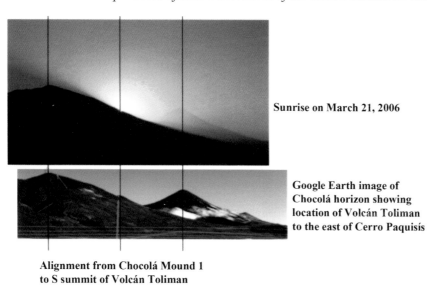

Sunrise on March 21, 2006

**Google Earth image of
Chocolá horizon showing
location of Volcán Toliman
to the east of Cerro Paquisís**

**Alignment from Chocolá Mound 1
to S summit of Volcán Toliman**

*Fig. 1.6. Comparison
of "first gleam" at
sunrise on March
21, 2006 with a
Google Earth image
of Chocolá's eastern
horizon illustrating
the location of Volcán
Toliman's south
summit in relation to
Mound 1*

*Fig. 1.7. Sunrises
(a) in the gap between
Cerro 2665 and
CerroPaquisís on April
30, 2006, and
(b) behind Volcán
Fuego on February 10,
2006 (photos by Byron
Lemus)*

309, 311). However, Thompson contended that the 260-day count was derived from a permutation of the numbers 13 and 20, and that any connection to the 260-day interval between zenith passages was "very unlikely" (Thompson 1950: 98–99).[19]

Thompson did not accept the suggestion that the 260-day cycle was chosen because it approximated the period of human gestation, considering the zenith passage derivation a "better explanation" but "very unlikely" due to "serious drawbacks" (*ibid.*). First, one must assume that "the cycle of 260 days originated on the periphery of the area in which it was current, and that, spreading northward and westward, it was eagerly adopted by peoples for whom it had no solar significance" (Thompson 1950: 98). However, the evidence of the extent to which the dates that bracket this interval at the latitude of Chocolá were commemorated in architecture all over Mesoamerica supports the conclusion that this is indeed what occurred (see below). Second, Thompson argued that if the 260-day interval had significance, "surely there would have been a complementary period of 105 days to maintain a correspondence with the solar phenomena." This presumes that a complete cycle must total the length of the tropical year, surely a Eurocentric assumption. In any event, the 265 days of the solar journey north of nadir passage and the 5 "uncounted" days highlight the asymmetries associated with those periods in contrast to the symmetry of the 260-day and 360-day periods. Further, the 105 days north of zenith passage to summer solstice and back (see Fig. 1.11) approximate the length of the rainy season cycle. Finally, Thompson contended that there was "absolutely no evidence" that the 260-day cycle originated "anywhere along latitude 14° 30' N, which is on the periphery of the area it covered." The solar phenomena marked at the eastern horizon at Chocolá provide such evidence.

Vincent Malmström argued against Copán as the place of origin of the 260-day almanac on both chronological and geographical grounds: Copán was founded too late to have been the birthplace of the 260-day count, and the observations of German naturalist Gadow that the day names commemorate lowland tropical animals persuaded Malmström that the 260-day count "must have been devised in a region where such creatures were present" (Malmström 1978: 106–107;

1973). Malmström concluded that only an ancient site situated in lowlands just south of latitude 15° N would meet all of the necessary criteria. "The only such site which exists in Mesoamerica is Izapa" (Malmström 1978: 107).[20] Malmström also asserted that the 260-day and 365-day counts were initiated at Izapa in 1358 BC and during the period 1323–1320 BC, respectively, based on his analysis of "the internal structures of the calendars themselves" (Malmström 1978: 107).[21] Both counts could have originated within the 35-year period, Malmström reasoned, from a "recognition of astronomical events which could be easily and repeatedly observed at Izapa," the astronomical events being the zenith passages separated by an interval of 260 days and the summer solstice sunrise marked at the summit of Volcán Tajumulco as viewed from Izapa (Malmström 1978: 109).[22] However, Malmström did not identify any solar horizon marker at Izapa other than Volcán Tajumulco, and the 260-day count would have been more easily identified from the more abundant and readily observable horizon markers at the eastern horizon of nearby Chocolá.

The evidence from the Chocolá horizon affords both a specific and an astronomical explanation of how and where the 260-day pan-Mesoamerican "sacred" count may have originated. It is a more precise explanation than has been previously offered, but one that also benefits from and is consistent with earlier ideas put forward by Thompson, Malmström, and Aveni.

While there is unlikely to be an "either/or" explanation for the origin of the 260-day count, a strong rationale for its adoption as the primary count disclosed by the Chocolá horizon data is that it is readily derived by observing the sun's path along the horizon south of the zenith passage marker (the prominent gap between Cerros 2665 and Paquisis), between the two days of the year when the sun reaches the center of the cosmos. While this is also true at Izapa (Malmström 1978), no horizon demarcating this solar journey has been identified there, as at Chocolá. Additionally, this is a path that is observedly symmetrical about the zenith "reference pole" (Aveni 1981): the sun takes 80 days (4 *winal*) to move from zenith passage to nadir passage; 100 days (5 *winal*) to advance from nadir passage to winter solstice and back to nadir passage; and another 80

Solar event	Date at Chocolá	Observation date	Time from previous event	
			Days	Winal.K'in
Winter solstice	Dec 21	Dec 20	50 (49)	2.10
Nadir passage	Feb 9	Feb 10	50 (51)	2.10
Nadir/equinox midpoint	Mar 1	Mar 3	20 (22)	1
Vernal equinox	Mar 21	Mar 21	20 (20)	1
Zenith/equinox midpoint	Apr 10	Apr 9	20 (19)	1
Zenith passage	Apr 30	Apr 30	20 (20)	1
Summer solstice	June 21	June 21	52 (52)	2.12
Zenith passage	Aug 13		53	2.13
Zenith/equinox midpoint	Sept 2		20	1
Autumnal equinox	Sept 22		20	1
Nadir/equinox midpoint	Oct 12		20	1
Nadir passage	Nov 1		20	1
Total			**365 (365)**	**18.5**
Trecena (13-day) marker	May 12		13	
Trecena (13-day) marker	July 31		−13	

Table 1.1 Summary of Chocolá horizon data

days (4 *winal*) to return from nadir passage to zenith passage, for a total of 260 days (13 *winal*)[23] (See Fig. 1.11). This new explanation manifests permutations of the numbers 13 and 20 (Thompson 1950: 98–99)

The 260-day count may also be a microcosm of the first 13 baktuns of the Maya era that commenced on August 13, 3114 BC, a day of southern zenith passage at the latitude of Chocolá. These 13 baktuns were completed on December 23, 2012 AD, two days after winter solstice,[24] a period of 20 *may* as well.[25] The 260-day count is the one solar cycle that can be said to consist of "20-day markers centered on a solar zenith passage date" and for which the zenith and nadir passages, marked at the horizon, are the fundamental reference poles (Aveni and Hartung 1991: 86; Aveni 1981). Of all of the solar events marked at the Chocolá horizon, zenith passage is the only event where the sun reaches the center of the sky at noon, becoming the "ruler of the cosmos" (B. Tedlock 1992: 19).

Additional support for the primacy of the 260-day count in Mesoamerica, as well as for its origination or confirmation at the Chocolá latitude, is provided by the fact that the zenith passage dates at that latitude (April 30 and August 13) are marked at the horizon or by architectural alignments at sites all over Mesoamerica, from Teotihuacan to Copán and from the Preclassic to the Postclassic. Building

Date of solar event	Horizon marker	Azimuth of horizon marker* (deg)	Azimuth of first light** (deg)	Azimuth difference (deg)
9 April 06	V. Fuego	104.6	105.6	−1.1
1 Mar 06	V. Atitlan	97.7	99.2	−1.5
10 Apr 06	C. Paquisis	82.2	83.8	−1.6
30 Apr 06	ZP Gap	77.3	76.3	+0.9
12 May 06	C. 2665	72.6	73.2	−0.5
31 July 06	C. 2665	72.6	73.2	−0.5
13 Aug 06	ZP Gap	77.3	76.5	+0.7
2 Sept 06	C. Paquisis	82.2	83.9	−1.8
12 Oct 06	V. Atitlan	97.7	99.1	−1.4
1 Nov 06	V. Fuego	104.6	105.5	−0.9

* Using UTM data from Instituto Geografico Nacional (Guatemala) topographical maps, 1960
** Using tables from the US Naval Observatory, adjusted for atmospheric refraction, earth's curvature, and elevation of horizon

Table 1.2 Comparison of azimuths of horizon markers and solar events (first light) from Chocolá (Mound 1)

orientations toward sunrise or sunset on April 30 and August 13 "occur with noteworthy frequency in Mesoamerica" (Broda 1993: 261–262). The Stirling complex at La Venta (900–600 BC) is oriented to sunset on April 30 and August 13 (Malmström 1978), as are the Pyramid of the Sun at Teotihuacan (*ibid.*; Aveni

Fig. 1.8. Sunrises (a) behind Cerro Paquisís on April 9, 2006, and (b) behind Volcán Atitlán on March 3, 2006 (photos by Byron Lemus)

Fig. 1.9. Sunrise behind Cerro 2665 on May 12, 2006 (photo by Byron Lemus)

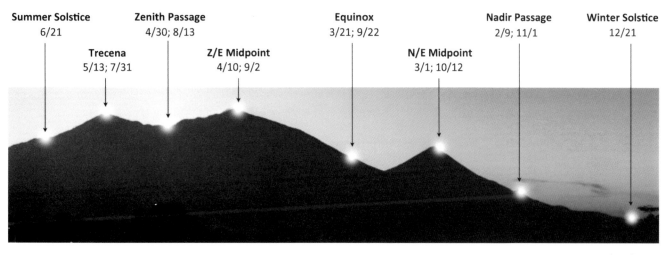

Summary of solar horizon markers labels:

Summer Solstice 6/21

Trecena 5/13; 7/31

Zenith Passage 4/30; 8/13

Z/E Midpoint 4/10; 9/2

Equinox 3/21; 9/22

N/E Midpoint 3/1; 10/12

Nadir Passage 2/9; 11/1

Winter Solstice 12/21

Fig. 1.10. Chocolá eastern horizon showing a summary of solar horizon markers

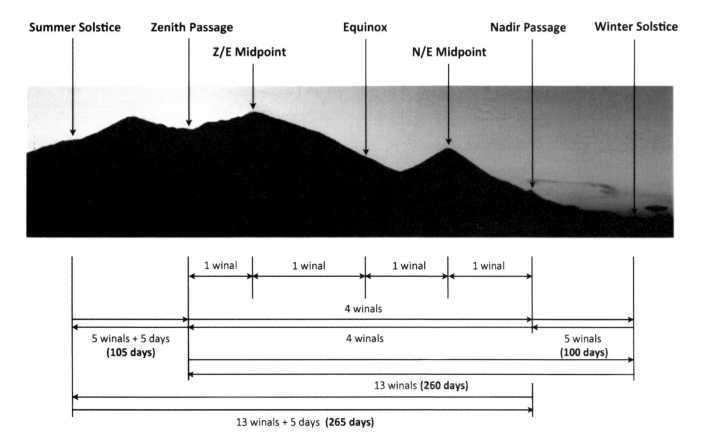

Labels: **Summer Solstice**, **Zenith Passage**, **Z/E Midpoint**, **Equinox**, **N/E Midpoint**, **Nadir Passage**, **Winter Solstice**

1 winal | 1 winal | 1 winal | 1 winal

4 winals

5 winals + 5 days **(105 days)** | 4 winals | 5 winals **(100 days)**

13 winals **(260 days)**

13 winals + 5 days **(265 days)**

Fig. 1.11. Chocolá horizon diagram with time periods expressed in winals

2001), the Cinco Pisos pyramid at Edzná, Campeche (Malmström 1978; 1991), and a solar marker in the Palace Tower at Palenque (Anderson *et al.* 1981), although April 30 and August 13 are not the dates of zenith passage at any of these sites. The alignment across the Classic Temple I and IV pyramids at Tikal, as well as the alignment of both window 1 of the Caracol at Chichén Itzá and the west door of the Round Tower at Mayapán, is to sunset on the zenith passage dates at Chocolá, not to the dates of zenith passage at Tikal, Chichén Itzá, or Mayapán (Malmström 1997: 166–173; Aveni *et al.* 2004). Underground chambers at Teotihuacan and "zenith tubes" at Xochicalco and Monte Alban mark not only the dates of local zenith passage but of the April 30 and August 13 zenith passages at the Chocolá latitude (Soruco Sáenz 1991; Morante 1993, 1996, 2001: 50, 2010; Broda 2000: 415, 2006: 190).

While Broda pointed to the "noteworthy frequency" with which August 13/April 30 sunrise orientations, such as that at the eastern horizon of Preclassic Cuicuilco, occur throughout Mesoamerica, she did not recognize that these orientations, including that at Cuicuilco, reflect the zenith passage sunrise dates at the latitude of the 260-day zenith passage interval where the Preclassic sites of Chocolá, Izapa and Tak'alik Ab'aj are located. Similarly, while Iwaniszewski noted that the alignments between Mount Tlaloc and the peaks of La Malinche and Pico de Orizaba, with bearings of 105–107° and marking sunrises on February 9–10/November 1–2, occur at a "great number of Mexican highland sites" (Iwaniszewski 1994: 166; see also Aveni and Gibbs 1976), he also did not recognize that these orientations, including that at Mount Tlaloc, reflect the nadir passage sunrise dates at the Chocolá latitude.

As Malmström was the first to observe, the significance of the pan-Mesoamerican commemoration of the August 13/April 30 zenith passage sunrise (or sunset) dates lies in the association between the 260-day zenith passage interval and the 260-day sacred count. The Chocolá data demonstrate how, very early on, the 260-day count, as well as the 20-day structure of both the 260-day and 360-day counts, could have been readily derived by observing the sun's path in relation to natural markers at the horizon. As Broda and

Iwaniszewski have documented (albeit without recognizing the association with the 260-day zenith passage interval), other sites such as Cuicuilco and Mount Tlaloc have been located where the 260-day zenith passage interval of the Chocolá latitude is marked at the horizon, even though the local zenith passage dates deviate significantly from August 13 and April 30.[26]

The 360-day cycle, and an astronomical explanation for the five "uncounted" days

The Chocolá horizon diagram (Fig. 1.11) also highlights the asymmetry of the sun's path north of zenith passage, as contrasted to the symmetrical path south of nadir passage. The sun's course south of nadir passage to winter solstice and back takes 5 *winal* (100 days) while that north of zenith passage to summer solstice and back requires 5 *winal* and 5 days (105 days). What disturbs the symmetry are the five "extra" days of the sun's journey north of zenith passage – the days regarded throughout Mesoamerica as "uncounted," "nameless," and "leftover" (Thompson 1950: 106, 117–118; León-Portilla 1988: 47, 145). Given the interest of the ancient Maya in finding symmetrical, harmonious and whole number relationships – that is, order – in nature (see Thompson 1950: 150–151; Carlson 1981; Farriss 1987; Powell 1997), ancient observers of the sun at the Chocolá horizon would likely have been impressed by the division of time between zenith and nadir passage into four 20-day (*winal*) periods, and by the symmetry of the 260-day (13 *winal*) journey to and from winter solstice in contrast to the asymmetry of the 265-day (13 *winal* + 5 *k'in*) journey north of nadir passage to and from summer solstice.

If it were not for these "leftover" days, the sun's annual cycle would be 360 days and would appear fully symmetrical about each of the solar axes (the solstices, equinoxes, and zenith and nadir passages) (Fig. 1.12). The sun's journey north of nadir passage would equal the 260-day cycle south of zenith passage. The five extra days in the north are what throw off the otherwise cosmic symmetry. It is this 5-day asymmetry of the solar cycles about the zenith and nadir reference poles that affords the first astronomical explanation for the "uncounted" and "nameless" characterization attributed to the five extra days. And the ancient Maya have left substantial evidence that they perceived a cosmic order in this symmetry of the idealized solar cycle of 360 days and embodied it in their other fundamental count, the period of 360 days, the *haab*'.[27]

As early as 1925, Long concluded from his examination of the Books of Chilam Balam and the Chronicle of Oxkutzcab that "haab" meant "the period of 360 days and nothing else, and ... there is no evidence of the existence of any name for the 365-day year" (Long 1925: 575). Thompson later reached a similar conclusion: "[A]ctually, there was no year of 365 days, but one of 360 days, to the end of which were added the five nameless days" (Thompson 1950: 121).[28] Landa states quite specifically that:

> although the characters and the days of their months are twenty, they have the habit of counting them from one to thirteen; after these thirteen, they turn back and begin with one, and they thus divide the days of the year into twenty-seven thirteenths and nine days, without counting the unlucky days. (Tozzer 1941: 149)[29]

> The Uayeb days are also called "*xma kaba kin*" "days without name," signifying their unlucky character and their being regarded ... as being outside of and as it were supplementary to the ordinary course of time. During such periods the whole course of life is considered suspended, and we know that the Maya observed Uayeb as a period of strict tabu in which they did as little as possible. (Long 1925: 577)

Leon-Portilla found the same to be true in the highlands of Chiapas: "Those five extra days were denominated 'nameless' days because they passed without being taken into account" (Leon-Portilla 1988: 145).

Girard describes the annual cycle of the Ch'orti' in terms of an agricultural cycle based upon a fixed calendar (which the Ch'orti' had by then adopted, likely due to European influence, but careful reading makes clear that the "traditional native calendar" was one "of 360 days, plus five unlucky days, called 'days of affliction'", and that the solar cycle was structured into "months of 20 days (*winal*) which ends with the five unlucky days" (Girard 1995: 15).

> In the thought of the Chorti theologians the imaginary line traced by the sun on the day of its first passage through the zenith, marks "the middle ground of the world," a line that divides the celestial quadrant into two sectors of equal dimensions, but of different quality and color. ...
> This cosmic bipartition is projected onto the calendar, which is divided into two periods corresponding to the mentioned seasons of the tropic: summer and winter. These are perfectly symmetrical time cycles like the cosmic models they reflect (180 days for each one). They total 360 days, a calendar wheel equivalent to the Tun of the ancient Maya. (Girard 1995: 101)

A most significant time of the solar cycle comprised the 80 days (4 *winal*) following "New Year" (February 8): the 40 days between "New Year" and "Equinox" (March 29) ("the first forty"), and the 40 days following Equinox ("the second forty") (Girard 1995: 69–71, 95). When this 80-day period is viewed astronomically in terms of the solar cycle, instead of in terms of the agricultural cycle within the fixed calendar of the Ch'orti', the Ch'orti' are describing, from observation of the interaction of the sun with "landmarks" on the "visible horizon," the period of time between the nadir and zenith passages at the latitude of Jocotan, Guatemala.[30] February 8, called "New Year" by the Ch'orti', is the date of solar nadir passage. Forty days from February 8 is March 20, vernal equinox (not March 29), and 40 days from equinox is the day of zenith passage on April 29 (see Aveni 2001: 249 and Note 22).

The 360-day count, or *haab*', was adopted as the "chronological unit" of the Long Count (Thompson 1950: 141; see also Closs 1977). The 360-day count is a multiple of 20, and with a 360-day idealized solar cycle the same "lord of the night" would always govern the same nights in each *haab*' (Thompson 1950: 151). Moreover, as Thompson observed, 13 360-day cycles equals 18 260-day cycles. While the Maya attributed a deity or "patron" to each of the 18 *winal* periods of the 360-day *haab*', no "patron" for the Wayeb period has ever been identified and, further, no Initial Series date "falling in the five unlucky days has yet been found" (Thompson 1950: 105).

As Long describes Landa's account of rituals relating to a new "year," an image made at the beginning of Wayeb to be placed at one of the four gates of the village during the forthcoming "year" was first taken to the gate belonging to the outgoing "year". It was then brought back into the village to be guarded throughout the Wayeb period, after which it was set at the gate belonging to the new "year" and left there.

> It is significant that there was no image on duty during Uayeb because we may take it that since at the beginning of it the new image was made, it had relieved the old one of its duties, but as soon as the new year came in the image was brought out and put at the

Idealized Cosmos of 360 Days

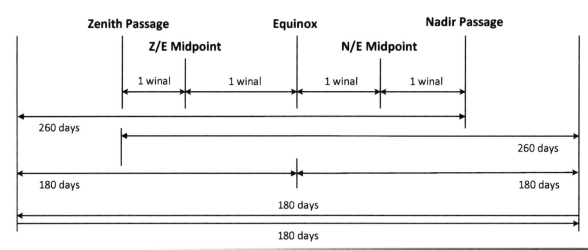

Fig. 1.12. The ordered, symmetrical cosmos of 360 days, without the five "uncounted" days

gate. It seems then that after the period of suspense, the Uayeb, they put the ahcuch haab, "he who bears the haab," at the gate to preside over the period from 0 Pop to the next 0 Uayeb, that is during a period of 360 days (... haab). It was called the bearer of this period [the 360-day *haab*] but there was no bearer of Uayeb. ... The Maya regarded the haab as being dormant during "uayeb haab," "the bed or repose of the haab," as is clearly shown by the meaning of the words. (Long 1925: 578)[31]

The "period from 0 Pop to the next 0 Uayeb" is, of course, not the "year" but the 360-day *haab'*, and the "bearer" that Landa and Long describe is not that of the "year" but of the *haab'*.

The completions of many of the successive 360-day periods that commenced with 4 Ajaw 8 Kumk'u were recorded during the Classic period as what are today referred to as "period endings" on stone monuments throughout the Maya area. However, recognition that stelae served to "commemorate" period endings in the Long Count "is far from an adequate explanation of why the Maya chose to emphasize these 'big stones' and other

types of monuments in their record-keeping" (Stuart 1996: 154).[32] While stelae served as "embodiments ... of time itself," those that featured royal portraits also conveyed the message that the image embodied the person or figure portrayed (Stuart 1996: 151, 158). By this juxtaposition:

> rulers were themselves embodiments of time and its passage – a role that was fundamental to the: cosmological underpinnings of divine kingship. ... Individual rulers were closely identified with the sun and its personified manifestation as the god *K'inich Ahaw*, 'sun-faced lord'. (Stuart 1996: 166–167)

In effect, the Classic Maya ruler, akin to the sun, was the ruler of the cosmos (Stuart 1996: 166; Tedlock 1992: 19).

All period ending dates fell on the last day of the 260-day count, Ajaw, and Ajaw was thus "the 'face' or 'lord' of the Period Ending" (Stuart 1996: 166).

> The cyclical reappearance of the Ahaw day at each Period Ending in the Long Count calendar was not only a renewal of cosmological time but also a

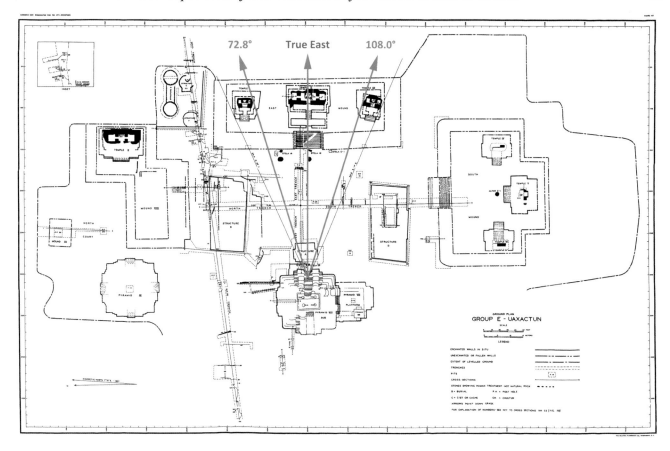

renewal, in effect, of the institution of kingship – an elaboration of the conceptual equation of the ruler and the sun …. (Stuart 1996: 167)

By his embodiment in the *lakam tuun*, or great stone (stela), the ruler "came to be explicitly identified with the temporal mechanisms of the cosmos" (Stuart 1996: 167–168).

Recalling from the Chocolá horizon data that a solar cycle in which the five extra days are not counted – the 360-day count — yields an idealized cosmos, where solar cycles are all symmetrical about all solar event axes, suggests an extension of Stuart's argument. For those portrait stelae erected in connection with commemoration of the end of successive *haab'* (360-day) periods, the stela embodies not merely abstract time, but a specific time period, the 360-day count. If the stela is not only the embodiment of that 360-day count but also of the ruler portrayed on the stela, then the ruler himself becomes the embodiment of the 360-day count (or multiple thereof) – that is, of the idealized cosmos, of cosmic order.[33] The "ritual in stone" that the Classic stela-altar

complex portrays is the ritual in which the ruler is not just the lord of abstract time, but the "ruler of the *haab'*," in which the ruler embodies the idealized solar cycle of 360-days that itself embodies the perceived order of the cosmos.

Given the early importance of zenith and nadir passages, a reconsideration of the purpose and function of the E-Group is in order

Lowland E-groups of the late Preclassic and early Classic have long been known to mark sunrises on the solstices and equinoxes. Why is it, then, that the eastern horizon observed by Chocolenses in the Preclassic, with distinct markers for zenith and nadir passage and chronological midpoint sunrises, does not appear to embody distinct natural markers for the winter and summer solstices or the equinoxes?[34]

The sun was perceived by the ancient Maya as a deity bearing a load (of time), much as the ancient Maya themselves had long borne loads

Fig. 1.13. Plan view of the Waxactun E-Group showing approximate sunrise positions on the zenith and nadir passage dates of May 9 and August 3, and February 1 and November 10, respectively (after Ricketson and Ricketson 1937: fig. 197)

supported by tumplines, as portrayed by the full-figure glyphs on Stela D at Copán (see Thompson 1950: 59–60).

> In conceiving and measuring the reality of the different periods in terms of their completeness, Maya thought achieved a new form of expression through this image of gods as bearers of time. Their arrival at the end of a journey ... is precisely the moment of the "weariness" of the gods. ... The new deities who in the same moment will take over the burdens of time will carry it on their backs until, overcome by fatigue, they arrive at another place of rest which is the completion of one cycle and the beginning of another. Understanding thus the measures of time as repose-completion, one of the roots from which the idea of cycles is derived may be perceived. (León-Portilla 1988: 51)

Chocolá's eastern horizon aptly represents this burden of the sun: at the endpoints of its endlessly repetitive northern and southern journeys (the solstices), the sun rests before reversing course; at the equinoxes, when the sun appears to be moving horizontally more rapidly than at any other time of year, it may be perceived as racing up (or down) the south slope of Paquisís bearing its load. The points where the sun appears to rest briefly as it surmounts a peak (or passes through a gap) are demarcated at important solar events: zenith and nadir passage and the chronological midpoints between equinox and zenith and equinox and nadir. Given the antiquity of the Chocolá site, it seems reasonable to propose that zenith and nadir passage sunrises (or sunsets) may also have been marked at lowland E-groups constructed much later.

Examining Ricketson's ground view map of the prototype E-group at Waxactun, the azimuth of a line from the stairs of E-VII-sub[35] to the south corner of the north building (E-I) is 72.8°, close to the azimuth of zenith passage sunrise at the horizon height of 3½°;[36] similarly, the azimuth of the north corner of the south building (E-III), as viewed from the stairs of E-VII-sub, is 108.0°, approximately 1.3° from the azimuth of nadir passage sunrise at that horizon (Ricketson and Ricketson 1937: fig. 197) (Fig. 1.13).[37] Thus, the Waxactun E-group could have been used to mark sunrises on the days of local zenith and nadir passage.

Only careful observation, measurement and documentation of zenith and nadir passage sunrises at the Waxactun E-group and possibly other lowland E-groups, can determine whether or not this hypothesis will be substantiated. But if ancient astronomers in the Middle Preclassic or earlier at Chocolá marked solar zenith and nadir passages at the horizon, it would seem likely, based upon "the flow of goods and ideas that moved from south to north" (Aveni and Hartung 1986: 67; 1991: 92), that E-groups constructed much later in the Peten would be used for these expanded, and arguably more important, observations as well.

Conclusion

While the evidence is not yet sufficient to conclude that the place where the 260-day cycle originated was Chocolá, as distinct from Izapa, Tak'alik Ab'aj, or another site (as yet unexplored or undiscovered) in the narrow latitudinal band of the 260-day interval, the Chocolá horizon is unique in marking significant events in the solar cycle and its equal has not been identified at any other site of comparable antiquity. Associations between between August 13 and April 30 alignments throughout Mesoamerica with the 260-day solar zenith passage interval at the latitude of Chocolá point to the derivation of that count from the Chocolá horizon or from another similar location in the narrow latitudinal band where the zenith passage interval is 260 days.

But for the five leftover, uncounted days, a 360-day solar cycle readily derived from the Chocolá horizon would have manifested symmetry about each solar event axis at Chocolá, similar to what the 260-day count does in relation to the zenith passage reference pole at that horizon. Associations between this idealized solar cycle, the chronological unit of the Long Count and the embodiment of the "ruler of the cosmos" in the "great stones" that mark the successive passages of 360-day periods throughout the Classic Maya period strongly suggest that the 360-day count may also have originated at Chocolá, given the manner in which the sun's movement is demarcated in "convenient 20-day blocks" during much of its cycle at that horizon. While the ancient Maya accommodated the reality of the 365-day "vague year," they adopted the idealized 360-day count that manifested a fully symmetrical, ordered cosmos as the Maya chronology unit, the foundation of the Long Count, and the temporal unit for recording period endings.

Although present evidence falls far short of establishing when these fundamental 260-day and 360-day calendrical counts were established, there are at least suggestions that it may have been significantly earlier than previously thought.[38] While it is by no means asserted here that the ancient people of Chocolá understood as much about the sun's initial journey along the eastern horizon in 3114 BC as may be implied here, an identical solar journey was repeated in 1607 BC,[39] not long before a "'Neolithic' revolution" occurred on the Pacific Coast between 1600 and 1100 BC, "the overture to the great Olmec symphony, to the origins of Mesoamerican civilization" (Coe 2006: 151). This was also only a short time before the rise of "the first simple chiefdom societies" about 1600 BC in the Pacific coastal lowlands (Hill and Clark 2001: 332; Clark 1997; Blake *et al.* 1995); the appearance of Barra phase (1550–1400 BC) ceramics evidencing "high quality of manufacture and wide range of decorative techniques" (Blake *et al.* 1995: 167; Lowe 1975); and the construction of Mesoamerica's oldest known ballcourt (Locona phase, 1400–1250 BC) at Paso de la Amada (Hill *et al.* 1998). By 1607 BC, the people in this coastal region were surely observing the sky and, in particular, the sun at the horizon,[40] and archaeologists working in the Pacific coast region may do well to keep in mind at least the possibility that fundamental Mesoamerican cosmological concepts were formulated this early. The evidence presented here does suggest that, given the completeness of the representation of fundamental elements of well-documented Maya cosmology derived from solar events marked at the Chocolá horizon, and the opportunity to confirm these elements early on at Chocolá[41] (and even at such early sites as Cuicuilco and Mount Tlaloc), that horizon may well have been used to confirm, if not originate, at least some of these elements.

The solar markers on the eastern horizon of the Middle Preclassic site of Chocolá provide evidence that may lead to a fuller understanding of the development of fundamental elements of ancient Maya cosmology and particularly of the system of timekeeping. This evidence suggests the early and central importance of zenith and nadir passages as reference poles in the development of fundamental 260-day and 360-day counts, as well as the emphasis on a perceived cosmic order that may underlie Maya kingship. And it not only supports the preliminary analysis of the potential importance of Chocolá as a regional center in the southern Maya area (Kaplan and Valdes 2004), but underscores the earlier views of Malmström and Girard that the origins of Maya cosmology would be found on the Pacific coast. While fertile soils and abundant water on the terraced slopes between the Rios Chocolá and Chichoy, as well as proximity to coastal and cross-mountain trade routes, surely influenced original site selection, Chocolá appears also to have been sited where it is for the reasons that the solar markers on the site's eastern horizon enabled derivation of the 260-day and 360-day counts so fundamental to calendrical development.

Acknowledgments

My grateful thanks to Jonathan Kaplan for his support throughout my work at Chocolá, and for his welcome suggestions for clarifying arguments; to Byron R. Lemus for his invaluable assistance in obtaining sunrise photographs; to Michael G. Rees for his help in developing the data for Table 1.2; and to Michael D. Coe and Anthony F. Aveni for their generosity in reviewing and making helpful comments on early drafts of this paper. Responsibility for any and all errors and omissions is solely mine.

Notes

1   At the latitude of Chocolá, the dates of zenith passage are August 13 and April 30, and the dates of nadir passage are February 9 and November 1. The chronological midpoints between zenith passage and equinox, and between equinox and nadir passage are, respectively, April 10 and September 2, and March 1 and October 12.

2   Another site within the narrow latitudinal band of the 260-day zenith passage interval may yet be found that has this characteristic.

3   This distinction "poses the question of the greater antiquity of this division of the year by means of the counting of the days instead of the precise observation of the astronomical equinoxes, which is rather difficult to make for early astronomers" (Broda 1993: 280).

4   The Chocolá data suggest a different interpretation of these horizon-marked sunrises and the significance of the related dates, as will be discussed below.

5   Broda further notes that "Cuicuilco seems to support the argument that the internal

structure of the Mesoamerican calendar (in its combination of the 260-day cycle and the 365-day solar year) might very well have Preclassic origins" (Broda 1993: 283). Aveni has noted that the Classic site of Copan "seems to have been deliberately arranged and oriented to reflect Maya calendric principles," specifically the division of the 40-day (2 *winal*) period between equinox and zenith passage at that latitude into equal *winal* periods by the Stela 12-10 baseline (Aveni 2001: 254, fig. 90). For an argument that the Postclassic site of Mayapan was deliberately situated at least in part for astronomical reasons, see Aldana 2003.

6   "[T]he chroniclers knew [Mount Tlaloc] to be perhaps the most important mountain in the landscape, for it was called 'Tlalocan,' the house of the rain god. In the Mexica religion, this mountain was said to be the origin of rain, mist, clouds, and snow" (Aveni *et al.* 1988: 298).

7   Given some deviation of solar events from horizon landmarks for some observations from Mound 1 (see Table 1.2), the possibility must be considered that another ancient mound could provide solar observations with more precise correspondence.

8   "Cerro 2665" is an unnamed peak on the 1:50,000 topographical map of the Instituto Geográfico Nacional of elevation 2665 m; it is designated here as "Cerro 2665" until its name can be ascertained.

9   Clouds prevented observation of sunrise on winter solstice, December 21, 2005. However, horizontal solar motion is not detectable with the naked eye within a day or so of the astronomical solstice (see Zeilik 1987: 26–27).

10 Of Tak'alik Ab'aj, Aveni and Hartung have said that "it is difficult to believe that the site location was not deliberately positioned to coincide with both mountain [Volcán Zunil] and solstice … ." (Aveni and Hartung 2000: 59; see also Malmström 1978: 112).

11 This assumes correctness of the GMT correlation constant.

12 104° 53.7' on February 9 and 104° 44.9' on November 1 (2006)(Anderson *et al.* 1999).

13 "It is very difficult for the authors to take the position that Preclassic people were not orienting to the solstice if the alignment we measure is off by 2–3° [4–6 solar diameters]" (Aveni and Hartung 2000: 64).

14 As viewed from Stela 12, sunset occurs behind Stela 10 across the Copán Valley on April 12 and September 1. The April sunset occurs 21 days after the vernal equinox and 19 days before the April zenith passage; the September sunset occurs 19 days after the August zenith passage

and 21 days before the autumnal equinox (Aveni 2001: 254).

15 Aveni postulated a hypothetical "solar horizon calendar" for Copán with the Stela 12-10 baseline dividing the time between the equinox and zenith passage into "convenient 20 day blocks," or *winals* (Aveni 2001: 254 and fig. 90).

16 Cloudy weather precluded sunrise observations on April 10.

17 Alignments to sunrises on these dates have been documented in central Mexico, but not explained. Iwaniszewski determined that the orientation of the southern wall of the ancient stone structure atop Mount Tlaloc was oriented to sunrise on March 1 and October 13 (Iwaniszewski 1994: 167–168), and an alignment from the Templo Mayor documented by Aveni *et al.* is to sunrise over Mount Telapon on March 1 and October 14 (Aveni *et al.* 1988: 302).

18 The morning of May 13, 2006 was so cloudy that sunrise was not visible. But from a comparison of sunrise photographs taken on May 11 and 12, it appears that sunrise, if visible on May 13, would have occurred directly behind Cerro 2665.

19 The referenced interpretations were made before the "Preclassic" had been extensively studied and the chronology more specifically delineated (see below, and references cited there).

20 Malmström did not mention either Takalik Abaj or Chocolá, or any other site in the latitudinal band where the interval between zenith passages is 260 days, nor did he explain why occupants of the Copán Valley prior to the Yax K'uk' Mo' dynasty could not have developed the 260-day count.

21 Malmström arrived at the 1323–1320 BC period for the initiation of the 365-day count by assuming that the count began when 0 Pop coincided with the summer solstice; he settled on the 1358 BC date for the initiation of the 260-day count by determining when 1 Imix fell on August 13, the date of southern zenith passage at the latitude of Izapa (14.8° N) (Malström 1978: 107–109). Both assumptions are speculative.

22 The site orientation is to Volcán Tacana on the north; Izapa Group B is oriented to sunrise atop Volcán Tajumulco on summer solstice (Malmström 1978).

23 At the equinox, where the horizontal speed of the sun is at its maximum, no distinct horizon marker is apparent. But Aveni has noted that "the sun sets in the same direction all over the Maya world on the days that fall two uinals before [and after] the zenith passage"(Aveni 2001: 249), which is on the equinoxes at the latitude of Chocolá.

24 The end of the current era, 13.0.0.0.0 4 Ajaw 3 Kank'in, will occur on December 21, AD 2012, using the GMT correlation constant of 584,283 (Aveni 2001: 210). Using the more widely accepted GMT constant of 584,285, the current era will end on December 23, AD 2012.

25 The *may* cycle consists of 260 360-day periods (as well as 360 260-day periods) (Rice 2004).

26 The zenith passage dates at Cuicuilco are May 16 and July 26 (294-day interval); at Mount Tlaloc they are May 15 and July 28 (291-day interval) (Anderson *et al.* 1999).

27 Maya epigraphers now agree that, for the Classic period, *tuun* (T528) means "stone" or "precious stone" such as were used to mark period endings, that is, the completion of successive 360-day cycles commencing with 13.0.0.0.0 4 Ajaw 8 Kumk'u, and *haab'* (T548) means "period of 360 days" (not necessarily related to a period ending) (Erik Boot, personal communication 2007). As Long noted long ago, "In no case do we find the word haab used by the Maya to show the number of the tun in the katun and similarly in no case is the word tun used with a numeral except to show the place of the tun in the katun. ... If a stone was put up to mark each tun-ending the use of the word is natural in that connection, but would be inappropriate to a distance number reckoned between any two points of time which were not period-endings, because there would not be 'stones' marking each 360 days of this" (Long 1925: 579).

28 Aveni *et al.* reached a similar conclusion from study of Mexica history. "It is well known from the written record that the Mesoamerican year was divided into 18 months, each consisting of 20 individually numbered days; and that each year so defined was separated from the next year by the five *nemontemi* or 'worthless' days" (Aveni *et al.* 1988: 289).

29 27 × 13 + 9 = 360.

30 Jocotan is at latitude 14° 49.1' N, longitude 91° 25.7' W.

31 See Tozzer 1941: 140–148.

32 *Lakam tuun* is the Classic Maya term for big or great stone, that is, stela.

33 "Time is part of the cosmic order. Indeed, for the Maya and the rest of Mesoamerica, time is cosmic order, its cyclical patterning the counterforce to the randomness of evil [chaos]" (Farriss 1987: 574).

34 There is the possibility that Volcán Tolimán, given its position directly behind the southern slope of Paquisís, as viewed from Chocolá's Mound 1, may have served as a natural marker for the equinoxes, as discussed above, but this hypothesis requires further study.

35 At Palenque, zenith passage sunrise was marked from the Temple of the Sun across the center of the roof comb of the Temple of the Cross, not at a corner of that structure (Mendez *et al.* 2005)

36 Aveni and Hartung have identified the middle of the first platform as the position where the "best fit" to a functioning observatory is achieved (Aveni and Hartung 1989: 444).

37 The dates of solar zenith passage at Waxactun (latitude 17.394° N, longitude 89.634° W) are May 9 and August 3; the dates of nadir passage are January 31 and November 11. The azimuths of zenith passage sunrise at Waxactun are 72.86° and 72.79° on May 9 and August 3, respectively; the azimuths of nadir passage sunrise are 109.39° and 109.53° on January 31 and November 11, respectively (Anderson *et al.* 1999).

38 Merrill speculated that the 260-day count was initiated on the day of southern zenith passage at Copán in "about 40 BC" (Merrill 1945: 311), but the later discoveries of Chiapa de Corzo Stela 2 and Tres Zapotes Stela C (dated to 7.16.3.2.13, December 8, 36 BC, and 7.16.6.16.18, September 3, 32 BC, respectively (Coe 2005: 64)) render this speculation dubious. Malmström opined that the 260-day count was initiated at Izapa when the first day of the count, 1 Imix, fell on August 13, the date of southern zenith passage, in 1358 BC (Malmström 1978: 108–109), but this is also speculative.

39 On August 13, 1607 BC, and again on August 13, 100 BC, zenith passage at Chocolá coincided with 4 Ajaw 8 Kumk'u (using the GMT constant 584,585); the associated Long Counts are 3.16.8.17.0 and 7.12.17.16.0.

40 San Lorenzo reached its peak development in the Gulf Coast region, where the "fully developed Olmec culture" was represented by "gigantic basalt sculptures fashioned in a distinctive style," from approximately 1200–900 BC (Coe 2005: 50–52). The mythology of the Hero Twins, the Maize God and the Creation appears to have been well formed by the first or second centuries BC at both Izapa and San Bartolo (Coe 1989; Laughton 1997; Saturno *et al.* 2005: 6–7).

41 Perhaps this confirmation occurred as late as 100 BC, when the second "renewal" of the sun's first journey of the current era along the Chocolá horizon took place (see Note 39).

References

Aldana, Gerardo, 2002. Solar Stelae and a Venus Window: Science and Royal Personality in Late Classic Copán *Archaeoastronomy* (supplement to the *Journal for the History of Astronomy*) 33, S29–S50.

Aldana, Gerardo, 2003. K'uk'ulkan at Mayapán: Venus and Postclassic Maya Statecraft. *Archaeoastronomy* (supplement to the *Journal for the History of Astronomy*) 34, S33–S51.

Anderson, Neil, Alfonso Morales and Moises Morales, 1981. Solar Alignment of the Palace Tower at Palenque. *Archaeoastronomy* (Bulletin of the Center for Archaeoastronomy) IV(3), 34–36.

Anderson, Tom, Peter Hanson and Ted Leckie, 1999. Starry Night Pro. Sienna Software, Inc. Toronto.

Apenes, Ola, 1936. Possible derivation of the 260 day period of the Maya calendar. *Ethnos* 1, 5–8.

Aveni, Anthony F., 1981. Tropical Archaeoastronomy. *Science* 213(4504), 161–171.

Aveni, Anthony F., 2001. *Skywatchers*. University of Texas Press, Austin.

Aveni, Anthony F. and Sharon L. Gibbs, 1976. On the Orientation of Precolumbian buildings in Central Mexico, *American Antiquity* 41(4), 510–517.

Aveni, Anthony F. and Horst Hartung, 1981. The Observation of the Sun at the Times of Passage Through the Zenith in Mesoamerica. *Archaeoastronomy* (Supplement to the *Journal for the History of Astronomy* 12(3)), S51–S70.

Aveni, Anthony F. and Horst Hartung, 1986. Maya City Planning and the Calendar. *Transactions of the American Philosophical Society* 76(7), 1–87.

Aveni, Anthony F. and Horst Hartung, 1989. Waxactun, Guatemala, Group E and Similar Assemblages: an Archaeoastronomical Reconsideration. *World Archaeoastronomy* (A. F. Aveni ed.). Cambridge University Press, Cambridge, 441–461.

Aveni, Anthony F. and Horst Hartung, 1991. Archaeoastronomy and the Puuc Sites. In *Arqueoastronomía y etnoastronomía en Mesoamérica* (J. Broda, S. Iwaniszewski and L. Maupomé eds). Universidad Nacional Autónoma de Mexico, Mexico, 65–96

Aveni, Anthony F. and Horst Hartung, 2000. Water, Mountain, Sky: the Evolution of Site Orientation in Southeastern Mesoamerica. In *Chalchihuitl in Quetzalli: Precious Greenstone, Precious Quetzal Feather: Mesoamerican Studies in Honor of Doris Heyden* (E. Quiñones Keber ed.). Labyrinthos, Lancaster, 55–65.

Aveni, Anthony F., E. E. Calnek and H. Hartung, 1988. Myth, Environment, and the Orientation of the Templo Mayor of Tenochtitlan. *American Antiquity* 53(2), 287–309.

Aveni, Anthony F., Susan Milbrath and Carlos Peraza Lope, 2004. Chichén Itzá's Legacy in the Astronomically Oriented Architecture of Mayapán. *Res* 45, 123–143.

Blake, Michael, John E. Clark, Barbara Voorhees, George Michaels, Michael W. Love, Mary E. Pye, Arthur A, Demarest and Barbara Arroyo, 1995. Radiocarbon Chronology for the Late Archaic and Formative Periods on the Pacific Coast of Southeastern Mesoamerica. *Ancient Mesoamerica* 6(2), 161–183.

Broda, Johanna, 1993. Astronomical Knowledge, Calendrics, and Sacred Geography in Ancient Mesoamerica. In *Astronomies and Cultures* (C. L. N. Ruggles and N. J. Saunders eds). University Press of Colorado, Niwot, 253–295.

Broda, Johanna, 2000. Calendrics and Ritual Landscape at Teotihuacán: Themes of Continuity in Mesoamerican Cosmovision. In *Mesoamerica's Classic Heritage*, (David Carrasco, Lindsay Jones and Scott Sessions eds). University Press of Colorado, Niwot, 397–432.

Broda, Johanna, 2006. Zenith Observations and the Conceptualization of Geographical Latitude in Ancient Mesoamerica: a Historical Interdisciplinary Approach. In *Viewing the Sky Through Present and Past Cultures*, (Todd W. Bostwick and Bryan Bates eds). City of Phoenix, 183–212.

Carlson, John B., 1981. Numerology and the Astronomy of the Maya. In *Archaeoastronomy in the Americas* (R. A. Williamson ed.). Ballena Press, Los Altos, 205–213.

Clark, John E., 1991. Beginnings of Mesoamerica: Apologia for the Soconusco Early Formative. In *The Formation of Complex Society in Southeastern Mesoamerica* (W. R. Fowler ed.). CRC Press, Boca Raton, pp. 13–26.

Clark, John E., 1997. The Arts of Government in Early Mesoamerica. *Annual Review of Anthropology* 26, 211–234.

Closs, Michael P., 1977. The Nature of the Maya Chronological Count. *American Antiquity* 42(1), 18–27.

Coe, Michael D., 1989 The Hero Twins: Myth and Image. In *The Maya Vase Book* Vol. 1 (J. Kerr, ed.). Kerr Associates, New York, 161–184.

Coe, Michael D., 2005. *The Maya* 7th edn. Thames & Hudson, New York.

Coe, Michael D., 2006. *Final Report: An Archaeologist Excavates His Past.* Thames & Hudson, New York.

Eliade, Mircea, 1954. *The Myth of the Eternal Return or, Cosmos and History.* Princeton University Press, Princeton.

Farriss, Nancy M., 1987. Remembering the Future, Anticipating the Past: History, Time, and Cosmology among the Maya of Yucatan. *Comparative Studies in Society and History* 29(3), 566–593.

Girard, Rafael, 1962. *Los Mayas Eternos.* Libro Mex Editores, Mexico, D. F.

Girard, Rafael, 1995. *People of the Chan.* Continuum Foundation, Chino Valley, AZ.

Hill, Warren D. and John E. Clark, 2001. Sports, Gambling, and Government: America's First Social Compact? *American Anthropologist* 103(2), 331–345.

Hill, Warren D., Michael Blake, and John E. Clark, 1998. Ball court design dates back 3400 years. *Nature* 392 (30 April), 878–879.

Iwaniszewski, Stanislaw, 1994. Archaeology and Archaeoastronomy of Mount Tlaloc: a Reconsideration. *Latin American Antiquity* 5(2), 158–176.

Kaplan, Johnathan, 2008. Hydraulics, Cacao, and Complex Developments at Preclassic Chocolá, Guatemala: Evidence and Implications. *Latin American Antiquity* 19(4), 399–413.

Kaplan, Jonathan and Juan Antonio Valdés, 2004. Chocolá, an Apparent Regional Capital in the Southern Maya Preclassic: Preliminary Findings from the Proyecto Arqueológico Chocolá (PACH). *Mexicon* 26, 77–86.

Kaplan, Jonathan, Juan Antonio Valdés and Frederico Paredes Umaña, 2006. Chocolá Archaeological Project: Report No. 2, Second Season 2004. www.famsi.org/reports/03033/section01.htm.

Larsen, Helga, 1936. The 260 day period as related to the agricultural life of the ancient Indian. *Ethnos* 1, 9–12

Laughton, Timothy B., 1997. Sculpture on the Threshhold: The Iconography of Izapa and Its Relationship to that of the Maya. PhD. Dissertation, University of Essex (British Thesis Service, British Library, London).

León–Portilla, Miguel, 1988. *Time and Reality in the Thought of the Maya.* 2nd edn. Beacon Press, Boston.

Long, Richard C. E., 1925. Some Maya time periods. In *Congres International des Americanistes* 21st Session Goteborg 1924 2, 574–580.

Lowe, Gareth W., 1975. The Early Preclassic Barra Phase of Altamira, Chiapas: A review with new data. *Papers of the New World Archaeological Foundation* 38, 13–14.

Malmström, Vincent H., 1973. Origin of the Mesoamerican 260-day calendar. *Science* 181(4103), 939–941.

Malmström, Vincent H., 1978. A Reconstruction of the Chronology of Mesoamerican Calendrical Systems. *Journal for the History of Astronomy* 9, 105–116.

Malmström, Vincent H., 1991. Edzná: earliest astronomical center of the Mayas. In *Arqueoastronomía y etnoastronomía en Mesoamerica* (J. Broda, S. Iwaniszewski, and L. Maupomé eds). Universidad Nacional Autonoma de Mexico, Mexico, 37–47.

Malmström, Vincent H., 1997. *Cycles of the Sun, Mysteries of the Moon: the Calendar in Mesoamerican Civilization.* University of Texas Press, Austin.

Mendez, Alonso, Edwin L. Barnhart, Christopher Powell and Carol Karasik, 2005. Astronomical Observations from the Temple of the Sun. *Archaeoastronomy* (*Journal of Astronomy in Culture*) XIX, 44–73.

Merrill, Robert H., 1945. Maya sun calendar dictum disproved. *American Antiquity* 10, 307–311.

Morante López, Rubén B., 1993. *Evidencias del Conocimiento Astronómico en Xochicalco, Morelos.* Master's thesis. ENAH, Mexico.

Morante López, Rubén B., 1996. *Evidencias del Conocimiento Astronómico en Teotihuacán.* Doctoral dissertation in Anthropology, Faculty of Philosophy and Letters. Universidad Nacional Autonoma de Mexico, Mexico.

Morante López, Rubén B., 2001. Las camaras astronómicas subterraneas. *Arqueología Mexicana* VIII(47), 46–52.

Morante López, Rubén B., 2010. *La Pirámide de Los Nichos de Tajín: Los Códigos del Tiempo.* Instituto de Investigaciones Estéticas, Universidad Nacional Autonoma de Mexico, Mexico.

Nuttall, Zelia, 1928. Nouvelles lumieres sur les civilisations americaines et le systeme du calendrier. *Proceedings of the 22nd International Congress of Americanists* (Rome 1928), 119–148.

Powell, Christopher, 1997. A New View on Maya Astronomy. Master's thesis published at the Maya Exploration Center website (http://www.mayaexploration.org/research_pubs.php).

Rice, Prudence M., 2004. *Maya Political Science: Time, Astronomy, and the Cosmos.* University of Texas Press, Austin.

Ricketson, Oliver G. and Edith B. Ricketson, 1937. *Uaxactún, Guatemala; Group E, 1926–1931.* Publication 477. Carnegie Institution of Washington, Washington, DC.

Saturno, William A., Karl A. Taube, David Stuart and Heather Hurst, 2005. The Murals of San Bartolo, El Petén, Guatemala. Part 1: the North Wall. *Ancient America* 7, 1–56.

Soruco Sáenz, Enrique, 1991. Una Cueva Ceremonial en Teotihuacán y Sus Implicaciones Astronómicas Religiosas. In *Arqueoastronomia y Etnoastronomia en Mesoamerica* (J. Broda, S. Iwaniszewski and L. Maupomé eds). pp. 461–500. Universidad Nacional Autonoma de Mexico, Mexico, 291–296.

Stuart, David, 1996. Kings of Stone: a Consideration of Stelae in Ancient Maya Ritual and Representation. *Res* 29/30, 149–171.

Tedlock, Barbara, 1992. The Road of Light: Theory and Practice of Mayan Skywatching. In *The Sky in Mayan Literature* (A. F. Aveni, ed.). Oxford University Press, Oxford, 18–42.

Thompson, J. Eric S., 1950. *Maya Hieroglyphic Writing: Introduction.* Publication 589. Carnegie Institution of Washington, Washington DC.

Tichy, Franz, 1981. Order and Relationship of Space and Time in Mesoamerica: Myth or Reality? In *Mesoamerican Sites and Worldviews* (E. P. Benson ed.). Dumbarton Oaks, Washington, DC, 217–245.

Tichy, Franz, 1990 Orientation Calendar in Mesoamerica: Hypothesis Concerning their Structure, Use and Distribution. *Estudios de cultura náhuatl* 20, 183–199.

Tozzer, Alfred M., 1941. *Landa's Relacion de las Cosas de Yucatan.* Papers of the Peabody Museum of American Archaeology and Ethnology 18. Harvard University, Cambridge Mass.

Valdés, Juan Antonio, Jonathan Kaplan, Oscar Gutierrez, Juan Pablo Herrera and Frederico Paredes Umaña, 2003. Chocolá: un centro intermedio entre la boca costa y el altiplano de Guatemala durante el Preclásico Tardío. In XVII *Simposio de Investigaciones Arqueológicas en Guatemala* (J. P. Laporte, B. Arroyo, H. L. Escobedo and H. E. Mejia eds). Instituo de Antropología e Historia Guatemala, Guatemala City, 426–438.

Zeilik, Michael, 1987. Anticipation in Ceremony: the Readiness of All. In *Astronomy and Ceremony in the Prehistoric Southwest* (J. B. Carlson and W. J. Judge eds). Papers of the Maxwell Museum of Anthropology 2, Albuquerque, 25–41.

2

Teotihuacan architectural alignments in the central Maya lowlands?

Ivan Šprajc

Introduction

Some of the most extensive gaps in the archaeological map of the Maya area were, until recently, located in the central parts of the Yucatan peninsula, particularly in the vast southeastern portion of the Mexican federal state of Campeche. Until the 1980s, when intensive research began in the area of Calakmul (Folan *et al.* 2001), Ruppert and Denison's monumental monograph (1943) was practically the only source of information on some archaeological sites in this region, but these were only a few of the largest and best preserved. As Adams (1981: 216) affirmed, the sites known until then in the area, except for El Palmar (Thompson 1936) "were all found by Ruppert and his Carnegie Institution surveys of the 1930s." In order to improve the situation, six field seasons of archaeological reconnaissance works have been carried out in southeastern Campeche since 1996 (Šprajc 2001a; 2002; 2003; 2002–2004; 2008a; Šprajc *et al.* 1997; 2005; Šprajc and Suárez 1998; Šprajc and Juárez 2003).[1] Being part of the central Maya Lowlands, the area is mostly covered with tropical forest. While the eastern part is sparsely populated, the rest of the territory belongs to the Calakmul Biosphere Reserve, which is now without permanent population.

In the course of our surveys, more than 70 formerly unknown archaeological sites have been recorded, and most of the sites that had been reported by Ruppert and Denison (1943), but were later lost again, have been relocated. Among the sites, which are mostly remains of settlements dating to the Late Preclassic and Classic periods (*c.* 300 BC–AD 900), there are several major centers with large complexes of civic and ceremonial architecture and sculpted stone monuments (Fig. 2.1).

Due to peculiarities of construction and aggressive tropical vegetation, standing architecture is seldom found, even at large sites. Architectural orientations can thus be rarely determined in the field: only occasionally sufficient portions of exposed walls are found, but most structures, even the largest pyramid temples, are nowadays reduced to mounds, whose size, irregular shapes provoked by collapses, and the dense vegetation cover make it impossible to determine their orientations in the field with any precision. However, I have been able to determine the most relevant orientations from our site maps based on total station surveying and oriented to true north.

The orientations at all the sites tend to be skewed clockwise from cardinal directions. This regularity, which is – in spite of exceptions

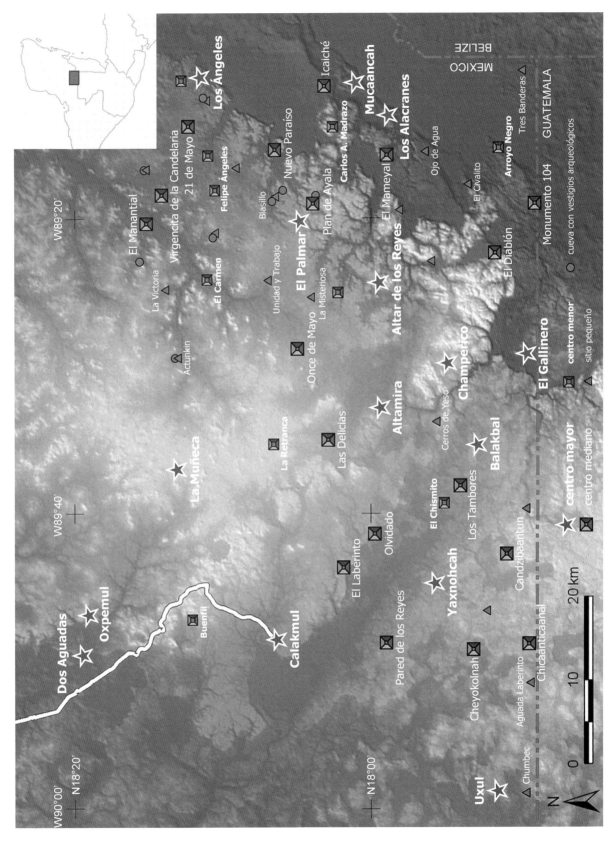

Fig. 2.1. Archaeological sites in southeastern Campeche, Mexico (digital elevation model: SRTM NASA; map elaborated by Žiga Kokalj)

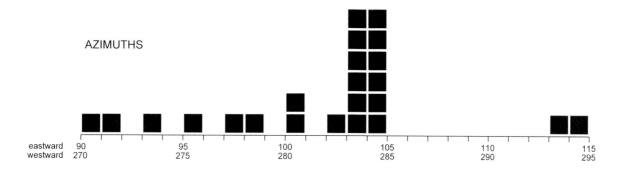

found in certain areas and periods – a well-known pan-Mesoamerican characteristic (*cf.* Aveni 2001: 233; Tichy 1991; Šprajc 2001b), is a first indicator suggesting an astronomical basis of these orientations: as stated by Aveni and Hartung (1986: 7f):

> if we find alignments that are confined to a narrow azimuthal range in a sample of buildings spread far apart in space […] there can be no conceivable way of actually laying out the chosen direction other than by the use of astronomical bodies at the horizon as reference objects.[2]

On the other hand, we can also observe that, in spite of the evident clockwise tendency, the buildings at every single site exhibit a range of orientations differing to a greater or lesser extent. Since it is, therefore, rather obvious that not all of the buildings at a site, even within its urban core, were used for astronomical observations, I assumed that only the most important civic and/or ceremonial buildings may have had this function. It may be added that these are normally the highest buildings, offering practically the only appropriate points for observations: the landscape is relatively flat and the height of the surrounding forest – even if a relatively high degree of deforestation should be assumed for the time of Maya florescence – allowed the horizon to be seen only from elevated spots. Where buildings composing a group exhibit similar orientations, one can presume, taking into account analogies from elsewhere (*cf.* Šprajc 2001b), that the orientation of the largest religious or civic structure was laid out accurately and on observational grounds, while the orientations of the surrounding smaller buildings roughly conformed to it, but were not observationally functional *per se*.

Since the ground plans of most buildings are roughly rectangular or composed of rectangular elements, the orientation of a structure can be described with two azimuths, which correspond to its north–south and east–west axes of symmetry or represent mean values of its north–south and east–west alignments. However, I only took into consideration the east–west orientation azimuths, assuming that the north-west alignments were not astronomically relevant. This assumption is warranted in the light of comparative data indicating that the Mesoamerican architectural orientations in most cases referred to the Sun's positions on the horizon. While the whole argument supporting this view can be found elsewhere (Šprajc 2001b: 25f), it is also noteworthy that all of the structures selected for the present orientation study have their east–west axes aligned within the angle of annual movement of the Sun along the horizon, which is a prevalent pattern throughout Mesoamerica (*ibid.*; Aveni and Hartung 1986: 59f; 2000: 55).

The orientations have been determined for 23 structures or architectural compounds[3] at 11 archaeological sites. In view of the present state of preservation of the buildings, and considering the uncertainties derived from map measurements, I estimate that the orientation azimuths that have been determined may be in error of up to ±½°. The azimuths are plotted in Figure 2.2 and the corresponding declinations in Figure 2.3. Horizon altitudes necessary for calculating declinations were determined on the basis of the available cartography; they were not measured in the field, both because of the problems of visibility and because in most cases the exact orientations were determined only after the site maps had been elaborated. While the distribution and possible meaning of all the orientations has been discussed in detail elsewhere (Šprajc 2008b), I will here focus only on the most numerous alignments, whose azimuths cluster around 104°/284°,

Fig. 2.2. Distribution of azimuths of the east–west architectural alignments in the archaeological sites of southeastern Campeche. Each square represents one azimuth corresponding to a structure or a group of adjacent structures sharing the same orientation. Azimuth values on the horizontal scale are spaced at 1° intervals (for example, all azimuths greater than 104° and smaller than or equal to 105° appear in a single column)

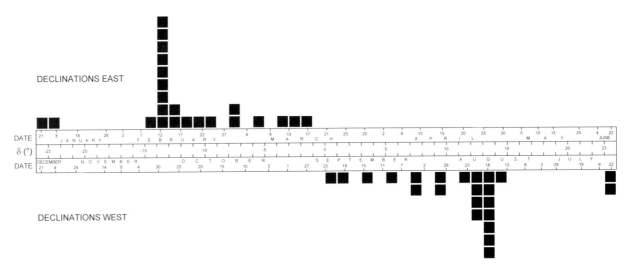

Fig. 2.3. Distribution of declinations corresponding to the east–west architectural alignments in the archaeological sites of southeastern Campeche. Declination values on the horizontal scale are spaced at 1° intervals (for example, all declinations greater than 13° and smaller than or equal to 14° appear in a single column). The declinations recorded on the eastern/western horizon are plotted upward/downward. Since all of them fall within the range of declinations attained by the Sun, the corresponding dates of the year are also shown; winter and spring dates appear above the declination scale and summer and autumn dates below it

corresponding to declinations of about −13°/+13° (Figs 2.2 and 2.3).

"Teotihuacan" alignments

The fact that the most numerous alignments cluster around the azimuth of 104°/284° does not come as a surprise, if we recall that, in the distribution of architectural alignments in Maya area in general, Aveni and Hartung (1986: 17; 2000: 55) observed a prominent peak centered at a deviation of 14° with respect to the cardinal directions. In view of the scarcity of systematic alignment studies in the Maya area, and considering that archaeologists tend to pay little attention to this aspect of urban planning, it is also worth noting that, according to Nalda (2004: 78ff), the orientations skewed around 13° east of astronomical north dominate a greater part of the urban layout at Kohunlich.

In southeastern Campeche, the alignments pertaining to this group are incorporated in structures I of Calakmul, 15-a of Champerico, 1-a of Cheyokolnah, 1 of Chicaanticaanal, A-1, B-1 and D-1 of El Gallinero, 2 of Las Delicias, and A-1, C-1, E-1 and E-6 of Yaxnohchah (Table 2.1; Figs 2.4–2.8; Šprajc 2002–2004; 2008a).

As one can observe in Figure 2.3, the declinations recorded by these orientations on the eastern and western horizon (around −13° and +13°) correspond to sunrises near February 12 and October 30 and to sunsets around April 25 and August 18. These alignments belong to one of the most widespread groups in Mesoamerica, the so-called 17°-family of orientations (Aveni 2001: 234).[4]

A systematic research accomplished in central Mexico disclosed that this alignment family is actually composed of two groups of slightly different orientations, which record different sets of dates.[5] Both groups occur simultaneously at several sites, most prominently at Teotihuacan and Xochicalco. The sunrise/sunset dates recorded by one group tend to be February 12 and October 30/April 30 and August 13. There is evidence suggesting an agricultural significance of the four dates, which marked four critical moments in the maize cultivation cycle: preparation of the fields (February), the onset of the rainy season and the time of planting (around May 1), the appearance of the first corn cobs or *elotes* (August), and the end of the rainy season and the beginning of harvest (around November 1). However, an additional peculiarity of the four dates is that they delimit intervals of 260 days (from February 12 to October 30, and from August 13 to April 30), equivalent to the length of the Mesoamerican ritual calendrical cycle. It has thus been argued that these dates must have been crucial moments of a *ritual* or *canonical* agricultural cycle (Šprajc 2000; 2001b: 79ff, 107ff).

Archaeoastronomical studies accomplished recently both in central Mexico and in other parts of Mesoamerica indicate that architectural orientations, in general, allowed the use of observational calendars composed of intervals that were predominantly multiples of 13 and 20 days, i.e. of the basic periods of Mesoamerican calendrical system. The placement in the tropical year of the most frequently recorded dates suggests that these observational calendars

Site	Structure, group	*A*	*h*	*δ*	\multicolumn{2}{c}{*Dates*}	
Calakmul	Structure 1	104°19'	0°12'	−13°42'	Feb 12	Oct 30
		284°19'	−0°09'	13°21'	Apr 25	Aug 17
Champerico	Structure 15-a	103°40'	1°10'	−12°44'	Feb 15	Oct 26
		283°40'	−0°06'	12°47'	Apr 23	Aug 19
Cheyokolnah	Structure 1-a	104°	0°	−13°29'	Feb 13	Oct 29
		284°	−0°08'	13°05'	Apr 25	Aug 19
Chicaanticaanal	Structure 1	104°	−0°09'	−13°33'	Feb 13	Oct 29
		284°	−0°08'	13°05'	Apr 25	Aug 19
El Gallinero	Structure A-1	104°40'	0°25'	−13°58'	Feb 12	Oct 30
		284°40'	0°55'	14°07'	Apr 28	Aug 15
	Structure B-1	104°16'	0°	−13°45'	Feb 12	Oct 30
		284°16'	0°41'	13°39'	Apr 26	Aug 17
	Structure D-1	104°07'	−0°16'	−13°42'	Feb 12	Oct 30
		284°07'	0°38'	13°29'	Apr 26	Aug 17
Las Delicias	Structure 2	104°20'	−0°07'	−13°50'	Feb 12	Oct 30
		284°20'	−0°08'	13°23'	Apr 25	Aug 17
Yaxnohcah	Structure A-1	103°50'	−0°10'	−13°23'	Feb 13	Oct 28
		283°50'	−0°10'	12°55'	Apr 24	Aug 19
	Structure C-1	104°35'	−0°02'	−14°03'	Feb 11	Oct 30
		284°35'	−0°08'	13°38'	apr 26	Aug 17
	Structure E-1	103°30'	−0°04'	−13°02'	Feb 14	Oct 27
		283°30'	−0°07'	12°37'	Apr 23	Aug 20
	Structure E-6	103°10'	−0°06'	−12°44'	Feb 15	Oct 26
		283°10'	−0°09'	12°17'	Apr 22	Aug 21

served for determining the most important moments of the annual climatic cycle and, consequently, for a proper scheduling of agricultural activities (*cf.* Aveni and Hartung 1986; Aveni *et al.* 2003; Šprajc 2001b; 2005); it should be recalled that, since the Mesoamerican calendrical year of 365 days, due to the lack of intercalations, did not keep in step with the tropical year of 365.2422 days, astronomical observations were essential for these purposes. The orientations, marking critical and canonized moments of the year of the seasons, not only allowed them to be determined through direct observations; if the observational calendars were composed of multiples of elementary periods of the calendrical system, it was relatively easy to *predict* the relevant dates, knowing the structure of the observational scheme and the mechanics of the formal calendar (Šprajc 2001b).[6]

In relation with this interpretation it should be pointed out that, according to Aimers and Rice (2006: 83), the Maya had no need to rely on astronomical phenomena to determine precise agricultural dates, because "weather and visible growth cycles clearly indicate

when it is time to perform certain tasks"; a similar opinion had been expressed formerly by Thompson (1974: 94f; *cf.* Aveni and Hartung 1986: 8). Nonetheless, the following ethnographic record obtained among the Maya of Quintana Roo casts doubt on such affirmations, suggesting that seasonal changes in the nature are not sufficiently exact and reliable indicators of the moments appropriate for initiating certain activities:

> El agricultor, por su parte, ha de procurar que la quema se lleve a cabo antes de que lleguen las primeras lluvias, pues, de lo contrario, quedaría imposibilitado para hacerlo, perdiendo así la ocasión de usar el terreno talado. Para preservarse de este peligro, el milpero suele acudir a alguno de los dos escribas que hay en el cacicazgo, el cual, usando un almanaque impreso en Mérida, le puede anunciar la clase de tiempo que ha de hacer en cada uno de los meses venideros. (Villa Rojas 1978: 315f)

If modern peasants, in spite of their knowledge about cyclical changes in natural environment, use a published almanac, it is obvious that, in prehispanic times, in the absence of a formal calendar maintaining a permanent concordance between the calendrical and tropical years, the regulation of agricultural works must have been based on astronomical observations.

Table 2.1. Data on architectural orientations with azimuths around 104°/284° in archaeological sites of southeastern Campeche

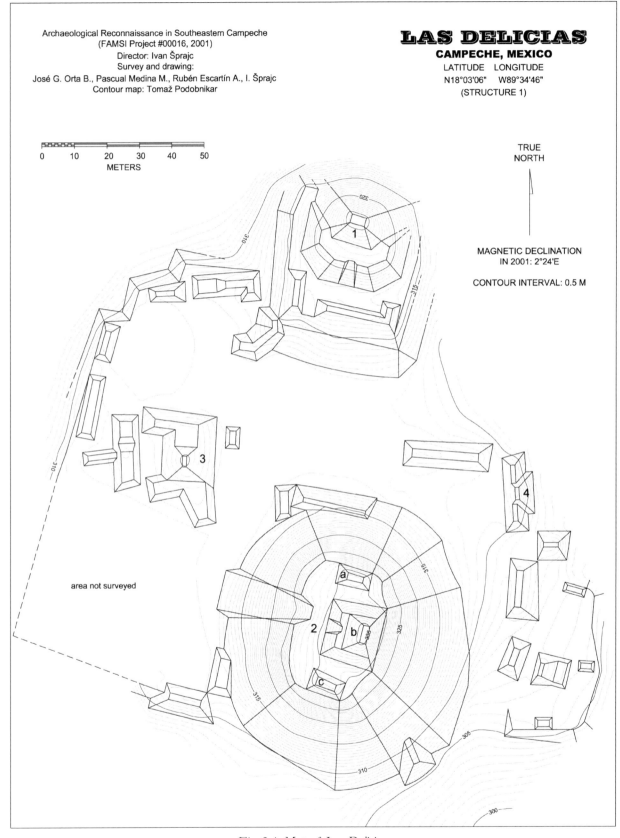

Fig. 2.4. Map of Las Delicias

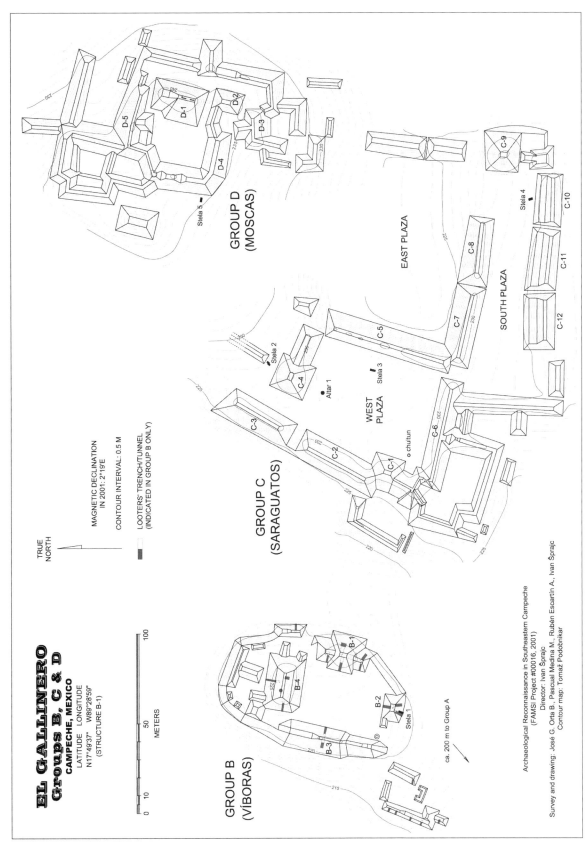

Fig. 2.5. El Gallinero, map of Groups B, C, and D

Nowadays, when practically all indigenous communities use Christian calendar, whose saints and feasts mark constantly the dates at which certain labors and associated ceremonies must be carried out, it may be difficult to assess or understand adequately the importance that astronomical observations must have had in practical life of prehispanic societies. However, the Quiché of Momostenango keep regulating their agricultural cycle on the basis of observations of celestial bodies (Tedlock 1991), and we could mention other ethnographically documented examples of the same practice (Girard 1948; 1949; Lincoln 1945; Remington 1980; *cf.* Šprajc 2001b: 151ff).

Returning to the orientations that correspond to sunrises on February 12 and October 30 and to sunsets on April 30 and August 13, it should be pointed out that, in central Mexico, in some cases the four dates are recorded by one and the same alignment. This is, however, not the case in southeastern Campeche:[7] while the sunrise dates recorded by the most numerous alignments tend to be February 12 and October 30, the sunset dates corresponding to the same orientations do not cluster around April 30 and August 13 but rather around April 25 and August 18. Since the interval separating April 25 and August 18 (115/250 days) does not seem significant, these orientations were likely intended to record only the sunrises on February 12 and October 30, separated by 260 days.[8]

Very interesting in this context is the spatial relationship existing between Structures C-1-a and E-1-a of Yaxnohcah, as well as the similarity of their orientations (Table 2.1). Based on the coordinates of both structures, determined by repeated GPS measurements in the field, it is possible to calculate that the azimuth of the straight line from Structure C-1-a (W89°44'52.9", N17°55'29.0") to Structure E-1-a, located a trifle more than 1 km to the southeast (W89°44'16.8", N17°55'20.3"), is 104°11' (Figs 2.7 and 2.8). The declination corresponding to this alignment (−13°40') reveals that, observing in front of Structure C-1-a, the Sun would have risen on February 12 and October 30 exactly above Structure E-1-a. There is no doubt the alignment could have been functional: the Chicanel ceramics found in Structure E-1 and the triadic groups characterizing

the two buildings (*cf.* Hansen 1998: 77ff; 2000: 95) suggest they both date to the Late Preclassic period and were, consequently, in use simultaneously, at least during a certain time-span. The intentionality of this alignment is further supported by the fact that its azimuth is practically identical to those determined for the east–west orientations of Structures C-1 and E-1 (Table 2.1).

Structures B-1 and C-1 of El Gallinero constitute a very similar case: the orientation of Structure B-1 corresponds, again, to sunrises on February 12 and October 30 (Table 2.1); furthermore, for the observer placed on top of Structure B-1, the Sun appeared on these dates above Structure C-1, located about 100 m to the southeast. Structure C-1 is relatively small and its present state of preservation does not allow its orientation to be reliably established; however, considering the layout of the mound, it may well have had the same orientation as Structure B-1 (Fig. 2.5).

Without having a larger number of similar cases, we obviously cannot generalize the idea that, beyond the orientations of particular buildings, also the alignments *between* structures of a site (or even among different sites) were dictated by astronomical considerations. However, the two examples mentioned above, as well as the alignments incorporated in the assemblages of Uaxactún-Group-E type (*cf.* Aveni *et al.* 2003), suggest that such motives, indeed, intervened in the placement of some buildings with respect to others.

The alignments at Yaxnohcah and El Gallinero referred to above – assuming they are not a product of a remarkable coincidence – reinforce the hypothesis about a special importance of the dates February 12 and October 30. Since the azimuths of both visual lines can be determined with considerable precision, the corresponding sunrise and sunset dates can also be accurately established: both alignments record the dates February 12 and October 30 on the eastern horizon, and April 26 and August 17 on the western horizon. Even if the possibility that these alignments were functional (also) in the western direction cannot be discarded, analogous cases from other parts of Mesoamerica do not support the idea: while numerous orientations in central Mexico record sunrises on February 12 and October 30, the importance of the dates April 26 and August 17 has not been attested (*cf.* Šprajc 2001b).

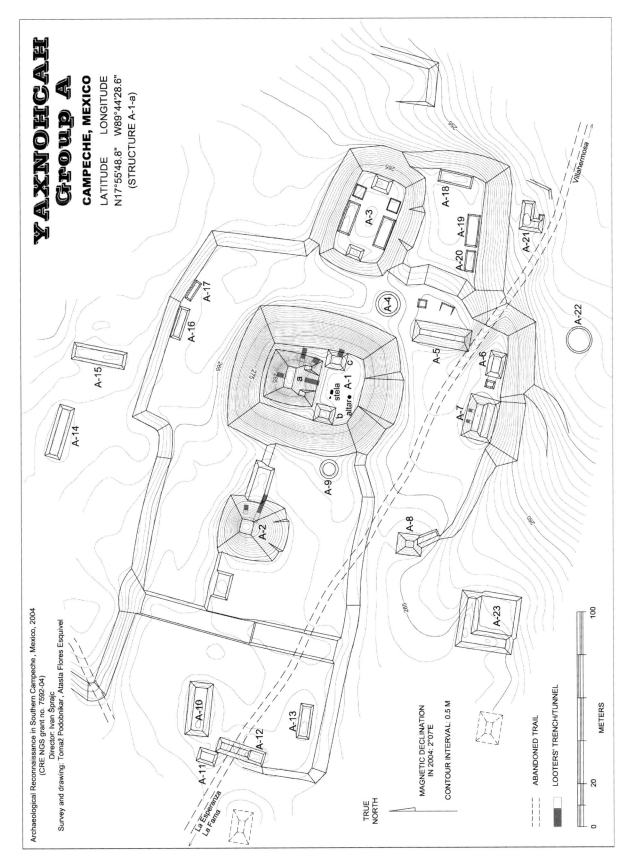

Fig. 2.6. Yaxnohcah, map of Group A

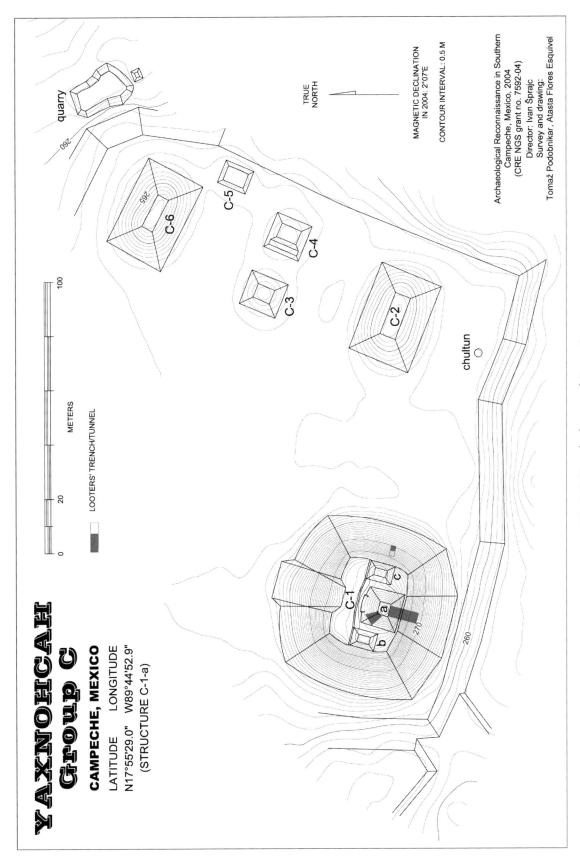

Fig. 2.7. Yaxnohcah, map of Group C

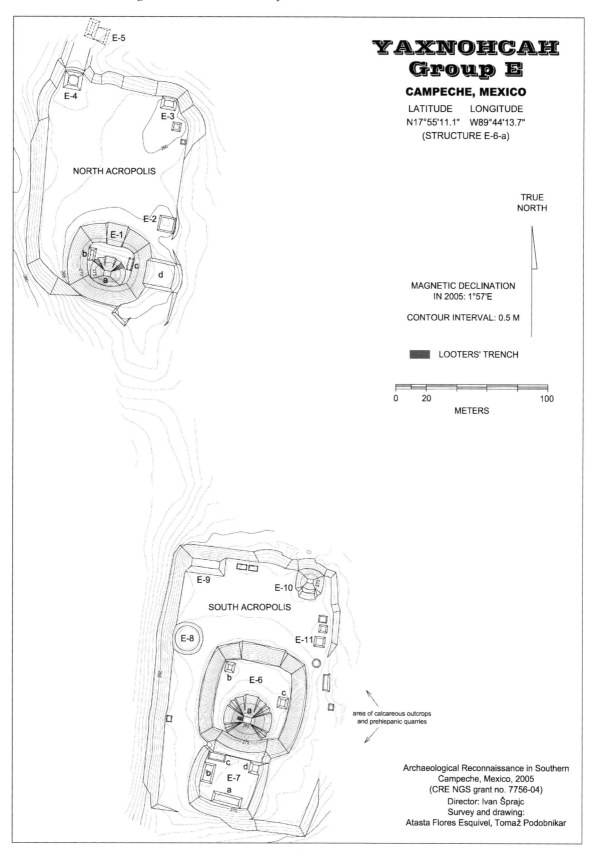

Fig. 2.8. Yaxnohcah, map of Group E

Problem of origins

The presence of this group of orientations in the Maya cities of southeastern Campeche has another very interesting implication. While several structures aligned this way pertain to the Classic period, others are earlier: Structure 2 of Las Delicias and Structures A-1, C-1 and E-1 at Yaxnohcah are pyramids with triadic groups (Figs 2.4–2.8), most probably dating to the Late Preclassic period (*cf.* Hansen 1998: 77ff; 2000: 95). In other words, they must have been built around the beginning of the current era, i.e. roughly at the time when the Pyramid of the Sun was erected in Teotihuacan, where the 17°-family of orientations, according to Aveni (2001: 234), may have originated.[9] Is it possible that these alignments, in fact, had their origin in the Maya area? This is certainly a question that should be borne in mind, particularly because recent measurements of orientations at El Mirador, Petén, Guatemala, revealed that orientations of this group are incorporated in some buildings dated to a time not later than the 2nd century BC and, therefore, definitely earlier than the Teotihuacan Sun Pyramid (Šprajc *et al.* 2009).

On the other hand, it is worth recalling that the alignments discussed above and found in southeastern Campeche (as well as those at El Mirador, Guatemala) appear to have been functional only to the east. Consequently, they seem to represent a simpler and, therefore, earlier version of the orientations that later evolved into the elaborate 17°-family of alignments, known from central Mexico and allowing the use of a complex observational calendar (Šprajc 2001b: 107ff).

Concluding remarks

The information recently collected in southeastern Campeche suggests that the role of architectural orientations in this part of the Maya area was quite similar to the one indicated by alignment data from other Mesoamerican regions: it is highly likely that observational schemes tied to agriculturally important dates and composed of calendrically significant intervals were in use. The most compelling evidence supporting this conclusion is undoubtedly the frequency of orientations recording sunrises on February 12 and October 30. The idea that the objective of these orientations was

precisely to record solar events on the eastern horizon is reinforced by comparative data from central Mexico. However, it is worth noting that the buildings exhibiting these orientations are looking with their main facades to the north, south, west, and rarely to the east. If we assumed that the placement of the access indicates the direction in which a building's orientation was functional, we would be forced to postulate that these structures recorded different phenomena. Such an idea is, however, highly unlikely, both because the orientations are very similar – the small differences in azimuth and declination values are likely to reflect measurement errors rather than deliberate variations – and because of analogies from central Mexico: if the orientations were functional to the north or south, referring to a star, we would observe, in the corresponding declinations, a consistent variation as a function of time, due to precessional shifts (*cf.* Aveni 2001: 100ff). In fact, it has been demonstrated that various central Mexican alignments of this group, which can be measured with high precision, record the same declinations during some 1500 years (at least since the foundation of Teotihuacan) and, therefore, evidently refer to solar events (Šprajc 2001b: 25f).

Consequently, we can conclude that the placement of the access or main facade of a building does not indicate the direction in which its astronomical orientation was functional. Analogous cases from central Mexico allow the same conclusion, which suggests that the placement of the access was rather dictated by the symbolism and ritual associated with a particular structure, as well as by general factors of urban planning (Šprajc 2001b: 69ff).

The study of architectural orientations may provide answers to a number of specific questions concerning the nature of underlying concepts, their meaning in the specific natural and cultural context, and their consequent role in the world view and political ideology (*cf.* Šprajc 2005). Furthermore, as exemplified by the problem of origin of the 17°-family of orientations, the study of alignment patterns, their development and similarities in different regions may contribute substantially to the understanding of the processes of cultural interaction in Mesoamerica, i.e. to the solution of problems of broader significance and general interest in Mesoamerican archaeology. Specifically, if some of the alignments discussed above are, indeed, earlier than their analogues in central Mexico, they will have to be added to the corpus of data that, as Marcus (2003: 91) points out, require a reconsideration of the alleged Teotihuacan influences in the Maya area.

Note Added in Proof

After this paper was submitted for publication, the idea about the directionality and origin of the alignment group discussed in this contribution, first inspired by orientations in southeastern Campeche, has been reinforced by further research. The orientations to sunrises on February 12 and October 30 have been found to constitute the most prominent alignment group all over the Maya Lowlands, while Late Preclassic buildings oriented this way have been identified not only in southeastern Campeche and El Mirador, but also at Tikal, Chakanbakan and Izamal (Sánchez and Šprajc 2012a; 2012b; Šprajc and Sánchez 2012; Šprajc et al. 2013).

Notes

1   The surveys have been supported by the Instituto Nacional de Antropología e Historia, Mexico, the Scientific Research Center of the Slovenian Academy of Sciences and Arts, the Foundation for the Advancement of Mesoamerican Studies, U.S.A. (grants 00016/2001 and 01014/2002), and the Committee for Research and Exploration of the National Geographic Society, U.S.A. (grants 7592-04, 7683-04 and 7756-04).

2   It should be pointed out that the astronomical argument is essential, but by itself not sufficient for explaining the clockwise skew of Mesoamerican architectural orientations. I have argued that this tendency can be accounted for by a combination of astronomical considerations and the symbolism related to the world directions or parts of the universe (Šprajc 2001b: 88ff; 2004).

3   If two or more prominent buildings pertaining to one architectural group were found to share the same orientation, the latter was considered in the analyses as a single alignment.

4   Referring to the approximate skew with regard to the cardinal directions, this has become a widely accepted and familiar label for these alignments (cf. Šprajc 2001b: 27).

5   The azimuths of these alignments exhibit considerable variations; depending on the dates recorded, as well as on the geographical latitude and the horizon altitude, they mainly vary between the values of 104°/284° and 108°/284°, being equivalent to clockwise skews of 14–18° from cardinal directions. Even if, therefore, the mean value of these deviations is not 17°, the designation for the "17°-family of orientations", whose origins can be sought in the pioneering stage of archaeoastronomical research in Mesoamerica (cf. Marquina and Ruiz 1932: 11; Šprajc 2001b: 27), has become conventional and widely accepted.

6   Sunrises and sunsets separated by 13-day intervals and their multiples occurred on dates with the same *trecena* numeral, while the events separated by 20-day periods and their multiples fell on dates having the same *veintena* sign of the 260-day count. The importance of intervalic time reckoning in Mesoamerica is attested both in central Mexican (Siarkiewicz 1995) and in the Maya codices (Aveni et al. 1995; 1996), hence the patterns of dates separated by certain intervals must have been well known to astronomers-priests. The mechanics of the 260-day count is even nowadays familiar to indigenous calendar-keepers in the Guatemala highlands, who use no written records; the knowledge possessed and the procedures employed by prehispanic full-time specialists were obviously far more sophisticated (cf. Šprajc 2001b: 151ff).

7   For the four dates to be recorded by one and the same orientation, appropriate horizon altitudes are required, such as those found in mountainous regions of central Mexico; in the Maya Lowlands, however, where horizon elevations are close to 0°, these four dates cannot be marked by a single alignment.

8   According to Malmström (1981; 1997), the motive underlying the orientations that recorded sunsets on August 13 (like the Sun Pyramid at Teotihuacan) was to commemorate the initial date of the Maya Long Count in 3114 BC. However, while Aveni et al. (2004) reported some orientations marking August 13 (and April 30) in the Terminal Classic and Postclassic architecture of Chichén Itzá and Mayapán, no such alignments have been found in the Late Preclassic and Classic period sites of southeastern Campeche.

9   Malmström (1981: 251f; 1997: 91ff) and Tichy (1991: 99) suggested an earlier origin of these alignments at other sites, but without giving precise alignment data.

References

Adams, Richard E. W., 1981. Settlement Patterns of the Central Yucatan and Southern Campeche Regions. In *Lowland Maya settlement patterns* (W. Ashmore ed.). School of American Research – University of New Mexico Press, Albuquerque, 211–257.

Aimers, James J. and Prudence M. Rice, 2006. Astronomy, Ritual, and the Interpretation of Maya "E-Group" Architectural Assemblages. *Ancient Mesoamerica* 17(1), 79–96.

Aveni, Anthony F., 2001. *Skywatchers: A Revised and Updated Version of Skywatchers of Ancient Mexico.* University of Texas Press, Austin.

Aveni, A. F. and H. Hartung, 1986. *Maya City Planning and the Calendar. Transactions of the American Philosophical Society* 76(7).

Aveni, Anthony and Horst Hartung, 2000. Water, Mountain, Sky: the Evolution of Site Orientations in Southeastern Mesoamerica. In *In Chalchihuitl in Quetzalli: Mesoamerican Studies in Honor of Doris Heyden* (E. Quiñones Keber ed.). Labyrinthos, Lancaster, 55–65.

Aveni, Anthony F., Anne S. Dowd and Benjamin Vining, 2003. Maya Calendrical Reform? Evidence from Orientations of Specialized Architectural Assemblages. *Latin American Antiquity* 14(2), 159–178.

Aveni, Anthony F., Susan Milbrath and Carlos Peraza Lope, 2004. Chichén Itzá's legacy in the Astronomically Oriented Architecture of Mayapán. *Res: Anthropology and Aesthetics* 45, 123–143.

Aveni, Anthony F., Steven J. Morandi and Polly A. Peterson, 1995. The Maya Number of Time: Intervalic Time Reckoning in the Maya Codices, part I. *Archaeoastronomy* 20 (*Journal for the History of Astronomy* Supplement to Vol. 26), S1–S28.

Aveni, Anthony F., Steven J. Morandi and Polly A. Peterson, 1996. The Maya Number of Time: Intervalic Time Reckoning in the Maya Codices, part II. *Archaeoastronomy* 21 (*Journal for the History of Astronomy*, Supplement to Vol. 27): S1–S32.

Folan, William J., Laraine A. Fletcher, Jacinto May Hau and Lynda Florey Folan, eds, 2001. *Las ruinas de Calakmul, Campeche, México: Un lugar central y su paisaje cultural.* Universidad Autónoma de Campeche, Campeche.

Girard, Rafael, 1948. *El calendario maya-mexica: Origen, función, desarrollo y lugar de procedencia.* Editorial Stylo, México.

Girard, Rafael, 1949. *Los chortis ante el problema maya,* Vol. II. Ministerio de Educación Pública, Guatemala.

Hansen, Richard D., 1998. Continuity and Disjunction: the Pre-Classic Antecedents of Classic Maya Architecture. In *Function and Meaning in Classic Maya Architecture* (S. D. Houston ed.). Dumbarton Oaks, Washington, 49–122.

Hansen, Richard D., 2000. Ideología y arquitectura: poder y dinámicas culturales de los mayas del periodo Preclásico en las tierras bajas. In *Arquitectura e ideología de los antiguos mayas: Memoria de la Segunda Mesa Redonda de Palenque* (S. Trejo ed.). Instituto Nacional de Antropología e Historia, México, 71–108.

Lincoln, Jackson Steward, 1945. *An Ethnological Study on the Ixil Indians of the Guatemala Highlands.* Microfilm Collection of Manuscripts on Middle American Cultural Anthropology 1, University of Chicago Library, Chicago.

Malmström, Vincent H., 1981. Architecture, Astronomy, and Calendrics in Pre-Columbian Mesoamerica. In *Archaeoastronomy in the Americas* (R. A. Williamson ed.). Ballena Press, Los Altos – The Center for Archaeoastronomy, College Park, 249–261.

Malmström, Vincent H., 1997. *Cycles of the Sun, Mysteries of the Moon: The Calendar in Mesoamerican Civilization.* University of Texas Press, Austin.

Marcus, Joyce, 2003. Recent Advances in Maya Archaeology. *Journal of Archaeological Research* 11(2), 71–148.

Marquina, Ignacio and Luis R. Ruiz, 1932. La orientación de las pirámides prehispánicas. *Universidad de México* 5, (25–26), 11–17.

Nalda, Enrique, 2004. *Kohunlich: Emplazamiento y desarrollo histórico.* Instituto Nacional de Antropología e Historia – Plaza y Valdés (Colección Científica 463), México.

Remington, Judith A., 1980. Prácticas astronómicas contemporáneas entre los mayas. In *Astronomía en la América antigua* (A. F. Aveni ed.) (orig.: *Native American Astronomy.* University of Texas Press, Austin, 1977). Siglo XXI, México, 105–120.

Ruppert, Karl and John H. Denison, Jr., 1943. *Archaeological Reconnaissance in Campeche, Quintana Roo, and Peten.* Carnegie Institution of Washington, Publication 543. Washington.

Sánchez Nava, Pedro Francisco, and Ivan Šprajc, 2012a. Arquitectura y planeación urbana en Calakmul, Campeche, México: astronomía, calendario y geografía simbólica." In: *Los Investigadores de la Cultura Maya* 20, tomo II: 93–110. Campeche: Universidad Autónoma de Campeche.

Sánchez Nava, Pedro Francisco, and Ivan Šprajc, 2012b. Orientaciones en la arquitectura maya: astronomía, calendario y agricultura. *Arqueología Mexicana* XIX, No. 118: 46–55.

Siarkiewicz, Elżbieta, 1995. *El tiempo en el tonalámatl.* Universytet Warszawski, Cátedra de Estudios Ibéricos (Monografías 3), Warszawa.

Šprajc, Ivan, 2000. Astronomical Alignments at Teotihuacan, Mexico. *Latin American Antiquity* 11(4), 403–415.

Šprajc, Ivan, 2001a. Archaeological Reconnaissance in Southeastern Campeche, México: 2001 Field Season Report; with an Appendix by Nikolai Grube. Report to Foundation for the Advancement of Mesoamerican Studies (www.famsi.org/reports/00016/index.html).

Šprajc, Ivan, 2001b. *Orientaciones astronómicas en la arquitectura prehispánica del centro de México.* Instituto Nacional de Antropología e Historia (Colección Científica 427), México.

Šprajc, Ivan, 2002. Archaeological Reconnaissance in Southeastern Campeche, Mexico: 2002 Field Season Report; with Appendices by Daniel Juárez Cossío and Adrián Baker Pedroza, and Nikolai Grube. Report to Foundation for the Advancement of Mesoamerican Studies (www.famsi.org/reports/01014/index.html).

Šprajc, Ivan, 2003. Reconocimiento arqueológico en el sureste de Campeche: temporada de 2002. In *Los Investigadores de la Cultura Maya* 11, Vol. I. Universidad Autónoma de Campeche, Campeche, 86–102.

Šprajc, Ivan, 2004. The South-of-East Skew of Mesoamerican Architectural Orientations: Astronomy and Directional Symbolism. In *Etno y arqueoastronomía en las Américas* (M. Boccas, J. Broda and G. Pereira eds). Memorias del Simposio ARQ-13 del 51° Congreso Internacional de Americanistas, Santiago de Chile, 161–176.

Šprajc, Ivan, 2002–2004. Maya Sites and Monuments in SE Campeche, Mexico. *Journal of Field Archaeology* 29(3–4), 385–407.

Šprajc, Ivan, 2005. More on Mesoamerican Cosmology and City Plans. *Latin American Antiquity* 16(2), 209–216.

Šprajc, Ivan, 2008a, ed. *Reconocimiento arqueológico en el sureste del estado de Campeche, México: 1996–2005*, BAR International Series 1742 (Paris Monographs in American Archaeology 19), Archaeopress, Oxford.

Šprajc, Ivan, 2008b. Alineamientos astronómicos en la arquitectura. In *Reconocimiento arqueológico en el sureste del estado de Campeche, México: 1996–2005* (I. Šprajc, ed.). BAR International Series 1742 (Paris Monographs in American Archaeology 19), Archaeopress, Oxford.

Šprajc, Ivan and Daniel Juárez Cossío, 2003. Altar de los Reyes, sitio del sureste de Campeche. *Arqueología Mexicana* X(59), 5.

Šprajc, Ivan, William J. Folan, and Raymundo González Heredia, 2005. Las ruinas de Oxpemul, Campeche: su redescubrimiento después de 70 años en el olvido (1934–2004). In *Los Investigadores de la Cultura Maya* 13, Vol. I. Universidad Autónoma de Campeche, Campeche, 20–27.

Šprajc, Ivan, Florentino García Cruz, and Héber Ojeda Mas, 1997. Reconocimiento arqueológico en el sureste de Campeche. *Arqueología: Revista de la Coordinación Nacional de Arqueología del INAH*, segunda época 18, 29–49.

Šprajc, Ivan, Carlos Morales-Aguilar, and Richard D. Hansen, 2009. Early Maya Astronomy and Urban Planning at El Mirador, Peten, Guatemala. *Anthropological Notebooks* 15(3), 79–101.

Šprajc, Ivan, Heinz-Dieter Richter, and Pedro Francisco Sánchez Nava, 2013. El tiempo registrado en el espacio urbano: alineamientos astronómicos en la arquitectura de Tikal, Petén, Guatemala. In: *XXVI Simposio de Investigaciones Arqueológicas En Guatemala*, Guatemala: Instituto de Antropología e Historia – Asociación Tikal.

Šprajc, Ivan, and Pedro Francisco Sánchez Nava, 2012. Orientaciones astronómicas en la arquitectura maya de las tierras bajas: nuevos datos e interpretaciones. In: *XXV Simposio de Investigaciones Arqueológicas En Guatemala*, Vol. 2: 977–996. Guatemala: Instituto de Antropología e Historia – Asociación Tikal.

Šprajc, Ivan, and Vicente Suárez Aguilar, 1998. Reconocimiento arqueológico en el sureste del estado de Campeche, México: temporada 1998. *Mexicon* 20: 104–109.

Tedlock, Barbara, 1991. La dialéctica de la agronomía y astronomía maya-quichés. In *Arqueoastronomía y etnoastronomía en Mesoamérica* (Johanna Broda, Stanislaw Iwaniszewski, and Lucrecia Maupomé, eds). Universidad Nacional Autónoma de México, Instituto de Investigaciones Históricas, México, 179–192.

Thompson, J. Eric S., 1936. Exploration in Campeche and Quitana [*sic!*] Roo and excavations at San Jose, British Honduras. *Carnegie Institution of Washington Year Book* 35, 125–128.

Thompson, J. E. S., 1974. Maya Astronomy. *Philosophical Transactions of the Royal Society of London* 276, 83–98.

Tichy, Franz, 1991. *Die geordnete Welt indianischer Völker: Ein Bespiel von Raumordnung und Zeitordnung im vorkolumbischen Mexiko*. Das Mexiko-Projekt der Deutschen Forschungsgemeinschaft 21. Franz Steiner Verlag, Stuttgart.

Villa Rojas, Alfonso, 1978. *Los elegidos de Dios: Etnografía de los mayas de Quintana Roo*. Instituto Nacional Indigenista, México.

3

The astronomical architecture of Palenque's Temple of the Sun

Alonso Mendez, Carol Karasik, Edwin L. Barnhart and Christopher Powell

During the solstices, equinoxes, zenith and nadir passages between the years 2002–2006, the authors observed distinctive patterns of sunlight inside the Temple of the Sun at Palenque. This article describes the recorded phenomena in detail and presents new evidence on the astronomical orientation of the temple. The second section puts forth a possible methodology for the architectural layout and design of the Temple of the Sun, whose geometric proportions and angles appear to correspond with the astronomical alignments of the temple. The final section discusses astronomical references in the text and in the iconography of the Tablet of the Sun.

Introduction

Maya architecture is a repository for ancient astronomical knowledge. To date, archeoastronomers have identified dozens of structures that were oriented to the Sun, stars, and planets rising and setting on the horizon. Astronomical observations formed the basis of the Classic Maya calendar, which eventually integrated the cycles of the Sun with the movements of the Moon and five visible planets. The calendar supported a religious system that linked the heavens with seasonal cycles and the agricultural rituals associated with them (Milbrath 1999: 1). Decipherments of carved inscriptions reveal that royal ceremonies and accessions also were timed to coincide with significant stations of the Sun or with rare planetary conjunctions (Aveni 2001: 163–214). The role of astronomy in agriculture, politics, and religion exemplifies the Maya penchant for interweaving nature, human society, and the divine. The night sky, with its infinite population of souls, gods, and monsters, presented a mirror image of the hidden underworld below. Alignments to celestial bodies expressed the bonds between earth and the many levels of the cosmos.

The ancient Maya exhibited their scientific and spiritual understanding of the cosmic realms through astronomical hierophanies (Aveni 2001: 220–221). As defined by the historian of religion Mircea Eliade (1958: 11), a hierophany is the manifestation of the sacred in an object or event in the material world. Archaeoastronomers have adopted the term to describe phenomena of sunlight and shadow that play across architectural features during important stations of the Sun. If accompanied by public ceremonies, these dazzling displays must have generated awe among the populace and confirmed the power of the divine ruler. Such spectacles rely on the precise alignment of monumental buildings with the Sun. In the Maya region the most renowned example takes place at Chich'en Itza during equinox when, in a dramatic play of light and shadow, the triangular pattern of a serpent appears on the balustrade of the pyramid, El Castillo.

While the Postclassic El Castillo is probably the best known, precedents for solar-oriented structures may be seen in the "Group E" complexes found at Waxaktun and at numerous other Early Classic sites (Aveni 2001: 288–292). Characteristically, the Group E complex contains a single temple, used for sighting, that stands directly west of three buildings, each of which mark winter solstice, equinox, and summer solstice sunrises. Because Group E complexes were primarily used to record the known positions of the Sun, rather than to obtain new astronomical information, they were not true observatories in the modern sense. Instead, the complexes served as stages for "ritual observations" that may have been the focus of public ceremonies (Krupp 1981: 249).

At Palenque, several buildings apparently designed for ritual purposes show celestial orientations (Carlson 1976; Aveni and Hartung 1978), namely: the alignment of the Temple of the Count to Sirius; the Temple of the Foliated Cross to Capella; and House A and the east side of the Palace to the Moon at maximum elongation. Considering the solar alignments of major buildings at the site, John Carlson (1976) was the first of several scholars (Aveni and Hartung 1978: 175; Milbrath 1999: 69) to hypothesize that the Temple of the Sun was oriented to face the rising Sun at winter solstice. Following the initial identification of these alignments, only a few researchers have witnessed hierophanies at the site.

Neal Anderson, Alfonso Morales, and Moises Morales (1981) demonstrated the existence of a specially designed chamber in the Tower of the Palace that made it possible for Maya astronomers and calendar keepers to monitor the Sun as its rays passed through the T-shaped window on the western façade of the Tower at summer solstice and zenith passages. They concluded that the Tower functioned as a working observatory, which allowed astronomers to divide the solar year into the 260-day ritual cycle and the 105-day agricultural cycle. This idealized growing season began at zenith passage on April 30 and ended at zenith passage on August 12 (Gregorian), the anniversary in the solar year of the date of Creation (Gregorian), 13.0.0.0.0 4 Ahaw 8 Kumk'u (Freidel *et al.* 1993: 97; Coggins 1996: 21; Malmström 1997: 52). As we have recently discovered and explain below, zenith passage also played a prominent role in the Creation myth and in the dynastic history of Palenque.

Two hierophanies, witnessed during winter solstice, have been associated with rites of divine kingship. While standing in the Tower of the Palace, Linda Schele observed that the "dying" Sun at winter solstice, setting over the ridge directly behind the Temple of the Inscriptions, appeared to enter the earth through the royal tomb of Janahb Pakal (Carlson 1976: 107). Schele interpreted this solar event as an annual re-enactment of Janahb Pakal's descent into the underworld, as depicted in the iconography on the sarcophagus lid. Soon after, Schele saw the setting winter solstice Sun send a shaft of light that slowly mounted the terraces of the Temple of the Cross and enter the temple (Carlson 1976: 107). Schele speculated that this phenomenon symbolized the transfer of royal power from Janahb Pakal to his son and heir Kan B'ahlam II.

Another dynamic relationship between the Temple of the Inscriptions and the Temple of the Cross has been described by Anderson and Morales (1981). At sunset during summer solstice, they noted that the light entering the western window of the anterior corridor of the Temple of the Inscriptions aligned with the eastern window directly across the corridor and then highlighted the upper platform of the Temple of the Cross, where Stela I once stood. Their findings reveal not only the longitudinal orientation of the Temple of the Inscriptions to the summer solstice, but also its remarkable alignment to the Temple of the Cross. Their observation also reinforces Schele's theory that the visual effects seen at the solstices represented the transfer of royal power from Janahb Pakal to Kan B'ahlam.

Schele's theory begins to address the metaphysical connection between astronomical phenomena and historical events recorded in the hieroglyphic inscriptions. In fact, on-site observations helped confirm her readings of two great historical moments: the heir-designation ceremony of Kan B'ahlam, held during summer solstice of AD 641, and the death and burial of his father, Janahb Pakal, some 40 years later. As it turns out, Schele's winter solstice observations require some correction; the Tower where she was standing was not erected until the eighth century (Hartung 1980: 76) and was therefore not the correct stage for watching the setting Sun. We have found that House E of the Palace, where Pakal was crowned, was the proper vantage point for viewing the winter solstice Sun sink behind the Temple of the Inscriptions where Pakal is buried. The connection between winter solstice and the Temple of the Inscriptions is provocative since the great pyramid was completed by Kan B'ahlam and dedicated on 9.12.16.12.19 10 Kawak 7 Pax, December 23, 688 (Stuart 2005 pers. comm.), two days after winter solstice. We still see the drama of birth, death, and royal succession written in light, for the last rays of the winter solstice Sun illuminate the Temple of the Cross, built by Kan B'ahlam to commemorate his accession to the throne. Years after his father designated him as heir, on the summer solstice, Kan B'ahlam continued to honor his father's interest in solstitial alignments.

Father and son also shared an intense preoccupation with the planets. Many scholars (Lounsbury 1989: 253–254; Aveni and Hotaling 1996) have noted that Pakal's katun-ending ceremonies were synchronized with the appearance of Venus at maximum elongation. As will be seen in the final section of this paper, the Moon and major planets also played a role in the timing of rituals conducted by Kan B'ahlam. Moreover, sometime during his reign, astronomers perfected the 819-day calendar, which took into account the cycles of Saturn and Jupiter (Lounsbury 1978; Powell 1996; Aldana 2004). Given the numerous allusions to astronomical phenomena in the art and literature, considerable speculation has gone into equating the rulers and patron gods of Palenque with specific planets (Kelley 1980; Lounsbury 1985; Schlak 1996).

In sum, on-site observations comprise a small part of the multi-disciplinary inquiries into the astronomical knowledge buried in the inscriptions, art, and architecture of Palenque. Aside from studies made by Milbrath (1988), little recognition has been given to the role of the anti-zenith, or nadir, passages in the Maya calendar. Venus, Jupiter, and Saturn have received enormous attention, but the Moon has been mysteriously slighted. Progress has been made in identifying the orientations of major buildings and their possible ritual and calendrical significance, but there has been little headway in discovering the overall cosmological scheme of the ceremonial center. Numerous observations from a significant vantage point are needed for a fuller appreciation of the alignments at Palenque. Our ongoing investigations show that the Cross Group, the Temple of the Inscriptions, and the Palace exhibit astronomical alignments that are fundamental to understanding their design, function, and interrelationships.

Observations from the Temple of the Sun

The Temple of the Sun is the westernmost building in the Cross Group, a complex of three temples erected on three hills rising above a small plaza (Baudez 1996: 121–124) (Fig. 3.1). Completed by Kan B'ahlam in AD 692, the Temples of the Cross, Foliated Cross, and Sun represent shrines to the three patron deities of Palenque, GI, GII, and GIII, respectively. Each temple contains tablets with texts that tie the history of Kan B'ahlam's lineage to those gods of Creation. Each tablet also commemorates major events in Kan B'ahlam's reign. With the Temple of the Cross on the tallest hill to the north, the Foliated Cross nestled at the base of the eastern mountain, and the Temple of the Sun on a low mound in the west, the temples represent a cosmogram of the Upper, Middle, and Lower Worlds. At the same time, the temples represent the three "hearthstones of creation" located at the center of the universe in the constellation of Orion (Freidel *et al.* 1993: 65–69). Sharing architectural and artistic styles as well as textual cross-references, the temples of the Cross Group are also interrelated in their alignments to one another as well as to the Sun and Moon.

The Temple of the Sun is the most intact structure in the Cross Group and therefore the most reliable focus for on-site observations. The hierophanies that occur inside the temple are characterized by thin rays of light that cross the temple floor at well-defined angles which, we propose, were determined by architectural features and by the position of the Sun.

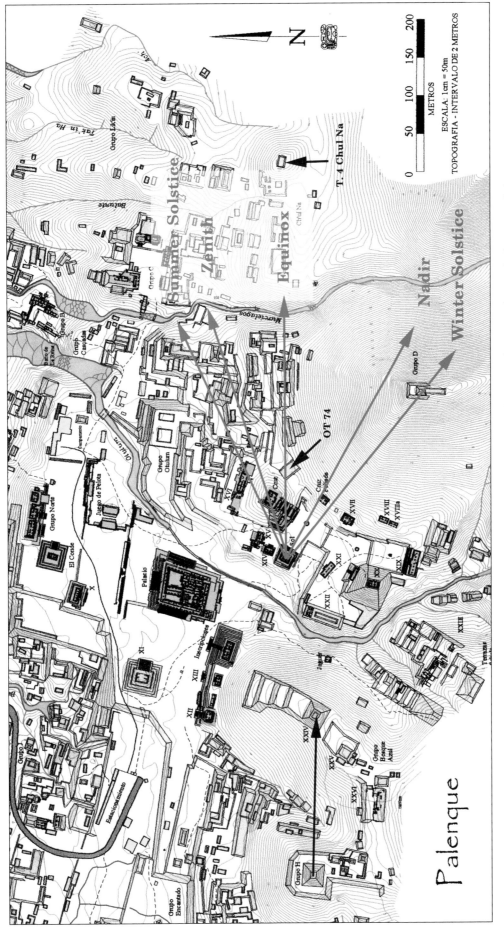

Fig. 3.1. Map of Palenque showing alignments from the Temple of the Sun (Edwin Barnhart and Alonso Mendez)

Fig. 3.2. Winter solstice sunrise over El Mirador as seen from the Temple of the Sun (photo by Alonso Mendez)

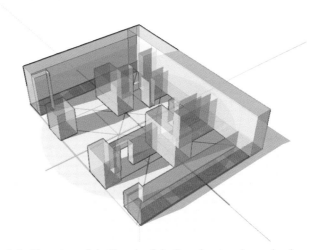

Fig. 3.3. Plan view of the Temple of the Sun showing the angle of light during winter solstice sunrise (drawing by Alonso Mendez)

Fig. 3.4. Equinox sunrise as seen from the Temple of the Sun (photo by Edwin Barnhart)

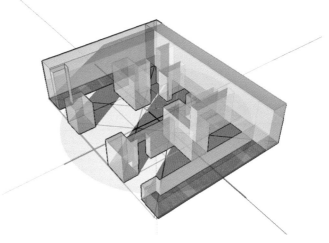

Fig. 3.5. Plan view of the Temple of the Sun showing angle of light during equinox sunrise (drawing by Alonso Mendez)

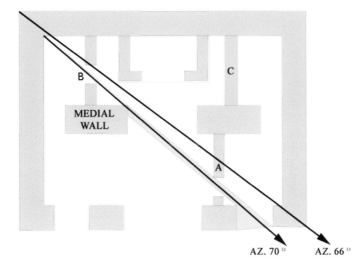

Fig. 3.6. Plan view of the Temple of the Sun showing the diagonal orientation of the temple and the angle of sunlight during summer solstice (drawing by Alonso Mendez)

The following descriptions of these solar events are based on naked-eye observations, corroborated by topographical measurements from the latest map of Palenque (Barnhart 2000) (see Fig. 3.1). Data for building azimuths are taken from Carlson (1976) and Aveni and Hartung (1978); solar azimuths and lunar information for Palenque's latitude were generated by the software Starry Night Deluxe (Andersen *et al.* 1997). All dates are Gregorian.

Winter solstice

It has long been held that the Temple of the Sun was oriented to face the rising Sun on the morning of the winter solstice. Calculating the orientation of the Temple of the Sun as 119° 46' and estimating a horizon line of 9° altitude, Carlson (1976: 110) predicted that the first rays of the Sun would enter the central doorway of the temple at a "directly perpendicular" angle.

Our observations did not confirm Carlson's hypothesis. At 9: 23 A.M. on December 21, the rising Sun broke the horizon at approximately 130° azimuth directly above El Mirador, the mountain under which the Cross Group was built (Fig. 3.2). At a vertical angle of 30°, the first rays shone through the central doorway of the temple at an angle 10° south of the transverse axis of 119°46' (Fig. 3.3). At that moment the light lined up along the back edges of the medial walls. That is the farthest the sunlight now reaches into the temple's interior during winter solstice.

On a flat horizon at Palenque's latitude of 17°28'N, the winter solstice sunrise occurs at an azimuth of 114°23'E and sunset at 245°36'W. As noted, the observed sunrise emerging over the peak of El Mirador is closer to 130°. Contrary to Carlson's predictions, the mountain completely blocks the Sun's visibility at a 9° altitude and prevents the early morning rays from entering the temple at a perpendicular angle. However, the fact that the Sun breaks from the peak of El Mirador is consistent with a recognized pattern of solstice orientations seen at numerous Mesoamerican sites with prominent topographical irregularities such as mountains or clefts between mountains (Malmström 1997).

If Carlson's hypothesis is not supported by direct observation, the problem remains: how do we account for the 119°46'E–299°46'W

alignment of the Temple of the Sun? One possible explanation is that the transverse axis of the temple closely matches the maximum elongations of the Moon. Like the Sun, the Moon has its maximum northern and southern rising and setting points. Called lunar standstills, they occur on the solstices, at full or new Moon, and repeat every 18⅔ years (Aveni 2001: 72–73). At Palenque's latitude, the Moon at its maximum southern extreme rises at 120° and at its maximum northern extreme sets at 300° on a flat horizon. The Moon rising at its maximum southern extreme on the eastern horizon would not have been visible from the central doorway of the Temple of the Sun; however, from the Temple of the Foliated Cross, the Moon at its maximum northern extreme would have been seen setting over the roof comb of the Temple of the Sun.

This correlation between the Temple of the Sun and the Moon lends weight to lunar interpretations of the iconography in the Tablet of the Sun (Bassie-Sweet 1991: 192–198). As we shall see, sunrise at nadir passage provides a decisive answer regarding the solar orientation of the temple.

Equinox

Equinox marks the midpoint between the solstices and corresponds to the time of year when the Sun rises and sets on the celestial equator. During vernal equinox, on March 21, and autumnal equinox, September 20, sunrise occurs at an azimuth of 90° due east and sunset at 270° due west.

Viewed from the Temple of the Sun on March 21, the Sun rises at a low point on the horizon, between El Mirador and the Temple of the Cross, at an azimuth of 91° (Fig. 3.4). At 6: 50 AM, sunlight enters the middle doorway of the temple at an oblique angle of 29° north of the transverse axis. The medial wall and sanctuary wall narrow the first ray until it becomes a thin knife of light reaching into the southwest corner of the central posterior chamber (Fig. 3.5). The light then retreats from the corner, and by 7:30 AM, it disappears completely.

It is worth emphasizing that this light pattern is not accidental. This corner, formed by secondary wall B and the back wall (Fig. 3.5), was apparently added to define the angle of sunlight at equinox. By observing the alignment of diagonal shafts of light in the far corner of the Temple of the Sun, Maya astronomers would have been able to recognize the exact days of vernal and autumnal equinoxes. This knowledge may have served to fix the dates for agricultural activities in the solar calendar (Aveni 2001: 293–294).

In contrast with equinox sightings made at sites with flat horizons, such as Chich'en Itza and Waxaktun, it is the low notch between El Mirador and the Temple of the Cross that defines the horizon at equinox. Our topographical surveys indicate that much of this low notch was manmade. Pending further exploration, structure OT74 and the terraces of the Otolum Group could prove to be the true markers for equinox sightings from the Temple of the Sun (see Fig. 3.1). Because they are related to the Cross Group and show alignments to equinox, these structures may eventually illustrate a concerted effort by Palencano builders to establish corridors of sightings. Given the hilly terrain, it is likely that astronomers made initial long-distance sightings of the Sun from high observation points, such as the hills crowned with standing structures that show definite equinox orientations to one another (e.g., between the Temple of the Cross and Temple IV in the Ch'ul Na Group and between Temple XXIV and Group H; see Fig. 3.1). These long-distance sightings would have decreased any margin of error in reading the slight differences in azimuth during the two successive days of equinox (Aveni 2001: 65–66). Readings taken from these lofty elevations could then be transferred to plazas or groups lacking clear views of the horizon. This was probably the case for the Temple of the Sun; modifications were made to the low notch as well as to the interior of the temple so that the building would better interact with the Sun at equinox. Future excavations as well as further investigations of ancient surveying techniques will no doubt shed light on the complex interrelationship between elevated sightings and plaza orientations.

Summer solstice

Summer solstice corresponds to the time of year when the Sun rises and sets at its maximum position in the most northerly position on the horizon. At Palenque's latitude, sunrise on a flat horizon occurs at an azimuth of 65°14'E and sunset at 294°44'W.

As we first observed in 2002, at 7:00 AM on June 21, the Sun, when viewed from the interior of the Temple of the Sun, rises from its northernmost point on the horizon, grazing the upper northwest terrace of the Temple of the Cross. Light enters the Temple of the Sun at an oblique angle of 50° north of the transverse axis, or approximately 70° azimuth.

The diagonal light entering the northeast doorway continues to steal across the temple floor. As it pierces the dark interior, the broad ray, blocked by consecutive wall edges, grows increasingly narrow until it becomes a thin beam of light striking the corner of the southwest chamber. By 7:30 AM the rays recede from the temple. As with the previous example, the angle of light seen within the temple appears to be the direct result of significant architectural details, which suggest that this solstice alignment was intentional. The northeast corner is set back 10 cm from the rest of the façade, a notable difference that allows the Sun to penetrate the interior at the desired angle. In order to permit the early morning rays to enter the front doorway at azimuths between 90° and 65°, the ancient architects left evidence that implies close attention to those particular angles of sunrise. Their concern is apparent in the addition of two interior walls (A and B) with doorways that precisely frame the light (see Fig. 3.6). Given the fact that the other secondary wall (C) does not have an opening, we must assume that the architects chose to capture the light that radiates from the northern part of the horizon. Careful alignment of the doorways to the medial wall permitted the ray of light to pass through the temple. By capturing sunlight through doorways at a diagonal, observers were also able to confirm the position of the Sun on the horizon with greater precision.

A final point needs to be made concerning the intentionality of design as well as the function of the temple. While the diagonal of the temple (66°14') is only one degree off the true azimuth for summer solstice sunrise (65°14'), it is the *visible light* entering the temple at 70° and its relationship to the transverse axis that mark the angle of the summer solstice (Fig. 3.6). This indicates knowledge of the solstitial azimuth prior to the construction of the temple; later design modifications reaffirm this knowledge both visually and conceptually. Based on these

Fig. 3.7. Zenith sunrise over the Temple of the Cross, as seen from the Temple of the Sun (photo by Alfonso Morales).

corresponds to the days when the Sun reaches a 90° vertical position from the horizon. At midday the Sun is directly overhead in the center of the sky.

Zenith varies according to latitude. At Palenque, the first zenith passage takes place on May 7 and the second on August 5, when the Sun rises at an azimuth of 72°2' and sets at an azimuth of 287°7'.

On the day of zenith passage, sunrise at Palenque occurs at about 6: 30 AM., but direct light is not visible from the Temple of the Sun until 8:00 AM. Seen from the central doorway of the temple, the Sun rises directly over the roof comb of the Temple of the Cross in a spectacular display of architectural alignment between the two buildings (Fig. 3.7).

Inside the Temple of the Sun, a wide beam of light enters the northeast doorway, as it does during summer solstice. Originally, Doorway A had a lintel that limited the maximum extension of the morning light. With the aid of a plumb rod marking the edge of the doorway and approximating the height of the door, we were able to observe a thin ray of light, defined by the width of the door and the angle of entry (approximately 45° north of the transverse axis), advancing toward the southeast corner of the sanctuary (Fig. 3.8).

Nadir passage

Nadir is the opposite of zenith. Like zenith passage, nadir passage varies according to latitude; the higher the latitude, the closer the distance between winter solstice and nadir passage, summer solstice and zenith passage. At the equator, nadir and zenith coincide with the equinoxes. At the 23° latitude of the Tropics, nadir and zenith correspond with the solstices. At Palenque's latitude of 17°28' N, nadir passage occurs at midnight on January 29 and November 9, when the Sun passes at 90° below the horizon.

The nightly passage of the Sun under the earth is described in contemporary cosmology and folk tales (Gossen 1974: 34; Karasik 1996: 232, 273). Additionally, ethnographers have found that modern Maya languages equate our cardinal directions of north and south with zenith, "up" or "above," and nadir, "down" or "below" (B. Tedlock 1992: 19–24). According to Coggins, the same was true for the ancient Maya (B. Tedlock 1992: 19).

Fig. 3.8. Plan view illustrating the angle of zenith sunlight in the Temple of the Sun (drawing by Alonso Mendez)

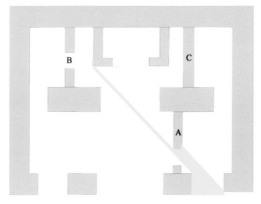

factors, we conclude that the temple functioned not so much as an instrument for collecting raw data but as a sacred space for conducting ritualized astronomical observations.

Zenith passage

Zenith passage occurs only within the limits of the Tropics of Cancer and Capricorn and

How did the ancient Maya determine the times of year when the Sun reached what they considered to be the center of the underworld? Nadir can be arrived at geometrically by measuring the angle between summer solstice and zenith sunrises and then transposing that angle to the known winter solstice azimuth and the presumed azimuth of nadir. Alternately, a straight line can be extended from the point on the horizon line where zenith sunrise occurred through the observer's location to a point opposite on the western horizon. The arithmetical solution is as simple. Astronomers at Palenque may have counted the number of days from summer solstice to zenith and then counted the same number of days from winter solstice to nadir. The results would have been fairly accurate. Astronomers could then correlate their findings by observing bright stars on the horizon. Sirius, the brightest star in the sky, would have been the logical marker for nadir passage. During the Late Classic period, Sirius rose at 106°26' and set at 253°33', remarkably close to the azimuths for the rising and setting nadir Sun (107°45'E–252°5'W) in the seventh century. Aveni and Hartung (1978: 176) have already noted that Palenque's Temple of the Count faces Sirius. It is possible that the temple also faced the rising Sun at nadir passage.

Milbrath's (1988: 26–28) identification of the east/west axis of El Castillo at Chich'en Itza is perhaps the first recognition of the relationship between zenith and nadir as seen in the alignment of a Maya temple. Milbrath mentions that the November nadir marked the beginning of the dry season while the January nadir marked the commencement of the agricultural season. In addition to its calendrical significance, Milbrath proposes that the November nadir announced the period of warfare.

At Palenque, the nadir Sun now rises and sets at an azimuth of 107°18'E–252°32'W. Viewed from the Temple of the Sun at 9:15 AM on November 9, the sunrise breaks the horizon at a vertical angle of 23° and a horizontal azimuth of 120°. Light floods the temple at a direct perpendicular angle, illuminates the room to the south of the sanctuary, and reaches the entrance to the inner sanctuary. The photograph in Figure 3.9, taken from the threshold of the sanctuary, shows the

Fig. 3.9. Nadir sunrise centered below the lintel of the middle doorway, Temple of the Sun (photo by Alonso Mendez)

centering of the Sun below the lintel of the middle doorway.

This is the effect that Carlson had predicted for winter solstice. Our observations establish that the transverse axis of the temple is oriented to the rising Sun at nadir.

As mentioned earlier, the transverse axis of the temple also marks the southern maximum extreme of the rising Moon as well as the northern maximum extreme of the setting Moon (300°), events which occur during the solstices every 18⅔ years. Although the moonrise at 120° is not visible from the Temple of the Sun, the alignment of the temple with the lunar standstills merits attention.

An astronomical blueprint for the layout and design of the Temple of the Sun

A nucleus of bedrock lies at the core of the Cross Group and forms the mass of the temples' substructures as well as the ravine between the major hills surrounding what would become the Cross Group Plaza (Hanna 1996: 5). First this deep ravine had to be leveled and the topsoil removed, in order to reach the bedrock carved by millennia of rains rushing down the mountainside. Then thousands of cubic meters of clay were laid down to insure that later flooding would never undermine the foundation of the Cross Group Plaza. Upon this foundation, construction of the Temples of the Sun, Cross, and Foliated Cross began. In this case, it was not necessary to move mountains but to "dress" them.

The builders of the Cross Group must have recognized the advantages of raising temples on natural elevations, one of which would face the rising Sun. While standing on the foundation for the future Temple of the Sun, the builders had observed the major stations of the Sun in relation to El Mirador. During winter solstice, the Sun rose directly over the peak; at equinox the Sun rose from the cleft between El Mirador and the ridge that would become the Temple of the Cross; at zenith the Sun rose directly above that same ridge; and at summer solstice, just north of the ridge. This information was all the builders needed for their preliminary design. The goal was to build two terraced platforms. The Temple of the Sun would serve as the solar observation point; the Temple of the Cross would serve as the back-sight for those observations.

Initially the taller platform of the Temple of the Cross was probably used for taking sightings that would orient the entire group. From this high vantage, surveyors were afforded a clear view of the eastern and western horizons. The primary observation would have been made during summer solstice, to establish the extreme northern position of the Sun. The surveyors drove a gnomon into the center of the stucco floor of the platform. Sunrise observations were recorded on the floor by tracing the shadow of the gnomon and connecting that painted line to a sighting stick aligned to the first rays of the Sun. The surveyors then waited until the Sun set in the west. A second line, painted over the evening shadow of the gnomon, ran toward a sighting stick aligned to the last rays of the Sun. In only one day of observations, it was possible for the surveyors to create two intersecting lines that crossed at approximately 50°, the angle of the solstices. By dividing these angles in half, they established the line of the equinox. This alignment was preserved in the diagonal orientation of the Temple of the Cross, which is less than one degree off due east–west (Fig. 3.10).

The longitudinal axis of the Temple of the Cross (119°E–301°W) coincides with the maximum excursions of the Moon. On a flat horizon at Palenque's latitude, the Moon, at its maximum southern position, rises and sets at an azimuth of 120°E–240°W and at 60°E–300°W at its maximum northern

position. The lunar azimuths also match the transverse axis of the Temple of the Sun (119°46'E–299° 46'W).

It was possible to project the measurements down to the platform of the Temple of the Sun with the aid of plumb bobs and sighting rods. Two crossed wooden sticks may have served as a rudimentary surveyor's transit. With this device, surveyors could project desired angles either vertically or horizontally (Aveni 2001: 65). Adjustments could then be made to the height of the platform, to bring the future temple into alignment with El Mirador, the low notch, and the Temple of the Cross.

After the solar angles were drawn on the platform of the Temple of the Sun, the builders began to lay out the geometric proportions of the temple. They probably relied on the same methods and the same tools traditionally employed in measuring houses made of wattle and daub (Anderson 2004, pers. comm.). In such case, braided henequen rope and wooden stakes were used for squaring the building from corner to corner. In effect, the temple builders repeated the actions of the Maker, Modeler of the *Popol Vuh* when they laid out the cosmos: "The fourfold siding, fourfold cornering, measuring, fourfold staking, halving the cord, stretching the cord in the sky, on the earth…" (D. Tedlock 1985: 72).

The repetitive measurements of halving the cord, then stretching or "doubling" the cord suggest that the Creators, like modern Maya house builders and farmers, began with a square (Vogt 1990: 17–18; Christenson 2003: 65). Next, the sides of the initial square were extended to produce a double square. This double square defined two larger squares, which, overlapping, produced a rectangle with a 3:4:5 ratio. The overlapping squares marked the two main piers of the temple façade, the width of the medial doorway, the façade of the sanctuary, and the secondary walls that framed the sanctuary. For the width of the walls, the builders stretched a cord from the center of the initial square to the outer rectangle and made a circle. The points where the radius intersected the major diagonals marked the interior corners of the temple. Three inner doorways eventually would allow sunlight to travel along the original sight lines that defined the interior space. Thus, a formula of progressive squares and rectangles produced a beautifully proportioned floor plan that also was in keeping with the principal solar orientations of the temple (Fig. 3.11).

The exterior dimensions of the temple were based on an integral right triangle with 3:4:5 proportions and interior angles of 90°, 53°, and 37° (Fig. 3.12). The 90° angle was inherent in the initial square, whose 45° diagonal was the angle between the observed sunrise at zenith and nadir passages. The 53° angle was the angle between summer solstice and nadir passage/maximum lunar excursion (Fig. 3.13). The observed sunlight entering the temple during summer solstice created a 50° angle with the transverse axis.

When the walls and vaults were raised, the roof comb was added. The side elevations conformed to the 3:4:5 principal proportion of the temple.

Astronomical elements in the text and iconography of the Temple of the Sun

The Temple of the Sun was originally named for the prominent "sun shield" displayed on the carved tablet in its inner sanctum (Fig. 3.14). In addition to the imagery, the hieroglyphic inscriptions on the tablet and *alfardas* contain numerous direct, and oblique, astronomical references. Floyd Lounsbury (1978; 1989), for instance, has provided brilliant mathematical insights into the Jupiter–Saturn periods related to the 819-day count, the Venus and Mars cycles, and the 1508-year tropical year drift cycle. Given the orientation of the temple, we now focus on the transits of the Sun and Moon alluded to in the Tablet of the Sun. (For correlations between calendrical data and astronomical phenomena we used the 584,285 GMT+2 standard and the Maya Date–Maya Calendric Calculator [see Bassett 1999]).

The text of the tablet begins with the birth of GIII on 1.18.5.3.6 13 Cimi 19 Ceh (A1-D6) (October 25, 2360 BC Gregorian). The second born of the Palenque Triad, GIII is named in the text as *Ahaw Kin*, "Lord Sun" (Lounsbury 1985: 50–51), though he is currently called *K'inich Ahaw*, "Sun-Faced Lord" (Miller and Taube 1993: 130; Ward 1999: 93; Montgomery 2002: 28). Long considered a solar deity, he is often associated with the Sun in the underworld (Kelley1976: 6). Dennis Tedlock (1985: 368; 1992: 264) identifies GIII with the younger Hero Twin,

Xbalanque, or "little jaguar sun," and equates him with the full Moon. It is interesting to note that a full Moon rose on his birthdate.

The later passages of the tablet cite important dates in Kan B'ahlam's life; those events are keyed to major astronomical phenomena. The first historical date, 9.12.18.5.16 2 Cib 14 Mol (D16-06) (AD July 23, 690), marks the dedication of the Cross Group, which corresponded with a rare Jupiter/Saturn/Mars conjunction. That night, Mars set at 252°45', less than a minute off the Sun's nadir position on the western horizon; Jupiter and Saturn set at 254°; and the Moon set at 250° 22'. In other words, this conjunction was amplified by the fact that the major planets entered the underworld through the portal of the nadir Sun.

Kan B'ahlam dedicated the *K'inich B'ahlam Kuk Nah* building (Houston 1996), the Temple of the Sun, on 9.12.18.5.17 3 Caban 15 Mol (N7-N8) (AD July 24, 690). That evening Venus rose within 3° of the Sun's summer solstice position. Like the Sun at that time of year, Venus would have been visible through the northeast doorway of the Temple of the Sun.

Following the dedication of the temple, Kan B'ahlam performed a blood-letting rite to the gods, on 9.12.19.5.19 5 Cauac 17 Mol (N13-N16) (AD July 26, 690). Apparently Kan B'ahlam had waited for the Moon to reach its southern extreme and to begin its northern journey when he conducted the blood-letting ritual. The anniversary of Janahb Pakal's accession to the throne, on July 29, five days prior to the Sun's zenith passage, fell immediately on the full Moon. The night before, the full Moon passed through the Sun's nadir position, rising at 106°9' and setting at 251°43'. Aveni and Hotaling (1996: 363) mention that Jupiter, Saturn, and Mars came within 4° on the anniversary of Janahb Pakal.

The inscription then moves back in time to record Kan B'ahlam's heir designation ceremony, which began on 9.10.8.9.3 9 Ak'bal 6 Xul (AD June 17, 641) and culminated five days later on the summer solstice. As the text states (Q5-Q10), *i-u-ti bolon Ak'bal wak Xul k'alwani u-ho'tal Ok-te K'in K'inich Kan B'ahlam B'aakel Wayal yi-chi-nal* GI: "After the fifth changeover [day] he is bound as the first Pillar of the Sun, the radiant Kan B'ahlam, the Bone Spirit, in the presence of GI" (Stuart

Fig. 3.10. Illustration of hypothetical methods used in aligning the Temple of the Cross to the Sun and Moon (drawing by Alonso Mendez)

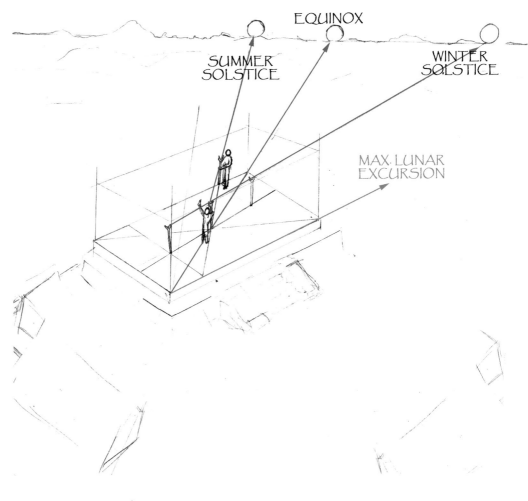

Fig. 3.11. Hypothetical geometric layout of the Temple of the Sun (drawing by Alonso Mendez after Merle Greene Robertson)

Fig. 3.12. Plan view of the Temple of the Sun showing its geometric proportions and respective angles (drawing by Alonso Mendez)

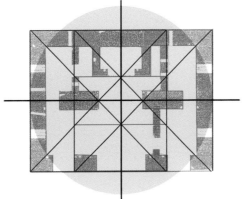

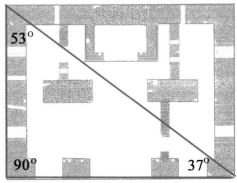

2005: 48). The heir-designation ceremony, culminating on the summer solstice, is perhaps the most critical of the solar allusions in the text as it defines the transfer of divine status from Janahb Pakal to his son Kan B'ahlam.

The final date on the tablet, 9.10.10.0.0 13 Ahaw 18 Kankin (P14-Q16)(AD December 6, 642), relates to a war event that coincided with a ten *tun* anniversary. As was customary, the six-year-old heir designate, or his father, was required to capture and sacrifice nobles from a rival kingdom (Schele and Freidel 1990: 236). Why was this date so propitious for war? Astronomically, this date fell close to a full Moon, which entered into a partial eclipse on December 14, perhaps an ideal time for

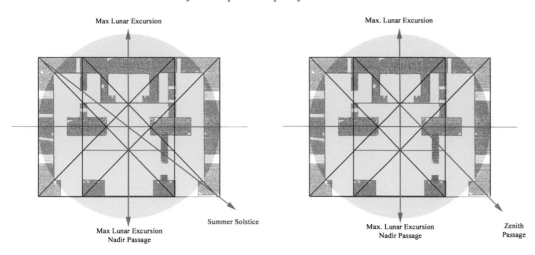

Fig. 3.13. Plan view of the Temple of the Sun showing the relationship between the temple's astronomical alignments and geometric proportions (drawing by Alonso Mendez after Merle Greene Robertson)

Fig. 3.14. Tablet of the Sun (drawing by Linda Schele)

a beheading. That night the Moon rising at 66°40', slightly more than one degree from the azimuth of summer solstice, seemed to be in direct opposition to the Sun, which set in the southwest at 245°37', only 10 minutes away from the azimuth of winter solstice.

A brief text prominently displayed above the center of the "sun shield" on the tablet records the accession of K'inich Kan B'ahlam II on 9.12.11.12.10 8 Oc 3 Kayab (L1-M6) (AD January 10, 684). At the ripe age of 48,

Kan B'ahlam waited 132 days after his father's death before he came to the throne (Schele and Freidel 1990: 240). A possible explanation may lie in the astronomical significance of this date. According to Lounsbury (1989), the event was timed to Jupiter's retrograde motion. But the Moon was far more prominent that evening. One day before full, and in conjunction with Mars, the Moon reached its maximum northern excursion, rising at 60° and setting at 299°39', less than one degree off the transverse

Glyph ID	L.C. *Tzolkin & Haab*	*Context*	GMT+2Correlation (854285) *All dates in Gregorian*	*Event*	*Proposed Astronomical Significance**
A1-B9	1.18.5.3.6 13 Cimi 19 Ceh	INSG Mythological date Tablet of the Sun	Oct 25, 2360 BC (Jul Nov 12, 2360 BC)	Birth of GIII	Full Moon at Zenith passage
D16-O6	9.12.18.5.16 2 Cib 14 Mol	Historical date Tablet of the Sun	AD July 23, 690	Dedication Temple of the Sun	Jupiter/Saturn/Mars/Moon (conjunction at nadir azimuth) Venus rises at 67° azimuth & A.M. G.E.**
N7-N8	9.12.18.5.17 3 Caban 15 Mol	Historical date Tablet of the Sun	AD July 24, 690	Dedication Temple of the Sun	Venus rises at 68° azimuth
N13-N16	9.12.18.5.19 5 Kawak 17 Mol	Historical date Tablet of the Sun	AD July 26, 690	Bloodletting rite	Full Moon rises at nadir azimuth Jupiter/Saturn/Mars conjunction at max. proximity
P6-Q6	9.10.8.9.3 9 Akbal 6 Xul	Historical date Tablet of the Sun	AD June 17, 641	Heir Designation Kan B'ahlam	New Moon Summer solstice Jupiter/Mars/Moon conjunction (25 June)
P14-Q15	9.10.10.0.0 13 Ahau 18 Kankin	Historical date Tablet of the Sun	AD Dec. 6, 642	War Event 10 Tun Completion	Full Moon/Partial lunar eclipse (Dec. 14)
L1-M6	9.12.11.12.10 8 Oc 3 Kayab	Historical date Tablet of the Sun	AD Jan. 10, 684	Accession Kan B'ahlam	Jupiter in Retrograde Full moon sets at 299° (max. northern excursion) Moon/Mars conjunction
A1-G2	9.12.19.14.12 5 Eb 5 Kayab	Historical date (*Alfardas*)	AD Jan. 10, 692	Dedication Sanctuary	Full Moon at 1° from Zenith azimuth (Jan 12)
H1-L2	9.13.0.0.0 8 Ahaw 8 Uo	Historical date (*Alfardas*)	AD Mar 18, 692	13th Katun Celebration	Vernal equinox Saturn/Mars/Moon conjunction Venus at nadir azimuth

Table 3.1. Dates from the Temple of the Sun and their proposed astronomical significance
* Astronomical data from Starry Night Deluxe (Julian)
** A.M. G.E. = Greatest elongation as Morning Star

axis of the Temple of the Sun. The placement of the accession text at the center of the tablet parallels the commemoration of this event in the central alignment of the temple. The visual and conceptual ramifications are profound. The Moon not only mirrored the position of the rising Sun during nadir passage, but also echoed the setting Sun at summer solstice, the time of Kan B'ahlam's heir-designation ceremony.

On the eighth anniversary of Kan B'ahlam's accession, he dedicated the sanctuary of the Temple of the Sun. According to a separate text recovered from the *alfardas* of the temple, this ceremony occurred on 9.12.19.14.12 5 Eb 5 Kayab (AD January 10, 692). The night before, a full Moon rose at an azimuth of 73°, only 1° from the Sun's position during zenith passage. Observed from the central doorway of the Temple of the Sun, the Moon would have been seen emerging directly from the center of the roof comb of the Temple of the Cross.

A few months later, Kan B'ahlam celebrated the completion of Katun 13 on the vernal equinox, 9.13.0.0.0 8 Ahau 8 Uo (H1-L2, *alfardas*) (AD March 18, 692). Saturn, Mars, the Moon, and Jupiter rose in alignment, within 2° and within two hours of one another. The planets would have been seen rising from the peak of El Mirador at the position of the rising Sun at winter solstice. Venus would have been visible from the Temple of the Sun directly centered in the doorway at 30° altitude and 120° azimuth, the Sun's nadir position on the horizon.

A series of dramatic lunar events surrounded

L.C. Tzolkin & Haab	Context	GMT+2 Correlation (854285) All dates in Gregorian	Event	Proposed astronomical significance
9.10.2.6.6 2 Cimi 19 Zotz	Temple of the Cross	AD May 23, 635	Birth of Kan B'ahlam	Moon at 1 day before new
		AD Jan 20, 702		Moon at 2.42 days before full Completion of one 18²/₃ year cycle of max. lunar excursion since Kan B'ahlam's Accession
9.13.10.1.5 6 Chichan 3 Pop	Zapata Panel	AD Feb 20, 702	Death of Kan B'ahlam	Full Moon rises at 1° from zenith azimuth
9.13.13.15.0 9 Ahaw 3 Kankin	Temple XIV Tablet	AD Nov 6, 705	Apotheosis of Kan B'ahlam	Sun at 4 nights before nadir passage, full Moon rises at zenith azimuth

Kan B'ahlam's death, recorded on the Zapata Panel as 9.13.10.1.5 6 Chikchan 3 Pop (AD February 20, 702). One month earlier, on January 20, the Moon reached its maximum northern excursion, completing the18²/₃ year cycle that began on the date of Kan B'ahlam's accession. Rising at an azimuth of 60° and setting at 300°, the full Moon would have been seen from the Temple of the Foliated Cross as it descended behind the Temple of the Sun, precisely along the line of the transverse axis. On the date of Kan B'ahlam's recorded death, the Moon, one day before full, rose in the sky in the zenith position (72° azimuth) and set at the position of the summer solstice Sun (285° azimuth). On AD April 20, 702, shortly before Kan B'ahlam's younger brother assumed office, a total lunar eclipse took place, and although it occurred just below the horizon at 103°, its red penumbra would still have been visible; by dawn the full Moon set at 254°, the nadir position of the sun. Two and a half years later, Kan B'ahlam's spirit is said to have risen from the underworld, on 9.13.13.15.0 9 Ahaw 3 Kankin, or AD November 6, 705 (Apotheosis Panel, Temple XIV). That evening the Sun set within one degree of nadir. The night before, the full Moon rose directly from the zenith position on the horizon, traveled across the height of the sky, and eclipsed the Pleiades before they descended into the horizon. Kan B'ahlam's life, death, and apotheosis were circumscribed by recurring patterns of the Sun and Moon (see Table 3.2).

Considerable debate surrounds the solar and lunar symbolism of the Tablet of the Sun, which ostensibly refers to war. The taller man, K'inich Kan B'ahlam II, offers a God K manikin, a symbol of royal lineage (Miller and Taube, 1997: 110–111) as well as blood sacrifice (Freidel *et al.* 1993: 194). The smaller figure, draped in "winding sheets," may represent Kan B'ahlam's dead father, K'inich Janahb Pakal (Schele and Freidel 1990: 254) or the young Kan B'ahlam before his accession to the throne (Milbrath 1999: 233; Martin and Grube 2000: 169). He offers a personified eccentric flint with flayed face shield: the *Tok Pakal*, an icon that denotes royal lineage as well as warrior status (Freidel *et al.* 1993: 305).

Both figures stand on the backs of sun deities and pay homage to the tablet's central motif, the "war stack" (Schele and Freidel 1990: 259): a shield in front of two crossed spears resting upon a platform adorned with the masks of a jaguar and two serpents. The face emblazoned on the shield has been identified as the Jaguar God of the Underworld, the Night Sun (Schele and Freidel 1990: 414), or the Jaguar War God, a deity associated with the Moon (Milbrath 1999: 123–125). Karen Bassie-Sweet (1991: 192–198) specifically associates what she calls the "Twisted Cord Jaguar" with the full Moon and then proposes that the jaguar is the zoomorphic form of GIII.

Although the platform upon which the sun shield rests appears to be a flat bar, it is most likely a throne with four sides (Bassie-Sweet 1991: 163). While the shield above the platform may represent the Sun on the horizon, it may also symbolize the seating of the ruler, K'inich Kan B'ahlam, on the throne.

Like many thrones seen in Classic Maya art, it is supported by two *Pauahtuns*, who hold up the throne with one hand and with the other, touch the band running across the bottom register of the panel. This band is composed of alternating glyph blocks: one reads *cab* or

Table 3.2. Dates for Kan B'ahlam's life and their proposed astronomical significance

"earth"; the second is a profile of God C, who signifies divinity or holiness (Taube 1992: 27–31).

The band terminates with the faces of GIII, and thus, it may represent the nightly passage of the Sun through the underworld (Baudez 1996: 123). Rather than the west to east path of the Sun beneath the earth, it may be more accurate to say that the band represents the horizon that lies between the points of maximum excursion. In any event, the band seems to serve as a symbol of transition. The gesture used by the *Pauahtuns* as they touch the band is reminiscent of the *u-pas-kab* or "hand above earth" glyph, interpreted as "to experience" or "to be born" (Lounsbury 1980: 113).

The underworld is a place of death, transformation, and rebirth. The presence of the underworld deity God L, the *Pauahtun* on the left, ties the scene on the tablet to the underworld. The floating toponyms on either side of the shield, referring to the "7 and 9 place," denote supernatural space (Miller and Taube 1993: 151; Martin and Grube 2000: 194); perhaps the 7 and 9 refer more specifically to the underworld. On the tablet located in the inner sanctuary – the *pib na*, "steambath" or "underground house" of GIII (Schele and Freidel 1990: 251; Houston 1996) – Kan B'ahlam is associated with the Jaguar War God, emblematic of the night Sun, the full Moon, and GIII seated in the underworld (Aldana 2004). The tablet thus resonates with metaphorical associations between warfare, the Moon, and the nadir Sun.

Multiple solar positions are implied on the tablet: the rising Sun at summer solstice, the Sun at or below the horizon, and the Sun in the underworld at nadir. The iconography of the tablet, although static, represents the myriad levels of the Maya universe.

This concept is embodied in the crossed spears poised above the throne. Milbrath (1999: 272) argues that the Temple of the Sun is oriented to a cross constellation in Sagittarius seen rising in the eastern sky just before Kan B'ahlam's accession and it is this constellation which was represented by the crossed spears in the tablet. A new hypothesis arises, though, with the results of this study. If we view the spears from a purely mathematical perspective, we discover yet another layer of interpretation. The angle of the spears is

53°. This angle is repeated in the 53° interior angle of the 3:4:5 proportions of the tablet. The angle of the crossed spears also coincides with the angle between the transverse axis and the diagonal of the temple. In other words, the angle of the spears commemorates the angle between summer solstice and nadir and between summer solstice and the maximum lunar extreme, a deft way of depicting the polarity between Sun and Moon. As it turned out, this angle encompassed Kan B'ahlam's life and death.

Conclusions

The Temple of the Sun was used to track major stations of the Sun as well as to mark important dates in the reign of Kan B'ahlam. Four new solar hierophanies have been identified within the temple. The morning light that enters the temple during equinox, summer solstice, and zenith passage is characterized by diagonal rays reaching back to interior corners. The broad beam of light entering the central doorway at nadir passage indicates the transverse axis of the temple.

The diagonal rays of light recorded at equinox, summer solstice, and zenith passage were observable only to a small group of astronomers dedicated to monitoring the passage of the Sun throughout the year. But at summer solstice, the dramatic morning light may have illuminated a noble personage standing in the center of the Temple of the Sun who would have been visible to a larger audience gathered in the plaza. This solar event may have played a part in the public pageantry celebrating the anniversary of Kan B'ahlam's heir-designation ceremony. These hierophanies would have strengthened the ties between the earthly and supernatural worlds that the ruler represented. As we have seen, the precision of the temple's original design and subsequent modifications suggests that the Temple of the Sun functioned as a commemorative structure for ritualized astronomical observations which served to reaffirm the ruler's central place in the cosmic order.

Hierophanies, both public and private, depended on the acute harmony between scientific observations and mathematical knowledge. The precision of the architectural design is apparent in the geometry of the temple, which is founded on the proportions of an integral right triangle. The use of the integral right triangle has been proposed as a significant design element in the layout of building groups at Palenque and Tikal (Harrison 1994: 243; Grube 2001: 230). The same proportion is repeated in the dimensions of the Tablet of the Sun. The patron proportion of the 3:4:5 integral right triangle contains interior angles that in turn relate to the angles of the Sun and Moon.

While the architecture continues to display alignments that apparently influenced the timing and expression of historical ceremonies, the iconography on the tablet is more difficult to read. The problem is that artists were trying to depict three-dimensional space on a two-dimensional field. For example, the earth band and throne define dual terrestrial planes or horizon lines, while the vertical figures and "war stack" either stand on earth or in the underworld below. How space is depicted in two-dimensional art remains a subject for further investigation.

The multiple views of space depicted in the art point to certain overlapping features in the architectural design. The most complex shifts relate to the constant variations between the azimuths of the building's alignment and the visible light, especially at summer solstice and at nadir. The unique setting of the site is responsible for this multi-dimensional perspective of space. Such a feat would not have been possible on a flat landscape. The mountainous environment of Palenque encouraged, rather than hindered, a profound examination of the horizon, and more profound solutions. Just as Palencano artists stretched the possibilities of multiple spatial references in their art, the builders of the Cross Group were cross-referencing horizon events.

Inherent in the brilliant, but problematic, interplay between the "ideal" and real horizons is the Maya concept of duality. Astronomically, that duality can best be appreciated in the synchronization of the lunar and solar cycles: the 120° moonrise every 19 years and the bi-annual nadir sunrise that mark the transverse axis of the Temple of the Sun; the full Moon setting at the solar nadir position on AD July 26, 690, the night before Kan B'ahlam's bloodletting rite; the full Moon rising at the zenith passage position on AD January 10, 692, when Kan B'ahlam dedicated the sanctuary; and finally the full Moon setting

at 300°, directly opposite the nadir sunrise position on AD January 10, 684, when Kan B'ahlam acceded to the throne.

The importance of nadir passage is now obvious in the alignment of the Temple of the Sun. Although no date is associated with the ceremony depicted on the tablet, it is possible that the central image represents the concept of nadir. At nadir, the morning Sun shone directly along the central axis of the temple; that night it illuminated the center of the underworld. This may have been an auspicious moment for communication with the other world through rituals associated with sacrifice, death, and renewal.

Just as the ruler acted as a conduit between worlds, the Sun's position at zenith and nadir passages served as a portal through which the Moon and outer planets passed. Viewed from the Temple of the Sun, the Moon and Sun appeared as complementary opposites whose interwoven cycles were the basis for keeping time and giving measure to space.

The alignment between the Temples of the Sun and Cross at zenith passages may lend support to theories that identify the gods of those temples with the twin protagonists of the *Popol Vuh*; that is, GI may represent the older Hero Twin, Hunahpu, the Sun, while GIII may represent the younger twin, Xbalanque, the Moon. In view of the astronomical complexities described in this article, we prefer to consider the complementary relationship empirically. The solstices, zenith and nadir passages, and maximum lunar excursions represent peak transitions in the courses of the Sun and the Moon. Solstices are the extreme extensions of the Sun on the horizon whereas zenith and nadir are the vertical extremes. These spatial positions demarcated the boundaries of the ecliptic and defined sky, earth, and underworld. As principal actors in the creation myth recorded in the Cross Group, GI and GIII established those cosmological boundaries. In playing out this paramount role, the divine brothers, like the Sun and the Moon, behaved as opposite yet complementary principles.

In the text and iconography of the Temple of the Sun, Kan B'ahlam aligned himself with GI and GIII. His affinities were marked by hierophanies in the heavens and on earth. The mathematical and astronomical precision seen in the architecture replicated the "cosmic principles of hierarchical order" that formed the basis of religious thought (Aveni 1986: 8). Linking the cosmos to earthly events was a powerful affirmation of the divine in a place and time.

References

Aldana, Gerardo, 2001. Oracular Science: Uncertainty in the History of Maya Astronomy, 500–1600. Doctoral thesis presented to the Department of the History of Science, Harvard University.

Aldana, Gerardo, 2004. El trabajo del alma de Janahb Pakal: la cuenta de 819 días y la política de Kan Balam. In *Culto Funerario en la Maya Clasico: IV Mesa Redonda de Palenque*. INAH, Mexico.

Anderson, Neal and Moises Morales, 1981. Solstitial Alignments of the Temple of the Inscriptions at Palenque. *Archaeoastronomy Bulletin* 4(3), 30–33.

Anderson, Neal, Alfonso Morales and Moises Morales, 1981. A Solar Alignment of the Palace Tower at Palenque. *Archaeoastronomy. The Bulletin of the Center for Archaeoastronomy* Vol. IV, No. 3, p. 34.

Andersen, Tom, Peter Hanson and Ted Leckie, 1997. Starry Night Deluxe. Sienna Software, Inc. Toronto.

Aveni, Anthony F., 1980. *Skywatchers of Ancient Mexico*. University of Texas Press, Austin.

Aveni, Anthony F., 2001. *Skywatchers*. University of Texas Press, Austin.

Aveni, Anthony F. and Horst Hartung, 1978. Some Suggestions about the Arrangement of Buildings at Palenque. In *Proceedings of the Third Palenque Round Table* (M. Greene Robertson ed.). Pre-Columbian Research Institute, San Francisco, 173–177.

Aveni, Anthony F. and Horst Hartung, 1986. *Maya City Planning and the Calendar. Transactions of the American Philosophical Society* 76(7).

Aveni, Anthony F. and Lorren D. Hotaling, 1996. Monumental Inscriptions and the Observational Basis of Mayan Planetary Astronomy. In *Eighth Palenque Round Table, 1993* (M. Greene Robertson ed.). Pre-Columbian Research Institute, San Francisco, 357–367.

Barnhart, Edwin L., 2000. The Palenque Mapping Project: Settlement and Urbanism at an Ancient Maya City, presented to the faculty of the graduate school of the University of Texas at Austin.

Bassett Leigh, 1999. Maya Date-Maya Calculator PO Box 2509, Laurel, MD. 20709 w3nlb@amsat.org

Bassie-Sweet, Karen, 1991. *From the Mouth of the Dark Cave*. University of Oklahoma Press, Norman.

Carlson, John B., 1976. Astronomical Investigations and Site Orientation Influences at Palenque. In *The Art, Iconography and Dynastic History of Palenque, Part III* (M. Greene Robertson ed.). The Robert Louis Stevenson School, Pebble Beach, CA, 107–117

Christenson, Allen J. 2003. *Popol Vuh: The Sacred Book of the Maya*. O Books, Winchester.

Coggins, Clemency, 1996. Creation Religion and the Numbers at Teotihuacan and Izapa. *Res* 29/30, 16–38.

Eliade, Mircea, 1958. *Patterns in Comparative Religion*. Sheed and Ward, New York

Freidel, David, Linda Schele and Joy Parker, 1993. *Maya*

Cosmos: *Three Thousand Years on the Shaman's Path*. William Morrow, New York.

Gossen, Gary H., 1974. *Chamulas in the World of the Sun: Time and Space in the Maya Oral Tradition*. Waveland Press, Prospect Heights.

Grube, Nikolai, 2001. *Mayas, Una Civilización Milenaria*.: Konemann Verlagsgesellschaft mbH, Cologne.

Hanna, William F., Claude E. Petrone, and others, 1996. Geophysical Surveys at Mayan Archaeological Sites: Palenque, Chiapas, Mexico. Hanna GPR Report.

Harrison, Peter, 1994. Spatial Geometry and Logic. In *Proceedings of the Seventh Palenque Round Table* (M. Greene Robertson ed.). The Pre-Columbian Art Research Institute, San Francisco, 243–252.

Hartung, Horst, 1980. Certain Visual Relations in the Palace at Palenque. In *Third Palenque Roundtable, 1978* (M. Greene Robertson ed.). University of Texas Press, Austin, 74–80.

Houston, Stephen, 1996. Symbolic Sweatbaths of the Maya: Architectural Meaning in the Cross Group at Palenque, Mexico. *Latin American Antiquity* 7(2), 132–151.

Karasik, Carol, ed., 1996. *Mayan Tales from Zinacantán: Dreams and Stories from the People of the Bat*, collected and translated by Robert M. Laughlin. Smithsonian Institution Press, Washington, D.C.

Kelley, David H., 1976. *Deciphering the Maya Script*. University of Texas Press, Austin.

Kelley, David H., 1980. Astronomical Identities of Mesoamerican Gods. *Archaeoastronomy* (Supplement to *Journal for the History of Astronomy*) 2, S1–S54.

Krupp, E. C. 1983. *Echoes of the Ancient Skies: the Astronomy of Lost Civilizations*. Harper and Row, New York.

Lounsbury, Floyd, 1978. Maya Numeration, Computation and Calendarical Astronomy. In *Dictionary of Scientific Biography*, 15, supplement 1 (C. Coulston-Gillispie ed.). Charles Scribner and Sons, New York.

Lounsbury, Floyd, 1980. Some Problems in the Interpretation of the Mythological Portion of the Hieroglyphic Text of the Temple of the Cross at Palenque. In *Third Palenque Roundtable, 1978*, Part 2 (M. Greene Robertson ed.). University of Texas Press, Austin, 99–115.

Lounsbury, Floyd, 1985. The Identities of the Mythological Figures in the Cross Group Inscriptions of Palenque. In *Fourth Palenque Round Table, 1980* (M. Greene Robertson ed). Pre-Columbian Art Research Institute, San Francisco, 45–58.

Lounsbury, Floyd, 1989. A Palenque King and the Planet Jupiter. In *World Archaeoastronomy: Selected Papers from the Second Oxford International Conference on Archaeoastronomy* (A. F. Aveni ed.). Cambridge University Press, Cambridge, 246–259.

Malmström, Vincent H., 1997. *Cycles of the Sun, Mysteries of the Moon: The Calendar in Mesoamerican Civilization*. University of Texas Press, Austin.

Martin, Simon and Nikolai Grube, 2000. *Chronicle of the Maya Kings and Queens*. Thames & Hudson, London.

Milbrath, Susan, 1988. Representación y orientación astronómica en la arquitectura de Chichen Itza. *Boletín de las Escuela de Ciencias Antropológicas de la Universidad de Yucatán* 89, 25–37.

Milbrath, Susan, 1999. *Star Gods of the Maya: Astronomy*

in Art, Folklore, and Calendars. University of Texas Press, Austin.

Miller, Mary and Karl Taube, 1996. *An Illustrated Dictionary of the Gods and Symbols of Ancient Mexico and the Maya.* Thames & Hudson, London.

Montgomery, John, 2002. *Dictionary of Maya Hieroglyphs.* Hippocrene Books, New York

Powell, Christopher, 1996. A New View of Maya Astronomy. Unpublished M.A. Thesis. University of Texas at Austin.

Robertson, Merle Greene, 1991. *The Sculptures of Palenque*, Vol. IV: *The Cross Group, The North Group, The Olvidado, and Other Pieces.* Princeton University Press, Princeton.

Schele, Linda, 1976. Accession Iconography in the Cross Group. In *Proceedings of the Second Mesa Redonda, 1974* (M. Greene Robertson ed.). The Robert Louis Stevenson School, Pebble Beach, CA.

Schele, Linda and David Freidel, 1990. *A Forest of Kings: The Untold Story of the Ancient Maya.* William Morrow, New York.

Schele, Linda and Peter Mathews, 1999. *The Code of Kings: The Language of Seven Sacred Maya Temples and Tombs.* Simon and Schuster, New York.

Schlak, Arthur, 1996. Venus, Mercury, and the Sun: GI, GII, and GIII of the Palenque Triad. *Res* 29/30, 180–202.

Stuart, David, 2002. The Hieroglyphic Inscriptions from Temple XIX at Palenque: A Commentary. Mesoweb.

Stuart, David, 2005. *Sourcebook for the 29th Maya Hieroglyphic Forum.* University of Texas at Austin.

Taube, Karl Andreas, 1992. *The Major Gods of Ancient Yucatan.* Dumbarton Oaks, Washington, D.C.

Tedlock, Barbara, 1992. The Road of Light: Theory and Practice of Mayan Skywatching. In *The Sky in Mayan Literature* (A. F. Aveni ed.). Oxford University Press, New York, 18–42.

Tedlock, Dennis, 1985. *Popol Vuh.* Simon and Schuster, New York.

Tedlock, Dennis, 1992. Myth, Math, and the Problem of Correlation in Mayan Book. In *The Sky in Mayan Literature* (A. F. Aveni ed.). Oxford University Press, New York.

Vogt, Evon Z., 1990. *The Zinacantecos of Mexico, A Modern Way of Life.* Holt Rinehart and Winston, Inc., Fort Worth.

Robert F. Wald, 1999. *A Palenque Triad* (P. Keeler ed.). The Maya Workshop Foundation, Austin.

4

An oracular hypothesis: the Dresden Codex Venus Table and the cultural translation of science

Gerardo Aldana y Villalobos

We must face it: so far as ends are concerned Maya astronomy is astrology.

(Thompson 1972: 77)

In the archaeology of ancient civilizations it is often difficult to humanize the producers and users of the remains we study. Linda Schele and Peter Mathews captured well some of this challenge in *The Code of Kings* through their discussion of the attribution of Tikal Structure 5D-46:

> Although feeling a bit of a fool, Linda went through an epiphany at that moment. The Central Acropolis ceased to be anonymous and became one of the most interesting buildings from the entire history of the Maya.
>
> Think of it! Toh-Chak-Ich'ak was a man like Alexander the Great or George Washington. He marked the history and identity of his city for the rest of its existence. His descendants preserved his house unchanged for over five hundred years – and that for a Maya building is an eternity. They built their own palaces around the enshrined house of their great ancestor, making it the most important and revered place in the entire kingdom. (1998: 94)

Schele's eureka moment of seeing an ancient Mayan ruler as an historical figure occurred after decades of study, when the glyphs she deciphered were associated with the patron of a palace and the owner of a ceramic vessel (see Fig. 4.1) Only then did this Mayan leader become mentally categorized with historical figures from "Western" culture.

Undoubtedly, a major factor here resides in the paucity of information we have available on any one individual from Classic Mayan times; we have no personal correspondence, no autobiographical journals. But just as important has to be the vast cultural gulf that prevents us from seeing ancient peoples' work and lives as familiar and their ideas as intellectually compelling – even more-so the esotera of elite culture. Eric Thompson's epigraph to this essay begins to address the latter issue, but does not address how the distinction becomes important. In this essay, I take up Thompson's inference explicitly and its relationship to Schele's eureka moment. Here, I nest this problem within the broader question of scientific endeavor and how scholars translate it across temporal and cultural divides.

Translations of the Dresden Codex

My entry into this endeavor comes by way of one aspect of the Venus Table – one that has given me pause since I first worked my

*Fig. 4.1. Decoration
on early Classic
ceramic vessel recording
the name of Chak Toh
Ich'ak. Drawing by
Linda Schele
© David Schele,
courtesy Foundation
for the Advancement of
Mesoamerican Studies,
Inc., www.famsi.org.*

way through Thompson's *Commentary on the Dresden Codex* some years ago. The Table itself has a long and mostly vaunted place within the historiography of Maya Studies, setting up astronomy as a central concern in interpretations of Mayan intellectual activity for much of the twentieth centurycentury (*cf.* Introduction, this volume). It has been tackled by several "big names," yet still proves elusive in some important aspects of its interpretation (Förstemann 1891; Seler 1904; Teeple 1930; Thompson 1972; Lounsbury 1978; Aveni 1980, 2001; Bricker and Bricker 2007). Regardless of any lingering issues, though, its capturing of the synodic period of Venus using the 260-day count has been hailed unequivocally as an impressive demonstration of Mayan scientific acumen.

Of the riddles it still presents to modern scholars, however, one ambiguity within the table has escaped concerted attention for some time: the table is far more accurate in the long term than it is in the short term. Thompson, for instance, noted only in passing that:

> after 65 VR [Venus Rounds], heliacal rising of Venus after inferior conjunction might be expected to be just over 5 days before 1 Ahau, the official *lub* (65 x .08 days), that is without taking into consideration the year-to-year variation in the VR which can fall to 581 or rise to 587 days. (1972: 62)

While he implicitly contrasts a 5-day accuracy over 104 years with a 6-day variation over a year and a half, Thompson avoids providing an explicit rationale for it.

For Floyd Lounsbury, however, the accuracy inconsistency did merit explicit consideration. In "Maya Numeration, Computation, and Calendrical Astronomy" Lounsbury wrote:

> [i]ts long-term accuracy is of course greater than its short-term accuracy. But even for short terms the accumulated error never exceeds the magnitude of the deviation of the planet's actual periods from their mean value. The table was probably used as a warning table, geared to anticipate the phenomena…. (1978: 789)

Thus, Lounsbury may have been the first to provide a rationale for this character, suggesting that the table compensated for its 6-day variability by anticipating the observable phenomena it predicted. His argument, therefore, is that the Venus Table did not have to predict planetary positions accurately in the short term if it predicted them far enough in advance and was capable of preserving its predictive ability into the long term.

In his 1980 and 2001 versions of *Skywatchers*, Anthony Aveni nominally suggested an interpretation not unlike Lounsbury's by comparing the Venus Table to the Dresden Codex Eclipse Table. In "general layout" and in "[i]ts function [the table] was likely the same as well — to serve as a warning table for the apparitions of Venus" (1980: 184; 2001: 184). But six pages into his elucidation of the table's operation, Aveni takes on a different tone to address the specific incongruity between the long-term and short-term characters of the Venus Table:

> the behavior of the Maya astronomer in the performance of his Venus calculations seems paradoxical. … fluctuations between the table and the observations could have varied by a few days on many occasions. In spite of the rigor with which the astronomers tallied the long-term average of their observation, their table gives no evidence that they paid any attention to the short-term deviations. To the modern mind this seems baffling, but evidently it did not bother the Maya. They seemed to be willing to falsify their short-term planetary observations in order to make the planetary motion fit the ritual calendar. We can think of their short-term calculations as mean motions. Their tables became true astronomical ephemeredes only when considered over long intervals". (1980: 190; 2001: 189–190, though in the earlier version, "rigor" is replaced with "seriousness" and "astronomer" is replaced with "priest")

Aveni elaborated on the possible motivation for falsification in his 1980 version by referring to the job duties of the "priest" who would have been using the Venus Table.

Aveni's is the most detailed attention paid to

the practitioner him/herself. He suggested that one of the uses of the table was to anticipate Venus events "for the purpose of staging the religious ceremonies and enunciating the prognostications that would have attended the Venus appearance and disappearance" (1980: 190–191). But in this task, Aveni's interpretation departs from Lounsbury's as he claimed that astronomers would have "distorted their Venus observations to fit the ritual calendar" (1980: 190).

> The celebration of actual Venus observations on special named days that may not necessarily coincide with the actual event is rather like our custom of officially assigning certain holidays (Memorial Day, Lincoln's birthday, etc.) to the Monday of the week in which they occur. (1980: 190–191)

Even more recently, Harvey and Victoria Bricker (2007) returned to Lounsbury's work to present yet another warning table hypothesis. Their principal goal was to determine when the Venus Table would have been most accurate in order to suggest when it was utilized. Bricker and Bricker noted that a determination between viable alternative interpretations must appeal to the function of the table, and that their own interpretation is in line with most others: "Our view, which is the same as that of Lounsbury (e.g., 1978: 789) and Aveni (2001: 184), to cite just two, is that it functioned as a *warning table* because there was danger to be anticipated and, if possible, avoided" (2007: 106). Of key concern for the Brickers was the dangerous character of Venus, inferred in part from the illustrations within the table itself.

> The violent theme shown in these pictures suggests that the heliacal rise of Venus as a morning star was an event dreaded by the Maya … This situation is quite different from what Barbara Tedlock (1999: 43) has described for the people of Momostenango, who regard the heliacal rise of Venus as morning star as a lucky event. In our view, then, the Dresden Venus instrument was primarily a warning table, providing advance warning of days that would be or might be dangerous for people; the middle and lower pictures show the dangerous characteristics or "actions" of Venus on that day. (2007: 109)

The Brickers thus re-invigorated Lounsbury's hypothesis mandating that it only would have been useful if the dates actually anticipated the observable phenomena. By the same token, the more benign role of facilitating the scheduling of ceremonies proposed by Aveni is downplayed.

Each of the above interpretations is reasonable, and we cannot easily look to a differential in utility to determine which might more accurately reflect the document's ancient usage. Yet in this case, neither can we appeal to a historical context since we know virtually nothing about its author, and we cannot even be sure of the specific provenance of the codex (Thompson 1972: 16). Worse, what we do know puts us further from the intent since in various places, the text suggests that the version left to our perusal is not the original but a copy of an earlier codex (Thompson 1972: 15; Aveni 2001: 169–170; Aldana 2005: 307–308).

In *Magic, Science, Religion and the Scope of Rationality*, Stanley Tambiah follows Jon Elster so that under the purview of rationality, one can often reconstruct various possible hypotheses for interpreting events or intents within other cultures (1990: 119). The real challenge, however is that rational argument can only exclude possible interpretations, it cannot select between rationally reconstructed alternatives (Tambiah 1990). Since by reason alone, we cannot differentiate the appropriateness of either Aveni's or Lounsbury's interpretations, without further constraints we would appear to be at a standstill.

On the other hand, the larger theoretical problem we confront here provides us with an alternate approach to tackling the issue. Tambiah provides a useful set of tools in furthering our cause by distinguishing between a "concept" and a "conception" (1990: 124). A conception, he states, does not already exist within a culture, but requires analogy or elucidation. In other words, we cannot assume that a concept recognized in one culture will necessarily find isomorphic representation in another culture. The difference he illustrates via example: "the concepts of *nirvana*, *dharma*, *karma* and so on… have no exact conceptual parallels in English, French and German" (1990: 125). Anglo-Americans from Kansas might have the *conception* of karma – it can be explained intelligibly to them – but they do not possess such a *concept* in their own culture (1990).

This allows us to bring a new level of analysis to the problem of interpreting the Venus Table and so getting at a more robust representation of its authors. We may now investigate whether or not a given interpretation exists as a concept within the target or originating culture as part

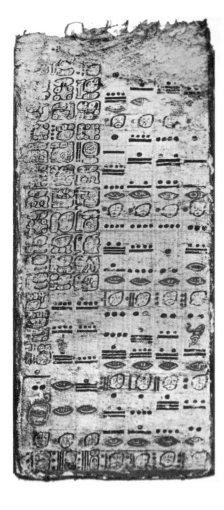
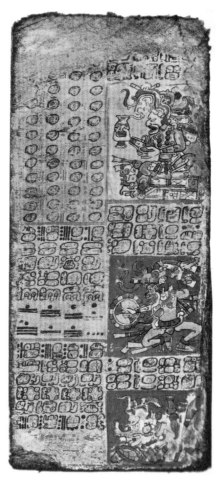

Fig. 4.2a, b and c. Pages 24, 46 and 47 of the Dresden Codex, the Preface and Pages 1 and 2 of the Table, respectively. From the Förstemann facsimile of the Dresden Codex.

of the assessment of its viability. In order to attempt such an analysis here, we first take a closer look at the Venus Table itself.

The Dresden Codex Venus Table

Since Ernst Förstemann's nineteenth-century achievements, much attention has been paid to the mathematical elegance of the Dresden Codex Venus Table. Indeed, there is much to find within the contrived Long Count dates and distance numbers in the Preface to the table, within the 584-day building blocks of its 37,960-day length coded in 260-day count dates, and in the real-time adjustment capability presented by the tropical year dates (see e.g. Aveni 2001: 184–196). (See Figs 4.2 and 4.3) Differing interpretations of these numerical patterns – 100 years after their cracking by Förstemann – still allow for further debate (see e.g. Bricker and Bricker 2007: 105, table 3.3). Yet there is also plenty of interest and ambiguity within the hieroglyphic text,

much of which has become more accessible with recent advances in the decipherment of the script.

One of the intriguing features of the hieroglyphic text, for example, is its emphasis on only one cosmic region. All of the text in the Preface and that framing the illustrations refers in some way to the East (see Fig. 4.2) The first pair of columns in the prefatory text (read in standard zigzag fashion) contains the phrase *'lak'in k'ahlaj'* (enclosed in the east) and then lists the names of five deities (Four Pawatun, Ix Uh Ajaw, Jun Ajaw, the "Star Caiman," and Kimil), each paired with Chak Ek' (Fig. 4.3: Glyph Blocks A4–B12, A13–A15). The same five deity names show up again in Glyph Blocks K17, S17, AA17, AI17, and AQ17, associated with the dates for the reappearance of Venus after its canonical eight days of occultation. These names also take up Glyph Blocks H21, P21, X22, AF22 and AN22, after the next set of tropical year base dates (although here in the columns for last morning appearance). Finally,

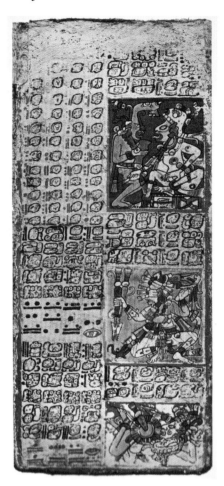

the figures at the top right hand side of each page are the referents of these five names (see Figs 4.2 and 4.3) Each of these figures sits on a celestial throne (skyband) indicating that they are probably residents of the sky.

The names of the other illustrated figures also are noted in the text and are similarly associated with the East. The third column of the prefatory text, Column C, provides the names of the figures illustrated in the bottom register on the right hand side of each page (see Fig. 4.2) Each of these figures is impaled through the midsection with a spear. Preceding the list of five names in Column C, two names are given (again paired with Chak Ek'), which correspond to the spearthrower-carrying figures in the middle register of the first two pages. The other three illustrated figures in the middle position (Tawiskal (ta-wi-si-ka-la; Tlahuizcalpantecuhtli), Chak Xiwitl (CHAK xi-wi-te-le; Xiuhtecuhtli), and Kaktonal (ka-ka-to-na-la)) are not listed possibly because they are Mayanized versions of Central

Mexican (Venus) deities (Schele and Grube 1997: 143).

This set of 15 illustrated figures and their associated texts seem to corroborate Eduard Seler's very early comparison to a quote from the Central Mexican sixteenth-century manuscript known as the Annals of Cuauhtitlan and maintain the relevance of the East. The Annals recount both mythological and historical events in a style that implies a narrative connection to codex records; Seler focused on the final passage within a recounting of Quetzalcoatl's life and apotheosis to suggest a connection to the Venus pages of the Codex Borgia:

> And as they (the ancients, the forefathers) learned
> When it appears (rises)
> According to the sign, in which it (rises)
> It strikes different classes of people with its rays
> Shoots them, casts its light upon them.
> When it appears in the (first)[1] sign, "1 alligator"
> It shoots the old men and women.
> Also in the (second) sign, "1 jaguar"
> In the (third) sign, "1 stag"
> In the (fourth) sign, "1 flower"

Fig. 4.2d, e and f. Pages 48, 49 and 50 of the Dresden Codex. From the Förstemann facsimile of the Dresden Codex.

Fig 4.3. (this page and the next five pages) Translation of Pages 24, 46–50 of the Dresden Codex.

PAGE 24						
A1	B1	C1	1			
A2	B2	8 Kumk'u	1	15	10	5
A3	CHAK EK'	C3	1	16	10	5
			14	6	16	8
			0	0	0	0
			(= 151,840 = 4×37,960)	(= 113,880 = 3×37,960)	(= 75,920 = 2×37,960)	(= 37,960 = 13×2,920)
east	k'ahlaj	Y1	1 Ajaw	1 Ajaw	1 Ajaw	1 Ajaw
CHAK EK'	X2	CHAK EK'	1			
CHAK EK'	X3	Y2	5	9	4	1
CHAK EK'	X4	CHAK EK'	14	11	12	5
			4	7	8	5
			0	0	0	0
			(= 185,120)	(= 68,900)	(= 33,280)	(= 9,100)
CHAK EK'	X5	Z1	1 Ajaw	1 Ajaw	1 Ajaw	1 Ajaw
CHAK EK'	X1	Z2	4	4	4	3
u muuk	B10	Z3	17	9	1	13
u muuk	B11	Z4	6	4	2	0
			0	0	0	0
			(= 12×2,920)	(= 11×2,920)	(= 10×2,920)	(= 9×2,920)
u muuk	B12	Z5	6 Ajaw	11 Ajaw	3 Ajaw	8 Ajaw
A13			3	2	2	2
A14	9	9	4	16	8	0
A15	9	9	16	14	12	10
	16	9	0	0	0	0
	0	16	(= 8×2,920)	(= 7×2,920)	(= 6×2,920)	(= 5×2,920)
6	0	0	13 Ajaw	5 Ajaw	10 Ajaw	2 Ajaw
2			1	1		
(0)			12	4	16	8
4 Ajaw	1 Ajaw	1 Ajaw	5	6	4	2
			0	0	0	0
			(= 4×2,920)	(= 3×2,920)	(= 2×2,920)	(= 1×2,920 = 5×584)
8 Kumk'u	18 K'ayab	18 Wo	7 Ajaw	12 Ajaw	4 Ajaw	9 Ajaw

It shoots the little children.
And in the (fifth) sign, "1 reed"
It shoots the kings.
Also in the (sixth) sign, "1 death."
And in the (seventh) sign, "1 rain"
It shoots the rain.
It will not rain.
And in the (thirteenth) sign, "1 movement"
It shoots the youths and maidens.
And in the (seventeenth) sign, "1 water"
There is universal drought.
(Seler 1904c: 384–385; Aveni 2001: 195–196; see also Bierhorst 1992: 36)

The parallel between the Annals passage and the Dresden Venus Table becomes even stronger when we consider the middle hieroglyphic text on the right hand side of each of the five pages (Glyph Blocks L13–O15, T13–W15, AB13–AE15, and AJ13–AM15). On each page, the text follows the same formula: *k'ahlaj lak'in* Y *Chak Ek'. Z u hul. U muuk* A_1, A_2, ... A_n (K'AL-ja la-K'IN-ni Y CHAK EK'. Z u JUL. u mu-ka A_1, A_2, ... A_n.) Because various translations of this text can still be found within the published literature, we here review each part separately.

The hieroglyphic passage begins with a logograph for the verb *k'al* (on all but one page with its derived intransitive suffix *-ja*, yielding *k'ahlaj* (Lacadena 2004)). As noted above, this is the same verb found in the first passage of the Preface (Page 24, Glyph Block A4) and at the beginning of each column of text in Glyph Blocks H15–K18, P15–S18, X15–AA18, AF15–AI18, and AN15–AQ18 of the table itself (see Figs 4.2 and 4.3) This is also the verb governing the only known explicit textual reference to Venus within the known corpus of Classic Mayan hieroglyphic

PAGE 46							
3 Kib	2 Kimi	5 Kib	13 K'an	L1	M1	N1	O1
11 Kib	10 Kimi	13 Kib	8 K'an	L2	M2	N2	O2
6 Kib	5 Kimi	8 Kib	3 K'an	L3	M3	N3	O3
1 Kib	13 Kimi	3 Kib	11 K'an				
9 Kib	8 Kimi	11 Kib	6 K'an				
4 Kib	3 Kimi	6 Kib	1 K'an				
12 Kib	11 Kimi	1 Kib	9 K'an				
7 Kib	6 Kimi	9 Kib	4 K'an		Illustration of X5		
2 Kib	1 Kimi	4 Kib	12 K'an				
10 Kib	9 Kimi	12 Kib	7 K'an				
5 Kib	4 Kimi	7 Kib	2 K'an				
13 Kib	12 Kimi	2 Kib	10 K'an				
8 Kib	7 Kimi	10 Kib	5 K'an	k'alaj	East	N13	O13
4 Yaxk'in	14 Sak	19 Tsek	7 Xul	Y1	Chak Ek'	u muuk	O14
k'al	k'al	k'al	k'al	Z1	u hul	N15	O15
North	West	South	East				
U1	V1	W1	X1				
Chak Ek'	Chak Ek'	Chak Ek'	Chak Ek'				
		1	1		Illustration of Y1		
11	16	10	11				
16	6	16	4				
(=236)	(=326)	(=576)	(=584)				
9 Sak	19 Muwan	4 Yax	12 Yax				
X5	U1	V1	W1	L21	u muuk	N21	O21
tse?-ya-ni	tse?-ya-ni	tse?-ya-ni	tse?-ya-ni	L22	u muuk	N22	O22
Chak Ek'	Chak Ek'	Chak Ek'	Chak Ek'				
East	North	West	South				
19 K'ayab	4 Sots'	14 Pax	2 K'ayab				
11	4	12	0		Illustration of Z1		
16	10	10	8				
(=236)	(=90)	(=250)	(=8)				

inscriptions. On the Northwest Tablet of Structure 10L–11 at Copan, the inscription closes with the phrase: "*u tzakaj* 5 *Kib* 10 *Pohp k'alwaniy Ajaw Chak Ek' u muuk*(?) *Jun Ajaw winik*" (u TZAK-aj 5 Kib 10 Pohp K'AL-wa-ni-ya AJAW CHAK EK. U ?-ka JUN AJAW (WINIK)) (Aldana 2001: 216, 2005) (see Fig. 4.4) Because the same root also very often is used in the accession statements of royalty (K'AL-HUUN) and in period-ending ceremonies (K'AL-TUUN-ni), it has generally been understood as "to tie," "to bind," or "to

PAGE 47							
2 Ajaw	1 Ok	4 Ajaw	12 Lamat	T1	U1	V1	W1
10 Ajaw	9 Ok	12 Ajaw	7 Lamat	T2	U2	V2	W2
5 Ajaw	4 Ok	7 Ajaw	2 Lamat	u muuk	U3	V3	W3
13 Ajaw	12 Ok	2 Ajaw	10 Lamat				
8 Ajaw	7 Ok	10 Ajaw	5 Lamat				
3 Ajaw	2 Ok	5 Ajaw	13 Lamat				
11 Ajaw	10 Ok	13 Ajaw	8 Lamat				
6 Ajaw	5 Ok	8 Ajaw	3 Lamat	Illustration of X_1			
1 Ajaw	13 Ok	3 Ajaw	11 Lamat				
9 Ajaw	8 Ok	11 Ajaw	6 Lamat				
4 Ajaw	3 Ok	6 Ajaw	1 Lamat				
12 Ajaw	11 Ok	1 Ajaw	9 Lamat				
7 Ajaw	6 Ok	9 Ajaw	4 Lamat	k'alaj	East	u muuk	W13
3 Kumk'u	8 Sots'	18 Pax	6 K'ayab	Y_2	Chak Ek'	V14	W14
k'alaj	k'alaj	k'alaj	k'alaj	Z_2	u hul	V15	W15
North	West	South	East				
U_2	V_2	W_2	X_2				
Chak Ek'	Chak Ek'	Chak Ek'	Ek'				
2	2	3	3	Illustration of Y_2			
5	9	4	4				
0	10	0	8				
(=820)	(=910)	(=1160)	(= 1168 = 2×584)				
3 Sots'	13 Mol	18 Wo	6 Sip				
X_1	U_2	V_2	W_2	T21	U21	u muuk	W21
Chak Ek'	Chak Ek'	Chak Ek'	Chak Ek'	T22	U22	u muuk	W22
East	North	West	South				
13 Yax	3 Muwan	8 Ch'en	16 Ch'en	Illustration of Z_2			
11	4	12	0				
16	10	10	8				
(=236)	(=90)	(=250)	(=8)				

fasten" (Barrera Vasquez 1995: 367–368). Yet in Yucatec (the language that creeps into the Dresden Codex) the term also carries the sense of "to enclose," or "to encompass" (Barrera Vasquez 1995: 368). The verb *K'al* is followed by "*lak'in*" within the table itself (though preceded by it in the preface), so that the translation often given is "is bound in the east," or "is tied in the east" (Schele and Grube 1997: 142, 146–156). More recently, I have followed the Yucatec to propose that the East is the patient of the intransitive verb (Aldana 2011). In this case, "the East is enclosed," hieroglyphically describing the concept depicted on the frontispiece to the Codex Féjérvary-Mayer.

PAGE 48							
1 K'an	13 Ix	3 K'an	11 Eb	AB1	AC1	AD1	AE1
9 K'an	8 Ix	11 K'an	6 Eb	AB2	AC2	AD2	AE2
4 K'an	3 Ix	6 K'an	1 Eb	AB3	AC3	u muuk	AE3
12 K'an	11 Ix	1 K'an	9 Eb	Illustration of X_2			
7 K'an	6 Ix	9 K'an	4 Eb				
2 K'an	1 Ix	4 K'an	12 Eb				
10 K'an	9 Ix	12 K'an	7 Eb				
5 K'an	4 Ix	7 K'an	2 Eb				
13 K'an	12 Ix	2 K'an	10 Eb				
8 K'an	7 Ix	10 K'an	5 Eb				
3 K'an	2 Ix	5 K'an	13 Eb				
11 K'an	10 Ix	13 K'an	8 Eb				
6 K'an	5 Ix	8 K'an	3 Eb	k'alaj	East	u muuk	AE13
17 Yax	7 Muwan	12 Ch'en	0 Yax	Y_3	Chak Ek'	AD14	AE14
k'alaj	k'alaj	k'alaj	k'alaj	Z_3	u hul	u muuk	AE15
North	West	South	East				
U_3	V_3	W_3	X_3				
Chak Ek'	Chak Ek'	Chak Ek'	Chak Ek'				
3	4	4	4	Illustration of Y_3			
16	2	15	15				
4	14	4	12				
(=1404)	(=1494)	(=1744)	(= 1752 = 3×584)				
2 Muwan	7 Pohp	17 Mak	5 K'ank'in	AB21	AC21	AD21	u muuk
tse?-ya-ni	tse?-ya-ni	tse?-ya-ni	tse?-ya-ni	u muuk	AC22	AD22	AE22
X_2	U_3	V_3	W_3				
East	North	West	South				
7 Sip	17 Yaxk'in	2 Wo	10 Wo	Illustration of Z_3			
11	4	12	0				
16	10	10	8				
(=236)	(=90)	(=250)	(=8)				

The first variable element in the textual formula, Y, directly follows the phrase "*k'al lak'in.*" Because Y is always followed by Chak Ek', scholars have taken these as the names of Venus in its heliacal rise form and identified them as the spearthrower-carrying figures (Bricker and Bricker 2007: 107–108; see also Taube and Bade 1991).

The next sentence is odd in grammatical construction, but does find corroboration in other parts of the codex. Its first part, Z is the name of the figure in the lower register of the right hand text – the speared figure. The glyph following Z appears to be a logograph *HUL* ("n. spear;" "v. to pierce, to spear" (Barrera Vasquez 1995: 242), composed of a *lu* syllabogram

PAGE 49							
13 Lamat	12 Etz'nab	2 Lamat	10 Kib	AJ1	AK1	AL1	AM1
8 Lamat	7 Etz'nab	10 Lamat	5 Kib	u muuk	AK2	AL2	AM2
3 Lamat	2 Etz'nab	5 Lamat	13 Kib	AJ3	AK3	AL3	AM3
11 Lamat	10 Etz'nab	13 Lamat	8 Kib				
6 Lamat	5 Etz'nab	8 Lamat	3 Kib				
1 Lamat	13 Etz'nab	3 Lamat	11 Kib				
9 Lamat	8 Etz'nab	11 Lamat	6 Kib				
4 Lamat	3 Etz'nab	6 Lamat	1 Kib		Illustration of X_3		
12 Lamat	11 Etz'nab	1 Lamat	9 Kib				
7 Lamat	6 Etz'nab	9 Lamat	4 Kib				
2 Lamat	1 Etz'nab	4 Lamat	12 Kib				
10 Lamat	9 Etz'nab	12 Lamat	7 Kib				
5 Lamat	4 Etz'nab	7 Lamat	2 Kib	k'alaj	East	u muuk	AM13
11 Sip	1 Mol	6 Wo	14 Wo	Y_4	Chak Ek'	u muuk	AM14
k'alaj	k'alaj	k'alaj	k'alaj	Z_4	u hul	u muuk	AM15
North	West	South	East				
U_4	V_4	W_4	X_4				
Chak Ek'	Chak Ek'	Chak Ek'	Chak Ek'				
5 / 9 / 8 (= 1988)	5 / 13 / 18 (= 2078)	6 / 8 / 4 (= 2328)	6 / 8 / 16 (= 2336 = 4×584)		Illustration of Y_4		
16 Yaxk'in	6 Keh	11 Xul	19 Xul	AJ21	AK21	u muuk	AM21
tse?-ya-ni	tse?-ya-ni	tse?-ya-ni	tse?-ya-ni	AJ22	AK22	u muuk	AM22
X_3	U_4	V_4	W_4				
Chak Ek'	Chak Ek'	Chak Ek'	Chak Ek'				
East	North	West	South				
6 K'ank'in	16 Kumk'u	1 Mak	9 Mak		Illustration of Z_4		
11 / 16 (=236)	4 / 10 (=90)	12 / 10 (=250)	0 / 8 (=8)				

pierced through by a pointed object (see Figs 4.2 and 4.3) The "*u*" prefix thus constructs the sentence: "s/he spears him/her/it," with the context making it clear that Y spears Z.

Finally, the last part of the middle text is controlled by the term constituted of the syllabograms mu and ka. In Yucatecan, *muk* is readily translated as a verb meaning "to cover," or "to bury," which is why Schele and Grube occasionally gave the translation of "A_1 is buried" (1997: 82, 148–156; see also Aveni 2001: 192–193). With a long vowel (possibly captured by its disharmonic spelling mu-ka (Stuart *et al.* 1999), *muuk* takes on the meaning of "news – either good or bad" (Barrera Vasquez: 1995: 534). The term's

PAGE 50							
12 Eb	11 Ik'	1 Eb	9 Ajaw	AR1	Chak Ek'	u muuk	AU1
7 Eb	6 Ik'	9 Eb	4 Ajaw	AR2	AS2	AT2	AU2
2 Eb	1 Ik'	4 Eb	12 Ajaw	AR3	AS3	u muuk	AU3
10 Eb	9 Ik'	12 Eb	7 Ajaw				
5 Eb	4 Ik'	7 Eb	2 Ajaw				
13 Eb	12 Ik'	2 Eb	10 Ajaw				
8 Eb	7 Ik'	10 Eb	5 Ajaw	Illustration of X_4 (with Z_3)			
3 Eb	2 Ik'	5 Eb	13 Ajaw				
11 Eb	10 Ik'	13 Eb	8 Ajaw				
6 Eb	5 Ik'	8 Eb	3 Ajaw				
1 Eb	13 Ik'	3 Eb	11 Ajaw				
9 Eb	8 Ik'	11 Eb	6 Ajaw				
4 Eb	3 Ik'	6 Eb	1 Ajaw	k'alaj	East	u muuk	AU13
10 K'ank'in	0 Wayeb	5 Mak	13 Mak	Y_5	Chak Ek'	u muuk	AU14
k'alaj	k'alaj	k'alaj	k'al	Z_5	u hul	u muuk	AU15
North	West	South	East				
U_5	V_5	W_5	X_5				
Chak Ek'	Chak Ek'	Chak Ek'	Chak Ek'				
7	7	8	8				
2	7	1	2	Illustration of Y_5			
12	2	12	0				
(= 2572)	(= 2662)	(= 2912)	(= 2920 = 5×584)				
15 Kumk'u	0 Tsek	10 K'ayab	18 K'ayab				
tse?-ya	tse?-ya-ni	tse?-ya-ni	tse?-ya-ni	AR21	u muuk	AT21	u muuk
X_4	U_5	V_5	W_5	AR22	u muuk	AT22	AU22
Chak Ek'	Chak Ek'	Chak Ek'	Chak Ek'				
East	North	West	South				
0 Yaxk'in	10 Sak	15 Tsek	3 Xul				
11	4	12	0	Illustration of Z_5			
16	10	10	8				
(=236)	(=90)	(=250)	(=8)				

extensive use throughout the entire codex makes it clear that the "news" translation – often rendered as "omen" – is better here (see also Mathews and Bíró (2005), which credits the "omen" meaning of *muk* to David Stuart and John Robertson and *mu'k* to Alfonso Lacadena and Soren Wichmann). Here, then, *u muuk* becomes "it is the omen of," or "it is

the news of," and the referents are the named entity or entities A_m.

Summarizing these translation results, it is easy to see the connections scholars have made to the passage from the Annals of Cuauhtitlan. The middle text on the right hand side of page 48, for example, would be read as: "The East is enclosed by Tawiskal and Chak Ek'. He speared

Fig. 4.5. Text from Page 47 above the warrior Fig.: k'ahlaj lak'in 10 Chan Chak Ek'

Ixim [the Maize God]. It is the omen of the east of the land, of the caves. It is the omen of [a place]."

Interpretive complications

With this overview and reading of the hieroglyphic text, both Aveni's and the Brickers' interpretations at this point appear to be corroborated and even extended. Spearings are multiply evidenced, for example, lending credence to the Brickers' emphasis on violence. Also, the consistent statement of omens in the hieroglyphic text follows Aveni's reference to prognostications; although, differing from the Brickers, Aveni leaves open the possibility that these omens could have been good or bad.

On the other hand, there are a number of complications that result from this close review of the data. Although the general layout of the Eclipse Table and the Venus Table may be similar as Aveni points out, they really would function differently as warning tables. The Eclipse Table, that is, gives a specific date on which an eclipse might happen (or

have happened). If inaccurate, it would have been off by one day (177–day cycle v. 178-day cycle; Aveni 2001: 181), not by as many as six or seven days. That is, an eclipse would either happen on the specified date or it would not. In Lounsbury's Venus Table warning model, though, the observable phenomena always occurred – the only variation was in how many days the prediction preceded the actual event. The dates in the table never actually predicted the observable event, but alerted the reader to a window of 1–6 days over which Venus would make its first visibility. Thus while the Eclipse Table and the Venus Table might both be considered warning tables, their actual functions are quite different.

Another complication comes via our reading of the hieroglyphic text. The attentive reader already may have noticed that the term Chak Ek' is in fact ambiguously linked to the name glyphs represented by Y. As we have seen, Glyph Blocks K17–18, S17–18, AA17–18, AI17–18, and AQ17–18 (as well as A4–B9) give the phrase including Venus as: "*k'ahlaj lak'in* **X** *Chak Ek'*." Yet in the middle passage, among the illustrations, Glyph Blocks L13–M14, T13–U14, AB13–AC14, and AJ13–AK14 give the phrase: "*k'ahlaj lak'in* **Y** *Chak Ek'*" (see Fig. 4.5) As noted above, X corresponds to the set of named figures in the upper tier of illustrations (the figure on the celestial throne) whereas Y represents the names of the middle figures (the ones holding spearthrowers). If we want to take Y as the name of Venus (as several scholars have argued (Schele and Grube 1997: 152–156; Bricker and Bricker 2007: 108)), then logically, we would also have to take X as its name as well. Is Venus now the celestially governing deity or the warrior deity? Perhaps it is neither? I have argued elsewhere (2011) that the reading above circumvents the problem entirely. "The East is enclosed by X and Chak Ek'" allows for both X and Y to participate in the activity without contradiction (Aldana 2010: 64–65). On the other hand, if this is the case, then we can no longer assume that Venus is inherently dangerous, for it is not strictly a warrior. Venus in this case is essentially neutral, working with a warrior and a celestial figure to "enclose" space and time.

Additionally, a careful reading raises the possibility that the violence referred to in the table is not always something to be feared. There is clearly a negative outcome for the entity who is speared, but that does not necessitate that the overall omen is a bad one for everyone. If the Maize God is speared, for example as on page 48, *we might expect* that it would have been interpreted as a failure of crops, which in turn would have been bad for the community of humans dependent on that corn. But what does it mean for Chak Balam (Great (or Red) Jaguar) to have been speared as on page 47? The text tells us that this spearing would have accompanied (or perhaps generated) "*u muuk yohl k'uh, k'uhul wayis ajaw*" – "the omen of the k'uh heart of the wayis ajaw." Is that something to be avoided or celebrated? The text does not tell us. Likewise, it is not clear why the spearing of the Maize God generates an omen for "the land and the caves of the east," whereas the spearing of an (undeciphered) deity is what generates *u muuk Ixim* – "the omen of the Maize God." That is, on page 50, Kaktunal spears a deity with an undeciphered name, but it is said to be the omen of the deities, of the ajaws, and of the Maize God. Clearly, we would have to know if the undeciphered deity were positive or negative to determine whether the people, the deities, and the Maize God would want him speared or not! (see Fig. 4.2e) Either way, no omen is a priori characterized as good or bad – it appears that the table provides the structure for generating the omen, but its character is determined by the specific event – and so open to interpretation by the astronomers/priests consulting the table.

Finally, and from a broader perspective, we should also exercise caution in the original interpretation of the *Anales* passage. Its most recent translator, John Bierhorst, notes explicitly in the introduction that the original author of the text held a negative bias against Precontact indigenous religion: "It will be noticed that the author … repeatedly disparages the old gods as 'sorcerers' or even 'devils'" (Bierhorst 1992: 1). It should be no surprise, then, that the passage notes only the negative doings of an Aztec deity. Because he notes only the negative, that does not require that Venus's effects were only negative.

Rather than take the *Anales* passage at face value, then, and allowing for the "omen" semantic value of "*muuk*," I suggest that an alternate interpretation of the Venus Table results from a reference to what we know about Mesoamerican "sorcerers."

Mayan ritual specialists

When we turn to descriptions of ritual specialists recorded in colonial times, divination is included as one of their specialties. A canonical reference, of course, is Diego de Landa's sixteenth-century *Relacion de las cosas de Yucatan*, in which he writes that:

> [t]he sciences which they taught were the computation of the years, months and days, the festivals and ceremonies, the administration of the sacraments, **the fateful days and seasons, their methods of divination and their prophecies**, events and the cures for diseases, and their antiquities and how to read and write with the letters and characters, with which they wrote, and drawings which illustrate the meaning of the writings. [emphasis added; Tozzer 1941: 27–28] (Zender 2004: 94)

Here the reference to "fateful days" and "their methods of divination" along with the specific "prophecies" appears quite suggestive relative to the content of the Dresden Codex.

Reflecting the persistence of these job duties even when confronted with Spanish colonialism, Andres de Avendaño wrote over a century later that the books utilized for songs also:

> están pintados por una parte y otra con variedad de figuras, y caracteres … **que indican no sólo la cuenta de los dichos días, meses y años, sino las edades, y las profecías** que sus ídolos y simulacros les anunciaron, o por mejor decir el demonio, mediante el culto, que en unas piedras le tributan… (emphasis added; 1997: 42; notes that the hieroglyphic books were largely concerned with "the count of the said days and months and years, but also [with] the ages and prophecies which their idols and images announced to them". (Zender 2004: 85–86)

This description also fits perfectly with the repository of knowledge assembled in the Dresden Codex.

In his recent review of the "Classic Maya Priesthood," Marc Zender refers to divination as the basis of priestly activity across specific titles:

> **In addition to** divination, most priests seem also to have been capable of performing healing rites, and the knowledge of herbs and curative bloodletting seems to have been a staple of recondite priestly knowledge (Chuchiak 2001: 136–142; Roys 1943: 88, 93–95; Thompson 1970: 312) (2004: 93).

Furthermore, Zender translates the Yucatecan term ajk'in – often rendered "daykeeper" – as "'diviner' (glyphic **AJ–K'IN-ni** for *ajk'in*, literally 'he of the forecasting')" (2004: 93), where he must be emphasizing the more abstract, temporal character of "k'in."

One of the goals of Zender's dissertation, though, was to push the basic job description back in time relative to those figures holding the titles of *ajk'uhuun*, *yajawk'ahk'*, and *ti'sakhuun* in historical hieroglyphic texts from the Classic period (2004: 123–226). For the present study, though, it would be more fruitful to move forward in time to consider the practice of divination within contemporary Mayan culture – specifically that utilizing the 260-day count. Here we turn to the results of Barbara Tedlock's fieldwork amongst the Momostenango K'iche'.

Divination

Barbara Tedlock's and Dennis Tedlock's ventures into K'iche' lands and cosmologies already have paid substantial dividends in various venues. Here, I would like to consider yet another opportunity not fully explored, although it has been hinted at by Aveni (1980: 190). Barbara Tedlock's ethnographic account records the activities performed by K'iche' ritual specialists in what she labels both shaman-priest and priest-shaman roles (1992: 47–53). Tedlock describes in detail a divination for a proposed marriage in part in order to challenge previous interpretations (for example by Charles Wagley, Oliver La Farge, and Benson Saler) that argued for conscious manipulations of the process or even dishonesty by the diviners (1992: 170–171).

The overall process involves:

i   taking a handful of seeds from a pile without regard to the specific number of seeds;
ii   partitioning these seeds into groups of four, with the remainder forming its own pile (with specific further conditions restricting the number of seeds in the final pile);
iii counting through the piles according to a progression through the chol qiij;
iv   addressing the days themselves as agents with "will";
v   listening for the blood "to speak" throughout the process.

The process is then repeated to ensure that the outcome of the divination can be verified.

In abridged form, Tedlock writes of a divination based on the manipulation of a pile of seeds:

> When all the seeds of the first arrangement have been set out, the diviner addresses the first group of seeds by the name of the day on which he is divining, for example, … 'Come here Lord 1 Quej, you are being spoken to' … After the first day has been addressed and summoned, the diviner will repeat or allude to the question being asked. In a marriage divination, one might say, … '1 Quej, you are being spoken to about the seven goodnesses, seven fatnesses.' … The counting may or may not be interrupted by the speaking of the blood. The moment it speaks, the diviner stops counting, noting the day name and stating the message. For example, if the blood moves in the right hand on the day 5 Batz', the diviner will say in a low voice: 'Already he has it grasped, it says' … Now there is a moment's pause. If the message does not come again in the same locale or in the paired place … then the diviner may ask 5 Batz' … 'Is it certain that it is you who speaks'? If the blood speaks again the message is confirmed. … Now the counting of the piles of seeds will resume. Let us say that in this case, it comes to 4 Ak'abal on the last group… This indicates that the marriage would seem to be certain, since one of the mnemonics for Ak'abal is *ak'abil* ('at dawn'), which would be the time of day to begin the asking. (Tedlock 1992: 162–168)

By considering this divination account with respect to the constraints on cultural translation considered by Tambiah, we are able to introduce an additional step into the interpretative process. Because this type of activity generally is dismissed as "superstitious" and intellectually bankrupt within the post-Enlightenment academy, the translation of an oracle from a concept in Mayan cultures to a concept in contemporary "Western" culture is stifled. In order to get around this obstacle, we must build a conception of an oracle in modern terms using contemporary scientific tools.

To do so, we first recognize that various synthetic and natural phenomena are brought together to constitute the oracle. That is, in the K'iche' case, this oracle comprises a stochastic component (the grabbing of an a priori indeterminate number of seeds), the element of repeatability (the seeds may be utilized indefinitely, and in fact the process is repeated to ensure that the reading is one of confidence (Tedlock 1992: 163–164)), a language for interpretation that simultaneously constrains the possible outcomes (the chol qiij), and an overlying layer of stochasticity in the "speaking blood." These factors together constitute the mechanism of a conception of an oracle.

A MODERN CONCEPTION OF MESOAMERICAN ORACLES
- a stochastic event
- repeatability
- interpretive language
- constraining mechanism
- additional stochastic aspects

It is important to emphasize, though, that such an interpretation is merely a conception within Western academic thought mapped over from a concept within Mayan thought. The difference, of course, is in the ontology behind each interpretation. The case is pointed to in Tedlock's divination description: the ritual specialist addresses the 260-day count dates (or better, the k'uh behind the dates) directly. The decision, or the will, of the dates is expressed in the speaking of the blood or the patterns made by the seeds. Without recognition of any such k'uh or entities behind the oracle, scientific observers attribute the "expressions" as chance events. I suggest that for contemporary scientific culture, the concept of chance or randomness is the result of an imperfect map from the concept of the oracle within K'iche' culture. What an indigenous conceptualization would characterize as the response of the oracle, contemporary scholarship attributes to a "random" outcome.

Clyde Kluckhohn has also made this point explicitly regarding his early twentieth century Diné consultants:

> The conception of "good luck" is hard to translate into the Navaho language. In their scheme of things one is not "lucky" or "unlucky." One has the requisite knowledge (sacred or profane) or one hasn't. Even in what European languages call "games of chance" the Navaho depends upon medicines, rites, and verbal formulas. The same is true with hunting. Getting a deer is never a matter of good fortune; it is a matter of ritual knowledge and one's relations with supernaturals which, again, are controllable (Kluckhohn, 1949: 362) (Blackburn 1975: 68).

That this is not simply a contemporary Mayan or Diné conceptualization is corroborated by divinations found in the historical record of Mesoamerica. One version bemoaned by a creole observer comes from Hernando Ruiz de Alarcón's *Treatise on the Heathen Superstitions That Today Live Among the Indians Native to This New Spain*. Here too the basic address and the dependence on "chance" are the same as the much more recent K'iche' example given above.

> They use this fortune telling in the following manner. From an ear of maize or from among a lot of maize,

the fortune-teller selects the most outstanding and beautiful kernels. … Having chosen the said kernels, the seer bites off their nibs with his teeth.
> …
> Without our lingering on the number, which is not to the point, and coming to the execution, the seer, after having arranged the kernels on the said cloth, begins his fraud with those that remain in his hand, shaking them in it and tossing them in the air and catching them again many times. And then he begins [an] invocation. …
> And at the time that he says the invocation he traverses the space that he has created with the stretched-out cloth at full speed with the hand in which he holds the kernels, moving his hand along the edge of the cloth over the maize kernels that he placed on it. **And the invocation is addressed to the maize kernels and to the fingers of his hands, as if attributing divinity to them.** After finishing the words of the incantation, he tosses the maize that he had in his hand into the middle of the cloth, and he judges the fortune according to how the maize kernels fall. The rule that they usually have in judging it is that, if the maize kernels fall face up, the fortune is good – for example, the medicine about which he is consulted will be good, or the lost person or thing that is being sought will show up – and the contrary if the maize kernels fall face down.
> …
> And they are believed like prophets… with all the basis for success being in whether the maize kernels fall face up or face down, and also in falling far from or near to the one who throws them. The first is chance, and the second the fortune-teller freely executes, throwing the maize kernels with more force or with less – less if he wants them to remain nearer (Ruiz de Alarcon 1629).

While this oracle has no association with the 260-day count, the dependence on "chance" and on a petition to "inanimate" entities is again fundamental. Furthermore, it follows the structure of a Western conception of an oracle: *stochasticity* – face-up or face down maize kernels after being tossed; *repeatability*; *language* – here only positive or negative.

The Venus Table as oracle

As evident in Figures 4.2 and 4.3, the Venus Table is broken up into canonical periods such that each row in each page will predict last evening, first morning, (something preceding) last morning, and first evening visibilities (Aveni 2001: 184–196). For the first row of dates on page 46, for example, Venus's first morning visibility would be expected on 13 K'an. According to warning table models, this date would signal that the observer should begin surveying the morning sky since the recorded event should transpire within a few days.

From an oracular perspective, though, the original concern expressed in this essay regarding the "accuracy" of the Dresden Codex Venus Table changes from being a liability of uncertainty into an asset. For the table as oracle in conception, the ajk'in consulting the Venus Table would desire a "bounded variability" in the short term, but extreme accuracy in the long run. One would prefer the predicted dates – those explicitly in the table – to sit right on the average of the planet's synodic period. In that way, the deviation would be equally positive and negative (i.e. on average, Chak Ek' would appear late as often as early). This variability, then, could have functioned as the "random" element in the oracle.

The other components map over as well so that in conception, the Venus Table can be considered an oracle as follows:

i   the outcome (Venus visibility) is stochastic about an expected date;
ii   "consultation" is repeatable (on 584-day intervals or sub-parts thereof);
iii there is a language through which a message can be read (the 260-day count); and
iv   an overlying layer of stochasticity is introduced by the weather.

The Venus Table as oracle, then, might work in one of a couple of different ways. It might be that first morning visibility was critical and if it fell on the predicted date, then the warrior deity speared the noted victim and the associated omens resulted. If first morning visibility did not fall on the predicted date, then there would have been no spearing and no omen. On the other hand, each Venus event may have constituted a consultation of the oracle. In this case, each event (fmv, lmv, fev, lev) was stochastic relative to its predicted date. For any given Chak Ek' event (any column in the table of dates), the table would be consulted to determine the expected omen. Deviation from the expected date still yields an omen since each date carries with it an associated meaning (as we saw in the K'iche' divination). Here, then, the calendar becomes the language through which the planet communicates with human observers.

Of course there are still other possibilities for the Venus Table's actual use as an oracle. The point is that these models for interpretation follow the conception of the Venus Table

in "Western" culture, but also map well into concepts in Classic Mayan elite culture. In fact, the framework also becomes productive in the interpretation of Mayan astronomy beyond the Dresden Codex Venus Table. The so-called "E-group" architectural constructions, for example, have long been recognized as markers of the solstices and equinoxes, yet they too could have served oracular functions. In this case, the major stochastic element would have been the weather. Was it possible on any given solstice to view sunrise at its marker? Or did fog or cloud cover prevent witness? The observation could be repeated annually, of course, but also subsequent days would confirm how close the predicted date would have been to the solar event. Finally, the 260-Day Count would have provided the language of interpretation, not unlike the Venus Table.

Another example might be the Venus window in Copan Structure 10L-22. Reconstructed to be useful in timing maize agricultural cycles by some scholars (Aveni 2001; Closs *et al.* 1984), I have argued elsewhere that it may have served an oracular function (Aldana 2002). At some level, then, this framework allows us to wrest free Mayan astronomy from characterization as a proto-"Western"-science. It now allows for meanings relevant to and within ancient elite Mayan culture itself. Accordingly, we now turn our attention to those historical figures who would have engaged these oracular constructs.

Priests and shamans

With this reconstruction, I suggest a new hypothesis for some Precontact Mayan ritual activity. Elite monumental construction was not produced for mundane purposes, but carried an esoteric character specific to roles in society. Parallel to the hieroglyphic inscriptions themselves, which meant radically different things to commoners versus elites, Mayan astronomy was driven as much by its potential social and political applications as by the insights it provided into the "nature" of the universe. At some level, this is no provocative proposal; Thompson long bemoaned the characterization of Mayan astronomy as "astrology."

I suggest that the specific formulation presented here resonates even more clearly with Precontact concepts of religion as exposed through Marc Zender's treatment of the Classic period ritual specialist title, ajk'uhuun and the history of its decipherment. Zender's insightful contribution is to go beyond previous interpretations by prioritizing consideration of the diachronic glyphic representations of the title in order to disambiguate its relevant components and then to recognize the linguistic link between the Classic Ch'olti'an term ajk'uhuun, and the Tzotzil *ch'uun* (2004: 181–182, 189). At end, Zender argues that:

> [b]oth Tzotzil *ch'u-un* (from Proto-Tzeltalan **ch'uh-un*, itself from pre-Tzeltalan ***k'uh-uun*) and Classic Ch'olti'an (i.e. hieroglyphic language) *k'uh-uun*, then, are best analyzed as derived transitive verbs with the core meaning "to worship". (Zender 2004: 190)

The final step, here, which is to translate these terms as "to worship," though, rests on previous translations and not on discernable job duties. And it is here that I suggest the problem of cultural translation arises again as evident in the examples that Zender used for his analysis. Regarding the root of the term, the noun k'uh, for instance, Zender notes that "the 17th century *Diccionario de Motul* provides the colonial Yucatec terms <ku> 'god', <kuul> 'to worship', <kuul cizin> 'to idolatrize' and <ah kul ciçin> 'idolator who worships the devil' …" (Zender 2004: 194). Thus in getting to the term "worshipper," the translation's origin in the perspective of a seventeenth-century scholar is going unproblematized. Certainly, however, this author – as that of the Annals of Cuauhtitlan along with other indigenous and European scholars writing for European audiences – would have characterized any type of Precontact priestly activity as the worship of idols or of the devil, for that is precisely what it meant to be "pagan" in their worldview. To accept a definition of k'uhuun as "worshipper," then is to suggest that the concept of worshipper in a European worldview maps directly to the same concept in a Mayan worldview.

Contrastingly, I argue that Zender's own linguistic analysis of *ajk'uhuun* provides better access to the indigenous concept. He breaks the term down (from its Late Classic glyphic representation) as follows:

AJ-K'UH-HUUN-(na)
Ajk'uh(h)uun
Aj-k'uh-uun
Agentive.prefix-GOD-denominative.transitivizer
"worshipper"
(Zender 2004: 192)

I would not pretend to challenge Zender's linguistic interpretation here, but I do think it is reasonable to reconsider the translation of k'uh/'god' as a derived-transitive verb as "to worship." And the link for me is the "deity" term.

Alfredo Barrera Vasquez's Yucatec Mayan Dictionary defines the term unambiguously: "**K'U** 1: Dios," and "deidad" according to the seventeenth-century Motul Dictionary and the more recent Diccionario Español-Maya by Ermilo Solís Alcalá (1995: 416). The issue, though, is that again, these are already translations into European concepts – and by sources that we should not hesitate in recognizing as significantly biased. We do encounter a somewhat different situation, though, when we venture outside of Mayan lands.

If we turn to the analogous term in Nahuatl, for instance, a less straightforward suggestion arises. Borrowing from written colonial sources as well as archaeological interpretation, Michael Smith warns us to take care in considering translations of "teotl," and not simply attribute a human personification to nature or natural phenomena/objects.

> The Nahuatl term *teotl* means "deity" or "sacred power." This is a complex and multifaceted concept that does not fit well with modern preconceptions of ancient polytheistic religion … Aztec gods … are better viewed as invisible spirits or forces whose roles, natures, and forms blended together. (Smith 2004: 199)

This "abstracted" personification reflects not only an Aztec or Mesoamerican concept, but one associated with a wide variety of Precontact indigenous people of the Western Hemisphere.

In his review of late-nineteenth and early-twentieth century Chumash mythology, for instance, Thomas Blackburn notes what he calls "homologies" across religious concepts of indigenous people throughout North America (1975: 66). In a sense, Blackburn is pushing the abstraction suggested by Smith still further, referring to 'causative agencies' rather than using the terms 'deity' or 'supernatural.'

> Because all causative agencies in the universe are personalized and endowed with such human qualities as will, intelligence, and emotionality, and because the beings so conceptualized are considered to have the potentiality for either positive or negative action, unpredictability is an essential aspect of all events and all phenomena (1975: 69).

There are at least three important points here that require emphasis: "causative agency," "positive or negative action," and "unpredictability."

The first point allows us to bring together the above considerations of k'uh and teotl: we might think of either of them more abstractly as "causative agencies." Such agencies can be construed to include rain (or better, the overall cause of rain), wind (or the cause of airflow – allowing it to be associated with "breath" and life as well) and even plant medicines (or causes of healing). The second point speaks directly to the term focused on above, *muuk*. As Tedlock makes clear, omens (and the entities generating them) can be either bad or good – in fact, they are virtually always both. And finally, because they are both positive and negative and they possess their own wills, any given outcome is unpredictable. Moreover, this framework allows us to see Chaak/Tlaloc as something other than a cross-Atlantic rain deity within a Mesoamerican pantheon.

If we now understand k'uh or "god" as a causative agency capable of unpredictable positive or negative activity, then we may return to the noble title that initiated this investigation with an alternative translation possibility. Now, the derived transitive form of k'uh, "to k'uh," as "to causative agentify" or "to empower" suggests a different translation from "to worship." If a god is a being of power, then "to god" something is to empower it, or to reveal its power. Such an interpretation suggests less that of worshipping and more that of revealing the power of the gods. In fact, ajk'uhuun might actually be a good translation for the double entendre within the term diviner: one who makes an entity divine by revealing its intent. By interpreting/divining the will of k'uh, the diviner gives that k'uh power. In this sense, the concept of a diviner might be homologous (in Blackburn's terms) to the concept of an ajk'uhuun across cultures (*cf.* Aldana 2011).

This review takes us back to Zender's suggestion that divination was basic to all priestly duties. His point bolsters our argument by again referring to Landa who wrote that "the duty of the Chilans was to give the replies of the gods to the people, and so much respect was shown to them that they carried them on their shoulders." (Zender 2004: 89; Tozzer 1941: 112) This is precisely the semantic meaning that Zender derives from a linguistic analysis of the term: *chilan*, from "chi'-il-a'n (speaker, user of language, prophet)" (2004: 89).

Results

At end, this essay at least argues for two practical results beside presenting an oracular hypothesis. First, it complicates further the real-time dating of the Dresden Codex through the Venus Table. If the table's intent was to balance error on both sides of the planet's average period, it would be difficult to determine when a given diviner would have realized that the table needed correcting. Here, the problem cannot be reduced to a question of "accuracy" in anticipation because from an oracular standpoint, a table that always anticipates the phenomenon is just as poor as one that is always late – neither provides a stochastic element. The upshot is that we cannot really hope to place the Dresden Codex Venus Table in real time by judging its accuracy. Rather, the accuracy should be used as a check on a placement derived by other means.

Second, and in line with Zender's conclusions (2004), this study further complicates attempts to distinguish between "priestly" and "shamanic" roles within Mayan religious ideology. In fact, it may render the sociological distinction meaningless. When we bring a radically different ontology into consideration, we seem to find that both "roles," would have been inextricably linked and requisite of any ritual specialist.

Moreover, the more abstract "causative agency" translation of k'uh suggests that it is not clear that all k'uhoob (all causative agencies) would be superior to humans. Indeed, humanity as a populace (as a collective entity) at least would have to be considered a causative agency – one among numerous others – which in turn provides insight into yet another noble title: *k'uhulajaw*, the term most often translated as the "ruler" of a given polity.

If ajaw derives from the Proto-Mixe-Zoquean "aj-aw" as suggested by Kaufmann (dictionary) meaning "one who shouts," then we confront a different conceptualization of Classic Mayan rulership. Paralleling the translation of the Nahuatl term for ruler, tlatoani (tlato – "to speak"; -ani – agentifier), a k'uhulajaw becomes (or gets translated as) a person who shouts with causative agency (among other causative agents). The k'uhulajaw in this formulation becomes the representative (as Gayatri Spivak delineates regarding *darstellung* and *vertreitung*) of the polity, interacting with other k'uhoob according to context. In other words, a k'uhulajaw can interact with his/her "subjects" in a rational/political way as with other k'uhulajawtaak. but the k'uhulajaw can also interact with the rain, Venus, or his/her royal ancestry (K'awiil) through other (k'uh) modes of discourse.

In the end, then, I am suggesting that – especially when we consider the products of intellectual communities – we spend more time on careful cultural translations, working more concertedly through concepts and conceptions in our interpretations of ancient Mayan cultures, including their sciences. In this case, I have argued that a cultural translation allows us to re-think and appreciate a subtle and rational ritual practice in the Dresden Codex, without dismissing it as "superstitious" or evolutionarily juvenile "proto-science." Likewise, I suggest that even though we may find evidence of oracular activity, it does not require that we consider all Mayan intellectual activity to be of the same character. Oracular knowledge may very well have sat alongside other forms of knowledge. Like revelation in Christianity, or portents in ancient China, oracle-produced knowledge probably fit within a broader political discourse, but it *did not have to dominate it* (see also Bielenstein 1950, 1984). Instead, the entire process may be recognized as just as complex as any more Modern ideology – it simply proceeded from a vastly different set of ontological assumptions. Indeed, it may be that taking seriously this subtlety of thought would do much more toward humanizing the members of ancient civilizations than identifying a person's name and associating it with the material culture s/he possessed.

Note

1 Seler's parenthetic count refers to a progression through the 260-day count "signs" by 13-day intervals.

References

Aldana, Gerardo, 2001. Oracular Science: Uncertainty in the History of Maya Astronomy. Ph.D dissertation, Harvard University, Cambridge, MA.

Aldana, Gerardo, 2005. Agency and the "Star War" Glyph: an Historical Reassessment of Classic Maya Astrology and Warfare. *Ancient Mesoamerica* 16, 2, 305–320.

Aldana, Gerardo, 2011. *Tying Headbands or Venus Appearing: new translations of /k'al/, the Dresden Codex Venus pages, and royal 'binding' rituals.* B.A.R. International Series 2239. Archaeopress, Oxford.

Aldana, Gerardo. 2011. On Deciphering Ancient Mesoamerican Foundational Texts: the Challenges of a non-Logos-based Creation Narrative. *Foundational Texts of World Literature*, Dominique Jullien, editor. Peter Lang Publishing, New York, pp. 47-68.

Aveni, Anthony, 1980. *Skywatchers of Ancient Mexico.* University of Texas Press, Austin.

Aveni, Anthony, 2001. *Skywatchers: A Revised and Updated Version of Skywatchers of Ancient Mexico.* University of Texas Press, Austin.

Barrera Vasquez, Alfredo, 1995. *Diccionario Maya, Tercera Edición.* Editorial Porrúa, México.

Bielenstein, Hans, 1950. An Interpretation of the Portents in the Ts'ien-Han Shu. *Bulletin of the Museum of Far Eastern Antiquities* 22, 127–143.

Bielenstein, Hans, 1984. Han Portents and Prognostications. *Museum of Far Eastern Antiquities Bulletin* 56, 97–112.

Bierhorst, John, 1992. *History and Mythology of the Aztecs: the Codex Chimalpopoca.* University of Arizona Press, Tucson.

Blackburn, Thomas, 1975. *December's Child: a Book of Chumash Oral Narratives.* University of California Press, Berkeley.

Bricker, Harvey and Victoria Bricker, 2007. When Was the Dresden Codex Venus Table Efficacious? *Skywatching in the Ancient Americas: New Perspectives in Cultural Astronomy.* University Press of Colorado, Boulder, 95–120.

Closs, Michael, Anthony Aveni and Bruce Crowley, 1984. The Planet Venus and Temple 22 at Copán. *Indiana* 9, 221–247.

Förstemann, Ernst, 1891. *Explanation of the Maya Manuscript of the Library of Dresden.* Translated by Nora Thomas, Bureau of Ethnology Library, Washington D.C.

Lounsbury, Floyd, 1978. Maya Numeration, Computation, and Calendrical Astronomy. In *Dictionary of Scientific Biography* (C. Coulson Gillispie ed.), Volume XV, Charles Scribner's Sons, New York, 759–818.

Mathews, Peter and Peter Bíró, 2005. Maya Hieroglyphic Dictionary. On-line dictionary at www.famsi.org

Ruiz de Alarcón, Hernando, 1629. *Treatise on the Heathen Superstitions That Today Live Among the Indians Native to This New Spain.*

Schele, Linda and Nikolai Grube, 1997. *Notebook for the XXIst Maya Hieroglyphic Workshop.* Department of Art and Art History, University of Texas, Austin.

Schele, Linda and Peter Mathews, 1998. *A Code of Kings.* Thames & Hudson, New York.

Seler, Eduard, 1904. Venus Period in the Picture Writings of the Borgian Codex Group. In *Mexican and Central American Antiquities, Calendar Systems, and History.* Bureau of Ethnology Bulletin 28, Smithsonian Institution, Washington D.C., 355–391.

Smith, Michael, 2004. *The Aztecs.* Thames & Hudson, New York.

Tambiah, Stanley, 1990. *Magic, Science, Religion and the Scope of Rationality.* Cambridge University Press, Cambridge.

Taube, Karl and Bonnie Bade, 1991. An Appearance of Xiuhtecuhtli in the Dresden Venus Pages. In *Research*

Reports on Ancient Maya Writing 35. Center for Maya Research, Washington D.C.

Tedlock, Barbara, 1992. *Time and the Highland Maya*. University of New Mexico Press, Albuquerque.

Teeple, John, 1931. *Maya Astronomy*. Contributions to American Archaeology 1(2). Carnegie Institution of Washington Publication 403, 29–116

Thompson, Eric, 1972. *A Commentary on the Dresden Codex: a Maya Hieroglyphic Book*. American Philosophical Society, Philadelphia.

Tozzer, Alfred, 1941. *Landa's Relación de las cosas de Yucatan: a translation*. Papers of the Peabody Museum of American Archaeology and Ethnology, Harvard University, Cambridge.

Zender, Marc, 2004. A Study of Classic Maya Priesthood. Ph.D. dissertation, University of Calgary, Alberta.

5

Centering the world: zenith and nadir passages at Palenque

Alonso Mendez and Carol Karasik

Introduction

Zenith and nadir passages are, by definition, polar opposites (Fig. 5.1). In northern latitudes, summer and winter solstices mark the waxing and waning of the solar year. In the tropical regions of Mesoamerica, zenith and nadir divide the rainy season from the dry (Milbrath 1999: 14). Like the summer and winter solstices, zenith and nadir are metaphors for the course of human life and the natural cycles of birth, death, and regeneration.

In the remote past, the Sun's position at the center of the noonday sky would have served as a primary constant. Although the dates of zenith and nadir passages vary at different latitudes, they are also fixed, on the horizon and in the sky, at any given locale in Mesoamerica. The Maya apparently understood this paradox in their search for a center that harmonized with calendrics, agriculture, and ritual.

Although much has been written about the world directions, the three-tiered conceptualization of the Maya universe, and their sophisticated system of horizon-based astronomy, ancient Maya methods of spatial reckoning remain a puzzle. The prominence of zenith and nadir within the cultural fabric, past and present, may provide some answers about how the Maya delineated space.

Among the modern Maya of Guatemala (B. Tedlock 1992a: 23–24), east and west are described as general locations where the Sun rises and sets. The same may have been true for the early Maya. Zenith and nadir, on the other hand, are firmly equated with up and down, above and below, north and south. As Barbara Tedlock (1992b: 178) points out:

> Mayan directions are not discrete cardinal or intercardinal compass points frozen in space, but rather are horizontal and vertical lines, sides, vectors or trajectories that are inseparable from the passage of time. They not only map out the flat world of the horizon astronomy, but open the sky to coordinate astronomy as well.

This chapter focuses on solar alignments recorded at Palenque during zenith and nadir passages and their relevance to the Creation story expressed in the texts and art at the site. These alignments suggest that the vertical opposition of zenith and nadir became the central axis that defined north and south as well as due east and west. This central axis also served as the pivot around which time and space revolved.

The relationship between zenith passage

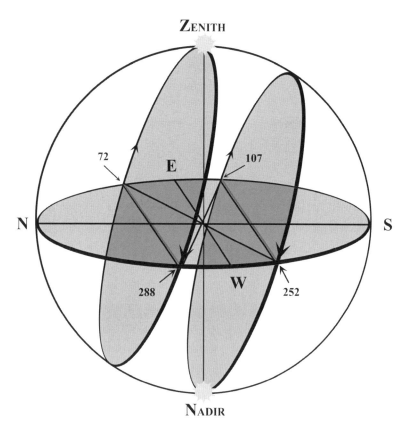

Fig. 5.1. Diagram showing the azimuths of zenith and nadir passages for Palenque's latitude of 17°28'N (drawing by Alonso Mendez)

local geography, history, seasonal cycles, and celestial activity. Underlying their cosmological scheme was a highly refined and accurate positional astronomy that allowed Palencanos to visualize the sky thousands of years in the past. As a result, astronomers were able to retrofit a mythology that would resound and harmonize with the lives of the city's great rulers.

Dennis Tedlock's translation of the *Popol Vuh* (1985) affirms that ancient Maya mythology conveyed significant astronomical information. Other evidence in the literature corroborates the ability of ancient astronomers to predict planetary cycles as well as the slow drift of the constellations in their almost imperceptible movement through the ages (Santillana 1969). The constellations, according to ethnographic sources, are, and were, of abiding concern as key markers for the changing seasons (B. Tedlock 1992a: 29; D. Tedlock 1985). In addition to playing a practical role in the agricultural cycle, constellations such as the Pleiades inevitably found their way into mythology and lore. As for the planets, the extraordinary astronomical records left behind by the Classic Maya have led to a general consensus that the Maya, despite having a geocentric perspective, achieved a profound understanding of synodic planetary movement (Lounsbury 1976; Milbrath 1999; Aveni 1992a: 7, 1992b, 1996, 2001; Aldana 2001, 2006). This astronomical knowledge, in concert with the solar and lunar calendars, gave the ancient Maya a solid framework from which to predict celestial events that would become powerful and integral elements of the religious and political system. More cogent to our discussion, recent hieroglyphic analysis of the Dresden Serpent Series, as well as mythological dates recorded at Palenque, indicate a concerted effort on the part of the elite to track the sidereal position of lunar eclipse cycles within the tropical year (Milbrath 1999: 259; Grofe 2007: 10; and McLeod 2007 pers. comm.). Together, these findings tell us that the Maya and their predecessors developed a system that permitted a skilled and informed astronomer to recreate the sky as it would have looked thousands of years in the past. This ancient system was much like the modern software programs that allow us to recreate the ancient Maya skies and to compare the evidence to written history and mythology. The Creation story, which integrated astronomy and mathematics with the acts of the gods, was

and the date of the Maya Creation has been discussed in a number of studies of other Mesoamerican sites (Freidel *et al.* 1993: 97; Coggins 1996: 21; Malmström 1997: 52; Broda 2006). According to Malmström, the Classic Maya calendar originated at the latitude of 15°N, where the Preclassic site of Izapa, in southern Mexico, is located. There, the 365-day solar year divides neatly between the zenith passages and solstices into the 260-day sacred calendar and the 105-day corn-growing cycle. The beginning of this cycle coincides with the date of Creation, 13.0.0.0.0 4 Ahaw 8 Kumk'u (August 13, 3114 BC Gregorian, September 8, 3114 BC Julian).

At 15°N latitude, the rising and setting positions of the Sun at zenith and nadir passages mark the midpoint between the equinoxes and the maximum northern and southern excursions of the Moon (Powell 2000 pers. comm.). When counting the days of the solar year at Palenque's latitude of 17°28'N, zenith and nadir passages mark the intermediary point between the equinoxes and solstices. With the knowledge that Palencanos inherited from the Olmec and Izapan civilizations, they developed a complex cosmology that took into account

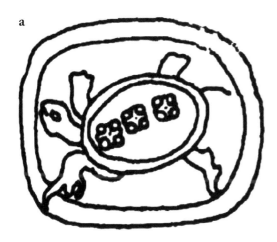

celebrated at Tikal, Copan, and other Classic Maya centers. Nowhere was it more evocative than its depiction at Palenque.

The Creation story at Palenque's Temple of the Cross

The three hearthstones

The first episode in the Creation story, as told on the Tablet of the Cross, was the setting of three stones in the "New Hearth Place" at *TI' Chan-na*, which Stuart (2006: 122) translates as the "Edge of the Sky". The three hearthstones seem to refer to three stars in the constellation of Orion. The modern Maya of Guatemala compare the triadic shape of their household hearths to the southern triangle formed by Alnitak, Saiph, and Rigel (B. Tedlock 1992b: 29). Indeed, Orion may be seen as a set of triads, the most prominent being the three stars of Orion's Belt, Mintaka, Alnitak, and Alnilam. It is probably these three that the ancient Maya depicted as three stars or stones inscribed on the back of a turtle representing Orion (Milbrath 1999: 253; Figs. 5.2a–b).

An analysis of the sky on the date of Creation confirms the identity of the three hearthstones. On September 8, 3114 BC (Julian), the Sun was at zenith passage, the Moon was full, and Mintaka, the leading star of Orion's Belt, reached the nadir of the night sky; that is, the center of the underworld. The setting up of the three stones may therefore refer to the centering of Orion in the underworld (Fig. 5.3). This epic moment has a direct biaxial relationship to the Sun's position in the center of the sky at zenith passage.

The presence of the Sun and Moon, also in direct biaxial positions at zenith and nadir passages, substantiates the importance of Heart of Sky-Zenith and Heart of Earth-Nadir as divine locations central to the creation of the cosmos and indivisible from the progenitor deities who resided in these locations. The primordial scene, together with astronomical data at the time of the Creation, is symbolized on a work of art portraying the birth of the Maize God from the carapace of the Earth/Turtle deity, which is subtly fused with the Turtle constellation, Orion, to depict Heart of Sky, Heart of Earth at the center of the cosmos (see Fig. 5.5a).

The round ceramic plate, like other ritual

Fig. 5.2. (a) Turtle constellation: Bonampak (after Miller); (b) Turtle: Madrid Codex (after Villacorta C. and Villacorta)

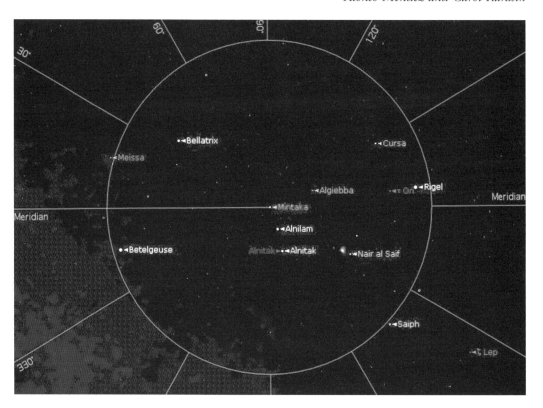

Fig. 5.3. Nadir position of Mintaka, in Orion's Belt, on the date of Creation (Starry Night Deluxe)

Fig. 5.4. Tablet of the Cross (drawing by Linda Schele)

servers of its kind, was known as a *Lak'in*, or Sun plate, and was associated with the eastern rising of the Sun. On opposite sides of the Turtle appear the Hero Twins, identified as the Sun and full Moon (see Mendez *et al.* this volume: 67, 73). Their physical placement, conforming to the position of both heavenly bodies during a full Moon, suggests that this

Classic Maya painted vessel represents the positions of the Sun, Moon, and Orion on the date of Creation. The plate is a veritable Rosetta Stone for understanding the celestial underpinnings of Maya mythology.

"Six-Sky House"

Five hundred and forty-two days later, on March 3, 3112 BC, GI created the *Wak Chan-Naahal*, the "Six-Skies House in the North." The Sun was now at nadir passage. In yet another instance of reflective opposition, the House in the North, or Zenith House, was established when the Sun was centered in the underworld, just as the three hearthstones were set up when the Sun was at zenith.

At the beginning of Creation, when earth and sky were one, the three hearthstones defined the center of the underworld sky. The "Six-Skies House" effectively separated the heavens from the earth, established the world directions, and defined the center of the upper sky. The central axis between them was the World Tree (Freidel *et al.* 1993: 71–73).

The World Tree

The Cross Group embodies the major themes of Creation. Its three temples may be earthly representations of the three hearthstones (Freidel *et al.* 1993: 65–69). The ancient name of the Temple of the Cross, or its inner sanctuary, is *Wak ? Chan na*, "Six ? Skies House" (Stuart 2006: 109), which is dedicated to GI, the first born of the three patron deities of Palenque. Inside his temple stands a magnificent depiction of the World Tree.

The Tablet of the Cross shows Pakal and K'an Bahlam extending offerings to the World Tree. Perched atop its jeweled branches is the Principal Bird Deity, Yax Na Itzamna, whom scholars have associated with the coming spring rains at zenith passage (Milbrath 1981: 270, 284). At the base of the tree lies the eastern head of the Cosmic Monster. The bowl infixed with the *kin* glyph that sits atop the monster's head is a key diagnostic symbol for GI and his association with the Sun, sky, and resurrection (Stuart 2006: 216). Stuart (2002: 142) reads the *kin* bowl as the sign for "east," with an associated meaning of "to rise" or "to come out." Thus, rising from its birthplace in the *kin* bowl, the Sun climbs the World Tree that is the central feature of the Tablet of the Cross. Specifically, the cross represents the ascent of

Fig. 5.5. (a) Birth of the Maize God, depicted on Classic Maya ceramic plate (drawing by Karl Taube); (b) Birth of Mixtec god from the World Tree. Codex Vienna (drawing by J. Furst)

the Sun at zenith passage (Mendez, *et al.* this volume 64; 2005: 56–57; Stuart 2006: 216)**.** Similarly, the hundreds of incense burners that were ritually interred in the terraces of the Temple of the Cross probably symbolized the first hearth as well as the journey of the Sun up the World Tree (Cuevas 2000: 56; Fig. 5.4).

This cosmic event is made manifest in the alignment of the Cross Group to the local zenith and nadir passages. During zenith passage on May 7 and August 5, the morning Sun, seen from the central doorway of the Temple of the Sun, rises directly out of the center of the roof comb of the Temple of the Cross (Mendez *et al.* this volume 64; 2005: 56). Because of the dramatic way the zenith Sun emerges from the center of the roof comb, it could be said that the temple as a whole portrays the establishment of zenith.

During nadir passage, on January 29 and November 9, the setting Sun, seen from the Temple of the Cross, sinks below Temple XXIV, directly behind the Temple of the Sun. The Temple of the Sun is dedicated to GIII, the god long associated with the night Sun (Kelley 1976: 6) and, as we have recently shown, the full Moon in the underworld (Mendez *et al.* this volume 72; 2005: 70, 71). This association is magnified by the Temple of the Sun's eastern alignment to nadir sunrise. On the anniversary of the day of Creation, the rising Sun emerges from the shrine dedicated to GI. The evening Sun at nadir sets over the temple dedicated to GIII. At sunrise during zenith and at sunset during nadir, the Sun itself manifests the World Tree in the center of the cosmos.

The birth of the Gods

The rebirth of the Maize God, from a crack in the cosmic turtle's shell during the August zenith passage (Freidel *et al.* 1993: 96–97), is depicted on numerous vessels from the Classic period. Other Mesoamerican deities are born from a cleft in the World Tree (Figs 5.5b). Although the Tablet of the Cross does not describe the manner of their births, the three patron deities of Palenque "touched the earth" in mid-November of 2360 BC. The youngest of the Triad, GII, Kawil, was born during nadir passage, November 28.

As Lounsbury (1978: 807) noted, the birthdates of the Palenque Triad, 754 years after Creation, actually refer to "the first calendar year since the beginning of the cycle where the equinoxes or solstices would be reversed with respect to the 365-day year." That is, hidden in the account of the birth of the gods is a subtle reference to the "tropical year drift cycle," which equals 2 × 754, or 1508 calendar years of 365 days. (It took 1508 *haabs* of 365 days to synchronize with 1507 tropical years of 365.2422 days.) During the first half cycle, from the date of Creation to the birth of the gods, the Sun drifted from its position at zenith to nadir passage. In other words, along with the reversal of the equinoxes and solstices was the reversal of the cosmic axis, zenith and nadir. This astute calculation on the part of Palenque's astronomers and mathematicians was followed by another: four cycles of 754 years after the divine births, in 2360 BC, bring us to AD 656, the height of Janahb Pakal's career.

Zenith and nadir in the dynastic history of Palenque

Following the birth of the gods, from whom the rulers of Palenque descended, the hieroglyphic texts recount the history of the royal dynasty. Six of Palenque rulers came to the throne during zenith or nadir passages.

Pakal's accession rites replicated the Creation story. His jaguar throne (along with the snake and shark thrones depicted on a number of tablets at Palenque) may have symbolized the first of the three hearthstones set up at the dawn of the new era (see Freidel *et al.* 1993: 66). Presiding over the fanfare surrounding Pakal's coronation was the radiant presence of the zenith Sun over the Palace (Fig. 5.6). These hierophanies aligned the ruler with the Sun and the grand cosmic scheme of creation.

Zenith and nadir observations in the Palace

Pakal's magnificent royal residence, built in successive stages beginning in AD 654 (Martin and Grube 2000: 163–164), incorporates solar alignments central to his dynasty. With the completion of House E, Houses C, B, and A eventually formed a dramatic inner courtyard that is both spacious and strangely askew. Along with House D, which was added later, the galleries, pillars, walls, and the T-shaped windows set inside them were carefully constructed with the Sun in mind.

At zenith passage, the setting Sun creates

perpendicular shadows along the western corridor of House C. Perpendicular shadows also play along the corridor of House D (Figs 5.7a–b).

At 6:00 PM the setting Sun, seen from the central doorway of House A, hovers above the center of the roof comb directly over the doorway of House C (Fig. 5.8). Several hieroglyphic passages found in House C associate this building with zenith (Schele 1994), which was dedicated five days after a zenith passage of the Sun on 9.11.6.16.11 7 Chuen 4 Chen (AD August 7, 659).

During nadir passage, the central doorways of Houses C and A are directly aligned with the rising Sun (Fig. 5.9). Equally dramatic is the zenith sunset seen through the central doorway of House A (Fig. 5.10). The use of natural light to illuminate ceremonies held in this doorway must have intensified the relationship between the Palace and the public spaces surrounding it, where nobles and commoners alike gathered to observe royal spectacles held on auspicious dates.

At both zenith and nadir, numerous alignments of the T-shaped windows may

be seen throughout the Palace. The T-shaped windows in House C and House D mark the position of the setting Sun at zenith (Fig. 5.11a). Three T-shaped windows in the western gallery of House E are aligned to zenith sunset and nadir sunrise (Fig. 5.11b).

House E was Pakal's coronation room, as is evident in his portrait above the throne. Although Pakal was crowned at zenith passage, he dedicated his house at nadir passage, AD November 9, 654.

Symbols related to zenith and nadir passages

Fig. 5.6. Palace orientation to zenith and nadir passages (drawing by Alonso Mendez after T. Maler)

Fig. 5.7 (a) Zenith sunset, House C, Palace; (b) Zenith sunset, House D, Palace (photos by Alonso Mendez)

*Fig. 5.8. Zenith sunset,
House C (photo by
Alonso Mendez)*

*Fig. 5.9. Nadir
sunrise, House C
(photo by Alonso
Mendez)*

appear above three doorways at the northern and southern ends of his house. The stucco bas-relief to the north depicts the double-headed Cosmic Serpent radiating from the central mask of the Principal Bird Deity, associated with zenith. At the southern end of the corridor, arching over the stairway leading down to the subterranean chambers, are two more images of the Cosmic Serpent: the first embellished with the Sun sign infixed in what may be a turtle

Fig. 5.10. Zenith sunset, east façade of House A (photo by Alonso Mendez)

Fig. 5.11 (a) Central window, House C; (b) T windows, House E (photos by Alonso Mendez)

Fig. 5.12 (a) Nadir sunrise, Temple of the Cross (photo by Carol Karasik); (b) Nadir sunrise, Temple of the Inscriptions (photo by Susan Prins)

shell, the second adorned with what may be the three hearthstones emitting volutes of fire or smoke. The dark passage bears the signature events of Creation that occurred in the center of the underworld.

Alignments between the Temple of the Cross and the Temple of the Inscriptions

Pakal's heir, K'inich Kan B'ahlam II, completed construction of the Temple of the Inscriptions and built the Cross Group *c.* AD 690. By aligning the Temples of the Cross and Inscriptions, the new king paid indelible homage to his dead father. During zenith passage, the evening Sun, viewed from the Temple of the Cross, sinks behind the Temple of the Inscriptions where Pakal is buried.

During nadir passage, the morning Sun, seen from the Temple of the Inscriptions, rises out of the roof comb of the Temple of the Cross (Fig. 5.12a). A dramatic ray of light pierces the eastern window of the Temple of the Inscriptions and marks the center of the

corridor (Fig. 5.12b). In the evening, the nadir Sun, seen from the Temple of the Cross, sets directly on the Inscriptions Prospect, just above the Temple of the Inscriptions.

The dialogue between father and son points to other incidents of cross-referencing between the two temples (See Mendez *et al.* this volume; 59). Of major interest is why the Temple of the Cross and the Temple of the Inscriptions share a diagonal alignment to equinox.

Finding the center

Pakal's sarcophagus lid is an elaborate portrait of cosmological events. At the base of the World Tree, the Quadripartite Badge, with its prominent *kin* sign, suggests a directional orientation to the eastern horizon. The figure of Pakal, poised on the *kin* bowl crowning the head of the Cosmic Monster, faces west. Rising like the Sun up the World Tree, he wears the attributes of the Maize God and around his neck the turtle carapace, symbol of Orion, out of which the Maize God was born.

Pakal was born on 9.8.9.1.3.0 8 Ajaw 13 Pop

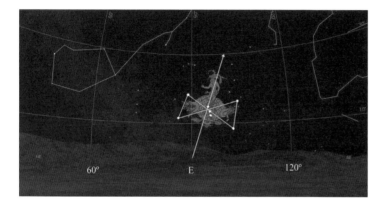

Fig. 5.14 The Maize God emerging from the hearthstones of Orion, seen as a set of equilateral triangles

(AD March 23, 603), the calendrical equinox. Though this date may have been contrived, his birth was linked numerologically to the mythical "Three-Stone Place" as well as to the birth of Palenque's Progenitor Deity, Muwan Mat, the Maize God, born on January 2, 3120 BC (see Coe 1993: 199). Projecting into the future, Muwan Mat's thirteenth baktun anniversary, on AD April 19, 2006, coincided with the *tzolkin* and *haab* anniversaries of Janahb Pakal's birthday. These calendrical acrobatics tell us with uncanny certainty that the divine king would be reborn as the new Maize God and Progenitor Deity. But the rebirth of the Maize God would not take place until the three stars of Orion's Belt – the three hearthstones of Creation – rose due east.

Beyond these mathematical computations, a grander design was at play. Geometrically, the sarcophagus lid is composed of two equilateral triangles that converge in the center (Fig. 5.13). The patron of the design is a square root 3 rectangle that outlines the ecliptic. Portrayed as the Cosmic Serpent (Freidel *et al.* 1993: 78), the ecliptic frames the

scene. Funerary art is appropriately "killed" by puncturing the center. In this case, the center was destroyed by breaking the corners of the lid. Thus, no one would be able to stretch two strings across to find the true center.

Herein lies a hidden meaning. The patron that defines the ecliptic is also present in the constellation of Orion (Fig. 5.14). The equilateral triangles formed by the outer stars of Orion echo the equilateral triangles of the ecliptic and converge in the central star of the Belt. As if the cosmic hearth had replicated itself on a vast scale, the sky is in harmony with the place of its own birth.

In time, the position of the central hearth would change. One full cycle of the Long Count was required for Orion to travel to its new location and the place of the Maize God's rebirth. Because of the precession of the equinoxes, the mythical hearth that was set up in the center of the underworld at zenith passage has now moving toward its new center at the close of this Creation. In 2012, Orion became an equinox marker, and its association with the midpoint of the year confirms that the intended

Fig. 5.15 The world directions (drawing by Alonso Mendez)

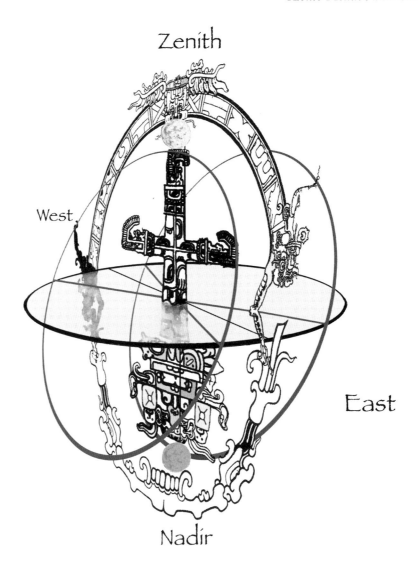

directional orientation of the Temples of the Cross and Inscriptions was, prophetically, to the equinox sunrise. The sarcophagus lid, in its eloquent depiction of Classic Maya cosmology, is therefore not a celebration of Pakal's moment of death but rather an apotheosis monument celebrating his rebirth.

Conclusions

Zenith and nadir mark significant dates in the lives of Palenque rulers. The Cross Group, Temple of the Inscriptions, and the Palace show major alignments to the Sun at zenith and nadir passages.

Brilliantly mirrored in the solar alignments witnessed at Palenque is the Maya myth of Creation. Our interpretation of the texts and iconography suggests that zenith and nadir passages were core motifs in the Creation story. They are repeated in the rulers' efforts, through art, written history, and the design of sacred space, to establish and perpetuate their divine power by identifying themselves as the pillar of the Sun, the World Tree.

The changing and changeless center was embodied in the person of the ruler, the "Founder Tree," whose roots in the primordial past spanned three cosmic realms and linked sky and earth, men and gods (Taube 1998). Centered in the eternal present, Pakal could trace his lineage back to – and be – Palenque's Progenitor Deity, Muwan Mat. He would also project forward to modern times: six years before the end of the thirteenth baktun, in 2012. In an indirect though mathematically prophetic statement, Pakal advanced himself as the Progenitor Deity for the next era. Aside from Tortugero Monument 6, this is the only Maya prophesy for the supposed "end date" of 2012. By aligning their temples to zenith and nadir passages, Pakal and Kan B'ahlam further assured their connection to the mythical past, as well as to the future, through cyclical astronomical phenomena. Their successions and reigns were therefore as inevitable as the cycles of time itself. Palenque's art and architectural alignments placed the Creation in their hands.

The polar opposition of zenith and nadir passages was the vertical pivot of the world. With the raising of the "Six-Skies House," it was possible to define the horizontal plane by marking the maximum excursions of the Sun at the solstices, and then, through geometrical division, find the orientation of true east and west on the horizon (Fig. 5.16). Zenith sunrise and nadir sunset were the nexus, the "place of change" (B. Tedlock 1992a: 28). Along with the solstices and equinoxes, the center moved through time and space.

As did the most prominent celestial markers. After the setting of the hearthstones, Orion gradually began shifting from its nadir position in the center of the underworld toward the center of the horizon. Orion reached its position at equinox in 2012, the end of one Great Round and the dawn of a new era. A society dependent on a harmonious system of timekeeping, astronomy, religion, and agriculture may have understood the principles of cosmic drift. Thus, zenith and nadir established their positions in the center of the sky and underworld as well as on the horizon, along with the Sun and constellations, forever fixed and changing in the grander cycle of precession.

References

Aldana, Gerardo V. 2001. *Oracular Science: Uncertainty in the History of Maya Astronomy 500–1600*. Ph.D. dissertation. Harvard University, Cambridge.

Aldana, Gerardo V. 2006. *The Apotheosis of Janahb Pakal: Science, History, and Religion at Classic Maya Palenque*. University Press of Colorado, Boulder.

Andersen, Tom, Peter Hanson, and Ted Leckie, 1997. Starry Night Deluxe. Sienna Software, Inc. Toronto.

Aveni, Anthony F. 1992a. Introduction: Making Time. In *The Sky in Mayan Literature* (A. F. Aveni ed.). Oxford University Press, New York, 3–17.

Aveni, Anthony F. 1992b. The Moon and the Venus Table: An Example of Commensuration in the Maya Calendar. In *The Sky in Mayan Literature* (A. F. Aveni ed.). Oxford University Press, New York, 87–101.

Aveni, Anthony F. 1996. Review of Maya Cosmos: Three Thousand Years on the Shaman's Path by David Freidel, Linda Schele, and Joy Parker. American Anthropologist, New Series, Vol. 98, No. 1, March, 1996, 197–198.

Aveni, Anthony F. 2001. *Skywatchers*. University of Texas Press, Austin.

Aveni, Anthony F., Harvey M. Bricker, and Victoria R. Bricker, 2003. Seeking the Sidereal: Observable Planetary Stations and the Ancient Maya Record. *Journal for the History of Astronomy* 34, 145–161.

Broda, Johanna, 2006. Zenith Observations and the Conceptualization of Geographical Latitude in Ancient Mesoamerica: A Historical and Inter-disciplinary Approach. In *Proceedings of the Oxford Seven Conference in Archaeoastronomy* (Todd Bostwick and Bryan Bates eds). Phoenix, 183–212.

Coe, Michael D. 1993. *The Maya*. Thames and Hudson, London.

Coggins, Clemency, 1996. Creation Religion and the Numbers at Teotihuacan and Izapa. *Res* 29/30. The Peabody Museum of Archaeology and Ethnology, Cambridge, 16–38.

Cuevas García, Martha, 2000. Los incensarios del Grupo de las Cruces, Palenque. In *Archaeologia Mexicana*, Vol. VIII, No. 45. Editorial Raices/Instituto Nacional de Antropología e Historia. Mexico, D.F., 54–61

Freidel, David, Linda Schele and Joy Parker, 1993. *Maya Cosmos: Three Thousand Years on the Shaman's Path*. William Morrow, New York.

Grofe, Michael John, 2007. *The Serpent Series: Precession in the Maya Dresden Codex*. Ph.D. Dissertation, University of California at Davis.

Grube, Nikolai, Simon Martin, and Marc Zender, 2002. *Palenque and Its Neighbors*. University of Texas Press, Austin.

Kelley, David H., 1976. *Deciphering the Maya Script*. University of Texas Press, Austin.

Lounsbury, Floyd, 1976. A Rationale for the Initial Date of the Temple of the Cross at Palenque. In *The Art, Iconography and Dynastic History of Palenque* (M. G. Robertson ed.). Pre-Columbian Art Research Institute, Pebble Beach, 211–224.

Lounsbury, Floyd, 1978. Maya Numeration, Computation and Calendarical Astronomy. In *Dictionary of Scientific Biography*, Volume 15, supplement 1 (Charles Coulston-Gillispie ed.). Charles Scribner and Sons, New York, 759–818.

Lounsbury, Floyd, 1980. Some Problems in the Interpretation of the Mythological Portion of the Hieroglyphic Text of the Temple of the Cross at Palenque. In *Third Palenque Round Table*, Part 2 (M. G. Robertson ed.). Pre-Columbian Art Research Institute, San Francisco, 99–115.

Malmström, Vincent H., 1997. *Cycles of the Sun, Mysteries of the Moon: The Calendar in Mesoamerican Civilization*. University of Texas Press, Austin.

Martin, Simon and Nikolai Grube, 2000. *Chronicle of the Maya Kings and Queens*. Thames and Hudson, London.

Mathews, Peter, 2005. *Palenque Dates, Long Counts, Who's Who*. FAMSI.

McLeod, Barbara, 2007. Pers. Comm.

Mendez, Alonso, Edwin L. Barnhart, Christopher Powell, and Carol Karasik, 2005. Astronomical Observations from the Temple of the Sun. *Archaeoastronomy,* Vol. XIX. University of Texas Press, Austin, 44–73.

Milbrath, Susan, 1981. Astronomical Imagery in the Serpent Sequence of the Madrid Codex. In *Archaeoastronomy in the Americas* (Ray Williamson ed). Ballena Press, Los Altos, CA., 263–294

Milbrath, Susan, 1999. *Star Gods of the Maya: Astronomy in Art, Folklore, and Calendars.* University of Texas Press, Austin.

Powell, Christopher, 2000. Pers. Comm.

Santillana, Giorgio de and Hertha von Dechend, 1969. *Hamlet's Mill: An Essay on Myth and the Frame of Time.* Gambit, Boston.

Schele, Linda, 1994. Some Thoughts on the Inscriptions of House C. In *Seventh Palenque Round Table* (Virginia M. Fields ed., M. G. Robertson gen. ed.), 1989. Pre-Columbian Art Research Institute, San Francisco, 1–10.

Schele, Linda and David Freidel, 1990. *A Forest of Kings: The Untold Story of the Ancient Maya.* William Morrow and Company, New York.

Stuart, David, 2002. The Hieroglyphic Inscriptions from Temple XIX at Palenque: A Commentary. Mesoweb.

Stuart, David, 2006. *Sourcebook for the 30th Maya Meetings.* The University of Texas at Austin.

Taube, Karl, 1998. The Jade Hearth: Centrality, Rulership, and the Classic Maya Temple. In *Function and Meaning in Classic Maya Architecture* (Stephen Houston ed.). Dumbarton Oaks Research Library and Collection, Washington, D.C., 427–478.

Tedlock, Barbara, 1992a. The Road of Light: Theory and Practice of Mayan Skywatching. In *The Sky in Mayan Literature* (Anthony F. Aveni ed.). Oxford University Press, New York, 18–42.

Tedlock, Barbara, 1992b. *Time and the Highland Maya.* University of New Mexico Press, Albuquerque.

Tedlock, Dennis, 1985. *Popol Vuh.* Simon and Schuster, New York.

6

The many faces of Venus in Mesoamerica

Susan Milbrath

Long term observations of Venus are encoded in an ancient Venus calendar that links five Venus cycles to eight years ($5 \times 584 = 8 \times 365$), which is an approximation of 99 lunar months (99×29.49). The eight-year Venus Almanac can be traced back to the Protoclassic period in Veracruz, as evidenced by the La Mojarra stela (Justeson and Kaufman 1993; Macri and Stark 1993: 6; Milbrath 1999: 192). The Venus Almanac is best known from Postclassic codices, such as the Dresden Codex and Codex Borgia, where the calendar periods are accompanied by a series of deities representing different manifestations of the planet Venus. In addition to these well-known representations of Venus, the Venus Almanac may be linked with more enigmatic representations, such as the rain god wearing a trapeze-and-ray headdress. This chapter explores the antiquity of the Venus Almanac and its various manifestations in Mesoamerican Venus imagery. Venus calendars and associated visual imagery are obvious references to the Venus Almanac, but it also seems to be expressed more subtly in certain symbols that can be associated with Venus in both Central Mexico and the northern Maya lowlands. The Venus Almanac seems to be a pan-Mesoamerican phenomenon, which can be recognized in a number of contexts through study of textual and iconographic records.

The Venus Almanac and Year Sign

Tracing the origins of certain designs that can be linked with the Venus Almanac may help define changes in form and meaning. The quincunx, a five-part design consisting

Fig. 6.1. Codex Borgia 19 (Milbrath 1999: fig. 5.6b)

Fig. 6.2. Codex Borgia 27 and 28 (Boone 2001)

of four dots or squares with a fifth in the center, is clearly used in the context of Venus imagery during the Postclassic period, in both glyphic symbols and the face painting of Tlahuizcalpantecuhtli ("lord of dawn"), one of the Venus gods in the Codex Borgia (Fig. 6.1). Quincunx face painting is an insignia of Postclassic Venus gods in the Codex Borgia and other Borgia Group codices, such as the Codex Fejervary-Mayer page 25 (Thompson 1957; Seler 1904). Quincunx face painting in the Codex Borgia shows four dots on profile faces, with the fifth dot on the cheek that is hidden from view (Fig. 6.1, Borgia 45). The quincunx design can be traced back to the Early Preclassic Olmec, where it might be an early expression of the five Venus cycles of the Venus Almanac (Milbrath 1999: 187, 211). In the Classic period the quincunx is associated with the rain god. Murals from Tepantitla depict a variant of the rain god known as "Tlaloc A" wearing a quincunx headdress, a form that seems to substitute for the Year Sign headdress more commonly worn by Tlaloc A (Pasztory 1974: 10, figs 5, 11).[1] Tetitla murals known as the "Jade Tlalocs" depict figures wearing a necklace with five pendants, each with the quincunx design (Pasztory 1974: fig. 12). A similar form appears in the first panel of the skyband in the center of Codex Madrid 11 (Fig. 6.3), and the same form is represented in the skyband on page 46 of the Venus almanac in the Dresden Codex (see Fig. 6.10). These designs are described by Ivan Šprajc (1996: 76, fig. 3.1) as Venus symbols related to Maya Venus glyphs. The Maya Venus symbol in glyphic writing has a somewhat different form, as seen on Dresden Codex page 46, where column F (sixth column from the left) shows a glyph compound with four dots or rings framing a cruciform design that is prefixed by Chak, read as Chak Ek' ("great star"). Chak also prefixes half versions of this glyph with two rings enclosed in an "M" design, each one marking transitions in the Venus cycle (Milbrath 1999: fig. 5.3a, line 18).

Another symbol apparently linked with Venus is the trapeze-and-ray design. This form makes its first appearance at Teotihuacan, where it has been connected with the eight-year Venus Almanac that regulated a cult of warfare (Carlson 1993: 204, 209, 212). This design appears as a headdress worn by Teotihuacan's rain/storm god, a counterpart of the Aztec rain god Tlaloc. Tlaloc with a trapeze-and-ray

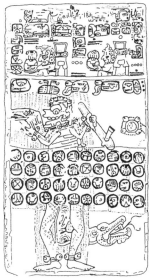

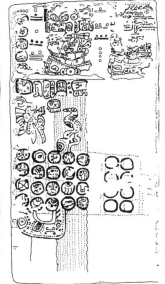

Fig. 6.3. Madrid Codex 12–18 (Milbrath 1999: fig. 7.3)

headdress actually appears more frequently in the southern Maya lowlands, where there is a clear link with dynastic and warrior images (Berlo 1984: 112; Milbrath 1999: 193–199; Nagao 1989: 88–89, 94–95; Stone 1989: 162, 165). For example, Classic Maya monuments from Aguateca and Dos Pilas depict the ruler as a warrior wearing a Tlaloc mask with a trapeze-and-ray headdress, imagery linked to "star wars" timed by the first appearance of the Evening Star, but also has been more broadly connected with the planets in general (Aveni and Hotaling 1994; Milbrath 1999: 195, fig. 5.8c, d; Schele and Freidel 1990: 444–446, fig. 4: 17).[2] Chac and Tlaloc both wear Year Sign

headdresses in Postclassic agricultural almanacs that can be related to Venus, as will be seen in the subsequent discussion (Figs 6.2 and 6.3).

In Postclassic contexts the trapeze-and-ray design was also used as a Year Sign marking yearbearer dates, as seen in the Codex Borgia (Fig. 6.2). In the Mixtec codices, the Year Sign more closely resembles a ray interlaced with an oval (the A-O sign) or a ray interlaced with a rectangle, as seen in the Codex Nuttall. Because the trapeze-and-ray and A-O sign both clearly designate the annual cycle and mark dates in the 52-year cycle in the Codex Borgia, they are truly "year" signs. Nonetheless, bearing in mind the possible origin of the trapeze-and-ray as a symbol of the Venus Almanac at Teotihuacan, it may also refer to Venus observations made in the context of the solar year, as seems to be the case on Borgia 27–28 (see below). And, since a double Calendar Round of 104 years integrates a repeating series of Venus events with the solar cycle (104 × 365 being divisible by 260 and 584), this larger cycle of time may be implied in contexts where the year sign is employed in iconography that has an apparent reference to Venus.

If the trapeze-and-ray Year Sign referred to the Venus cycle in an early Venus Almanac at Teotihuacan, it may have referenced a count of years referred to the Venus cycle, and this meaning may have carried forward over time. Tlaloc and the trapeze-and-ray "year signs" reappear in Maya art in the late seventh century and early eighth century, where they seem to be linked with astronomical stations in the synodical periods of Venus and Jupiter (Kowalski 2007: 257; Schele and Freidel 1990: 130–131, 438 n. 3, 444–446, n. 47).

Terminal Classic Puuc architecture often represents sets of five Chacs, which may allude to the five Venus cycles equated with eight solar years. At the Puuc site of Uxmal, the North Structure of the Nunnery shows a stack of masks with the uppermost mask representing Tlaloc with a Year Sign in his mouth. Jeff Kowalski (2007: 295, fig. 2) links the Nunnery Tlaloc masks to Teotihuacan-related religious beliefs and imagery associated with a cult of Venus-sanctioned warfare. Stacks of five Chac masks are common at Uxmal, some with Maya style Venus glyphs below the eyes (Aveni 2001: 286), but on the North Structure, the fifth Chac is replaced by Tlaloc (Milbrath 1999: 201, fig. 5.9g). Although the Chac masks have been recently reinterpreted as *witz* monsters representing mountains, this designation in the context of the Uxmal upper façade would not seem appropriate. Not only are they part of a stack of masks that include Tlaloc in his role as a sky god controlling storms (the Storm God of the Classic period) and the trapeze-and-ray that is associated with both Tlaloc and Chac imagery as on Madrid Codex 11 (Fig. 6.3). In fact, Linda Schele and Peter Matthews (1998: 270–271) reinterpreted the Chac masks on the North building as Itzamna, a god who often has celestial associations, noting an association with representations of clouds and the "sky house" (*kan-nah*). On the House of the

Governors all four sides of the shows Chac in sets of five with the Venus glyph infixed under his eyes, probably alluding to the five-ness of Venus; the House of the Governors also has corner masks with the number 8, representing either the eight-day underworld sojourn of the Venus in inferior conjunction or the eight-year interval of the Venus Almanac (Aveni 2001: 286; Milbrath 1999: 204). Whether Chac is a manifestation of Venus or somehow symbolizes an aspect of Venus linked with the rainy season remains uncertain, but this deity clearly has a connection with the Venus Almanac (Milbrath 1999: 204–205).

Venus and the Chicchan Serpent Almanac in the Madrid Codex 12b–18b

The Codex Madrid (12b) shows Chac, the Maya counterpart for Tlaloc, wearing a stylized Year Sign headdress in the preface to an *in extenso* almanac recording a 260-day cycle (Fig. 6.3; Milbrath 1999: 259, fig. 7.3; Just 2004). Apart from the sequence of Day Signs in the 260-day almanac on pages 13b–18b, there are relatively few glyphs and the sequence of 260 days remains incomplete. There are unfinished Day Signs on 18b, and another entire page would be required to finish the complete count of 260 days. The arrangement of four rows implies four sets of 65 days, a format useful in calculations involving Venus events, because dropping down one row and moving back one place, leads to the Day Signs that would coincide with the next period of 584 days. And, if we consider that there are numeral coefficients implied by the positioning of the Day Signs in a row, there is an even greater precision in the Venus calculations. For example moving from 11 Kan on page 15b to 10 Lamat (one down one back) allows a quick calculation of the interval of a 584-day Venus Round (584 = 64 + 2 × 260 days). The synchronicity of the Venus Almanac breaks down over time because the average synodic cycle of Venus (583.92 days) falls short of 584 days, but this could be accommodated by dropping back one more day when necessary to keep track of the Venus dates.

The dominant figure on pages 12b–18b is the Chicchan serpent, a crested snake that Karl Taube (1992: 140; fig. 76e) links with Quetzalcoatl, the "feathered serpent," widely identified as a manifestation of Venus (Aveni

2001: 26; Šprajc 1996; Milbrath 1999: 177–186). In the Madrid Codex, the serpent often appears with Chac (pp. 12b, 13b, 17b), the Yucatec Maya rain god. The pairing of Chac and the Feathered Serpent seems to echo representations pairing the feathered serpent and Tlaloc at Teotihuacan, as in the miniature temple in the painted Patio 2 of Atetelco (Miller 1973: fig. 346). The Year Sign headdress worn by Chac on Madrid 12b recalls images of Tlaloc wearing the Year Sign headdress, which may have developed as a symbol of the Venus Almanac at Teotihuacan. It is noteworthy that there are a total of five Chacs in the imagery on pages 12b–18b, just as there are five Chicchan serpents. This may be linked with a pattern that Anthony Aveni (1991: 315, 317) has described as the "fiveness" of Venus.

Chac and the Chicchan Serpent appear in sets of five even today. In a contemporary Maya account from Quintana Roo, there are four Chacs at the four corners of the sky who ride horses that represent clouds, and they are guided by an archangel who represents the fifth Chac in the center (Milbrath 1999: 202). A more authentically Maya combination is represented by the Chorti Chicchan serpents. Half-feathered and half-human, they are found in sets of four or five, and they control rainfall, like the Chacs and their horses in Quintana Roo (Milbrath 1999: 36).

The Chicchan Serpent in the Codex Madrid, apparently depicting Venus as a celestial serpent, also has stellar attributes when pictured as a rattlesnake. This suggests that a number of different celestial cycles are incorporated in the imagery, ones that integrate Venus events with the tropical year, marked by both solar and stellar events involving the Pleiades. In previous publications, I interpreted the Madrid Codex Chicchan serpent as a rattlesnake constellation representing the Pleiades, called "the rattlesnake's rattle" in Yucatan. This constellation represented as a rattlesnake in the Paris Codex zodiac (Bricker and Bricker 1992; Milbrath 1999: 258). I proposed that the 260-day calendar on Codex Madrid 12b–18b refers to an agricultural almanac that focused on the position of the Pleiades during a 260-day agricultural cycle running from early February through late October, a cycle still evident among the Chorti today (Girard 1962). The Chicchan

serpent has rattles in the first two pages of the *in extenso* almanac (13b, 14b), but thereafter the serpent reverses course and loses its rattles (Milbrath 1999: 259–262). The serpent with rattles in the first two images can be related to the descent of the Pleiades at a time of year that preparation for planting begins in February through March; the subsequent representations show the serpent without rattles (15b–16b), which can be linked to the disappearance of the Pleiades in the evening sky when the rains begin in May through June (Milbrath 1999: fig. 7.3). Added support for this interpretation is seen in seasonal imagery, such as the male deer without antlers on page 14b, symbolizing the month of March, when the deer shed their antlers, and specific images that can be linked with the seasonal cycle evident in the Yucatec Maya festival calendar (Milbrath 1999: 61–62).

Developing this idea further, I proposed that the Day Signs on each page could also be used as "counters" much like the system in Central Mexico, where round dots are used to represent intervals of days (Milbrath 1999: 61). This means that not only could the Day Signs be read in a traditional sense in rows of 65 days (here foreshortened to 52), but they could literally be used as counters to give the total number of days on each page, without regard to the sequencing. The Codex Madrid Day Signs arranged in horizontal rows and vertical columns on each page, form groups of days, ranging from 32 days to 40 days (Fig. 6.3). Counting the number of Day Signs on each page, I noted that the intervals represented by the placement of eclipse glyphs on pages 13b and 17b seemed to be related to eclipse intervals. Counting the number of days from page 13b through page 16b results in a 148-days period (reached by adding 32, 36, 40, and 40), and page 17b itself adds another 40 days for a total of 188 days, a period that could embrace a second eclipse interval of 177 or 178 days, intervals all noted as eclipse intervals in the Dresden Codex (Milbrath 1999: 61).[3] The idealized intervals could denote that if a solar eclipse were to occur in the period covered by page 13 (February through early March), another eclipse would be expected 148 days later. There may have been agricultural auguries that would be linked with this eclipse patterning. Counting the days signs on each page also helps define subdivisions of the agricultural almanac in the Codex Madrid

(Milbrath 1999: 61, fig. 7.3). Three pages involve sets of 40 days, a subdivision also seen in the 260-day agricultural cycle surviving today among the Chorti, which also begins in early February and covers approximately the same period (Girard 1962).

Another line of evidence not adequately explored in my previous publications is the glyphs in the augural glyphs in a band dividing each page. The band on pages 13b–16b includes fire glyphs, which could refer to burning the fields in preparation for planting in February through May. The two pages (17b–18b) at the end of the sequence have augural glyphs (III.567: 130) that originally were seen as a reference to an abundance of food in the Dresden Codex (Thompson 1972). The interpretation of these glyphs as references to maize seems to be supported in subsequent research on the Dresden Codex (Bricker and Bricker 2011). These glyphs are appropriate to the latter part of the agricultural season, a period spanning from July through October when the maize matures. Although Chac is represented repeatedly in the imagery on pages 12b–17b, his name glyph first appears in the augural band on page 16b, a page referring to the period from late May to early July, when the rains grow increasingly heavy.

The image of Chac with the Year Sign on page 12b seems to introduce an almanac that integrates Venus with the annual cycle of solar and stellar events. Observations of Venus in relation to the annual cycle invariably involve repeated stellar positions. For example, in its sidereal cycle of just under 225 days, Venus passes by the Pleiades only in March through June, overlapping with the beginning of the rainy season, a pattern that has been evident for more than 2000 years (Milbrath 1999: 262).[4] Integrating the solar cycle and dusk observations of the Pleiades defines an agricultural almanac of approximately 260 days, but adding observations of Venus incorporates the Venus Almanac in the seasonal cycle. Given the placement of the agricultural almanac in early February through late October, the serpent rattles appear only on those pages that represent periods when the Pleiades were visible at dusk. Looking for seasonal patterns when Venus was near the Pleiades at dusk, places Venus in the Evening Star phase, which seems appropriate because the imagery of rainfall in the agricultural almanac evokes the

widespread link between agricultural fertility and the Evening Star documented by Ivan Šprajc (1993a; 1993b; 1996).

Over the course of a little more than a century (a double Calendar Round) there were 65 different periods when the Evening Star was visible, so if we want to determine the placement of the Madrid almanac, we must narrow the choices to more specific criteria. The placement of pages 13b–14b in early February through mid-April helps narrow the search. Given the fact that Venus passes by the Pleiades only in March through June, and the Venus serpent "wears" the Pleiades rattles on pages that represent a period that partially overlaps this interval, the best fit may be a time when the Evening Star in proximity to the Pleiades in March through April. Based on the 15th century date for the Madrid Codex proposed by a number of scholars (Aveni and Vail 2004: 19–20), Bryant Tuckerman's (1964) tables given in geocentric positions (tropic celestial longitudes and latitudes with respect to the mean equinox of date) provides a means to study when Venus passes by a specific star group. Focusing on times when the Evening Star was located around 50° longitude, which marked the position of the Pleiades during the fifteenth century, a number of solutions resulted. In the year AD 1403 Venus was positioned near the Pleiades in March and April for a relatively long time, as it moved in retrograde motion before disappearing as the Evening Star in April (ELast 4/13/1403 O.S., 4/23/1403 N.S.; calculated by the PLSV3.1 program; Lange and Swerdlow 2006). Since these events would repeat around the same time every eight years, other possible solutions include AD 1411, 1419, 1427, etc. Iconographic support for this model is seen in the sequence of events on pages 13b–15b (Fig. 6.3). The reconstructed 260-day agricultural almanac begins on page 13b with a 32 day period running from February 8 (N.S.; 1/31/1403 O.S.) to March 11, followed by a 36-day period from March 12 through April 16 on page 14b, and a 40-day period from April 16–May 26 on page 15b, a period when both the Pleiades and Venus disappeared (ELast 4/13 O.S., 4/22/1403 N.S). The imagery on page 15b shows the serpent has lost its rattles and reversed course, which could symbolize that the disappearance of the Pleiades, at the time Venus disappeared and reversed course, moving from the western sky at dusk to the eastern sky at dawn.

An alternate solution is presented by the seasonal patterning at eight-year intervals centered on the year 1468, when EFirst occurred in early February, and Venus passed by the Pleiades around April 10 (O.S. or 4/19 N.S.) and remained visible for almost 260 days, overlapping with the dates ascribed to pages 13b–18b (EFirst occurred on February 11 O.S. and ELast on October 22 O.S.). The 1468 EFirst event may also be recorded in the Codex Borgia, as discussed below (see also Milbrath 2007). Another possible pattern is presented by the years 1464–1465, when EFirst occurred on or near November 29, 1464 (O.S., 12/8 N.S) and Venus was visible as the Evening Star until August 9, 1465 (ELast O.S.). In 1465, Venus passed right by the Pleiades on March 28 (O.S., 4/6 N.S.), and hovered in its vicinity for some weeks. Placing the events in 1465 would account for a 1 Imix date that Harvey Bricker (*et al.* 1997) and his colleagues have identified on page 13b. The date 1 Imix date on 13b could refer to the Calendar Round 1 Imix 4 Yax (2/6/1465 O.S. or 2/15/1465 N.S.), which is close to the early February date I originally proposed for the beginning of the agricultural cycle on that page. No other fifteenth-century Calendar Round date places a 1 Imix date in early February, but in the early sixteenth century the two correlates for 1 Imix 4 Yax fall in 1512 and 1517 (2/3/1517 N.S., 1/25 O.S. and 2/10/1512 N.S., 1/31 O.S.). Only the 1512 date coincides with the Evening Star, but Venus was more than 60° longitude away from the Pleiades in early March and did not pass by the constellation until early June. The 1465 solution best fits the parameters of a 1 Imix date corresponding to early February when Venus was the Evening Star in proximity to the Pleiades, but Venus was about 30° longitude away from the Pleiades in early March, and did not pass by the Pleiades until about a month later (3/27 O.S., 4/5 N.S.). This presents a good fit but not a perfect one if page 13b covers the period from February 8 through March 11, N.S. In this scenario, the image of the Chicchan Serpent wearing rattles would have to refer to a period when the Evening Star was in the approximate vicinity of the Pleiades, whereas the next page (14), covering March 12 to April 16 would coincide with the time that Venus passed right by the Pleiades.

If the 1 Imix date as a date that is merely intended to show an idealized beginning for the agricultural almanac, we have a number of different possibilities, but if we take the 1 Imix date as a real record, only the 1465 date fits the parameters designated by the model explored here. None of the proposed solutions correlates with dates correspond to eclipses events that could be observed in Yucatan (nor does the solution proposed by Bricker *et al.* 1997). The dates recorded could serve a different role more specifically linked with the Venus cycle, for not only do we find a unique solution to the 15th century 1 Imix date in early February corresponding to the Evening Star, but the dates would be used to easily calculate the 584-day Venus cycle by dropping down one row and moving back one day. My current research indicates a link with the Evening Star and eclipse pairs in 1452 (Milbrath n.d.).

Venus and the annual cycle in Codex Borgia 27–28

We can now turn to other examples of Venus Almanacs that have only recently been recognized. Imagery of the rain god represented in relation to the Venus cycle appears in the Codex Borgia, a manuscript that has a number of parallels with the Codex Madrid (Vail and Aveni 2004). Tlaloc with a Year Sign headdress is featured prominently in two agricultural almanacs in the Postclassic Codex Borgia, both apparently integrating the Venus cycle with agricultural events (Fig. 6.2). Recent breakthroughs in our understanding of these almanacs involve placing the Calendar Round dates in real time, and linking these dates with events with Venus events (Aveni 1999; Bricker 2001; Hernández 2006). Page 28 represents a detailed view of a five-year period that may incorporate dates coinciding with a number of planetary events, including dates for two Efirsts (2/5/1468 and 5/12/1471 O.S.; Aveni 1999: tables, 3–4).[5] Page 28 has three calendar glyphs but none of the numbers is well-preserved, and only one day sign is clearly present (Motion). Nonetheless, both Aveni and Hernández agree that the first date is the day 5 Motion in the year 1 Reed, a date from the 52-year cycle, which by convention is designated with the year first and the tonalpohualli date second (1 Reed 5 Motion). Page 28 initiates a five-year cycle with EFirst in early Feburary and records

Fig. 6.4. Codex Borgia 29–30 (Milbrath 2007: fig. 5.1)

pattern of rainfall and five Chacs corresponding to the five Tlalocs.

On page 27, Tlaloc with a Year Sign headdress appears in a 52-year Almanac that begins on 1 Reed 1 Crocodile, marking Elast in March of 1467, and the subsequent dates cover a 52-year period AD 1467–1519, with all the Calendar Round dates falling in March (O.S.), indicating a ritual cycle in preparation for planting and the onset of the rains (Aveni 1999: table 2; Hernández 2006; Hernández and Bricker 2004: 313, table 10.1). My recent research indicates that the second occurrence of 1 Crocodile in the year 1 Reed is an equally important date, coinciding with December 20, 1467 (Dec. 11 O.S.), the full moon on the winter solstice (Milbrath 2013). The focus on E-last and the winter solstice falling 1 Crocodile in the year 1 Reed (but 260-days apart), is noteworthy because the section that follows (Borgia 29–46) seems to begin some 28 years later with another correspondence between these two events, namely the disappearance of the evening star shortly after the winter solstice. The focus on imagery and dates that tie important Venus events to solar events is standard fare in the Venus almanac, as seen in the Dresden Codex which links the end of an eight-year Venus almanac with the summer solstice in the year 1227 (Milbrath 1999: 172, table 5.2).

Venus and the annual festival cycle in Codex Borgia 29–46

Pages 27 and 28 preface an 18-page narrative sequence that sets Venus events in the context of the 18 months or *veintenas* of the Central Mexican calendar, representing 1/8th of the full length of a Venus almanac (Milbrath 1989; 1999: 180; 2007). Dating the sequence of events in the Codex Borgia has been possible through study of the festival calendar embedded in the 18-page sequence. The visual imagery and inherent structure records an 18-month festival calendar, like that documented among the Aztecs and neighboring Tlaxcala, the probable origin point of the Codex Borgia (Milbrath 2013). The entire narrative section of the codex is designed to be read from top to bottom, a pattern also seen in the festival calendar of Sahagún's *Primeros Memoriales* (Milbrath 2013). And each festival is represented on a separate page, a pattern seen in most Aztec

rainfall patterns synchronized with agricultural events. The early February date is also one of the proposed solutions for the placement of Madrid 12b–18b, which similarly shows a

codices (Codex Telleriano-Remensis, Codex Tudela, Tovar Calendar, *etc.*). A number of festivals can be identified in the visual imagery based on images and descriptions of Central Mexican festivals. For example, the fifth page in the sequence (33) depicts the Tlacaxipehualiztli festival, representing the sacrifice of Xipe, who is shown lying on the stone of sacrifice in the center of the scene (Fig. 6.5). Because page 33 depicts the Tlacaxipehualiztli festival and each page represents a 20-day period, the first page

in the narrative sequence (29) must refer to Atemotzli, the festival of the winter solstice at the time of the conquest (Caso 1971: table 4).

Study of the patterning indicates that the Venus Almanac was significant in the sequence of events. Venus events are shown over the course of one year, beginning with the disappearance of the Evening Star (ELast) on page 29 (Fig. 6.4; Milbrath 2007). Page 29 shows a skeletal god, wearing a "bow-tie" headband like the Venus god, Tlahuizcalpantecuhtli

Fig. 6.5. (left) Codex Borgia 33–34 (Milbrath 2007: fig. 5.2)

Fig. 6.6. (right) Codex Borgia 39–40 (Milbrath 2007: fig. 5.3)

*Fig. 6.7. Detail Codex
Borgia 46 (Milbrath
2007: fig. 5.7)*

(Borgia 19). He is burned in a jade bowl designed to hold the hearts of sacrificial victims, echoing descriptions in the *Anales de Cuauhtitlan* that recount that Quetzalcoatl set himself on fire and was transformed into the Tlahuizcalpantecuhtli, the Morning Star, after eight days in the underworld (Bierhorst 1992: 36; Milbrath 2007: 192). The transformation of the skeletal Venus god is implied by starry Ehecatl serpents emerging from the ashes, and the small figures of Ehecatl that emerge from the serpent jaws. Ehecatl is widely recognized as the wind god manifestation of Quetzalcoatl, the feathered serpent embodying Venus (Milbrath 1999: 177–180).

On page 30, the Morning Star is represented more graphically as a rayed disk not unlike the rayed headdress worn by Ehecatl-Quetzalcoatl and Quetzalcoatl on Codex Borgia 19 and 62 (Fig. 6.4). The sequence of Venus imagery tracks the Venus cycle through the emergence of the Evening Star on page 46 (Figs 6.5–6.7).

Here Quetzalcoatl is burned in a fire and emerges transformed into the Evening Star. He drills a fire on the back of the fire serpent, an image representing the fire ceremony described in the festival of Panquetzaliztli (Milbrath 2007; 2013).

This unique narrative sequence tracks Venus from its disappearance as the Evening Star to its re-emergence as the Evening star (ELast to EFirst). This pattern of solar and Venus events would be expected to repeat at intervals of eight years, but the actual layout of Venus events in relation to the solar year involves determining the specific year that best fits the following parameters: 1) a year when ELast occurred in Atemoztli, 2) and EFirst took place in Panquetzaliztli. We can narrow the search for an ideal fit by recognizing that Codex Borgia 27 and 28 serve as a preface to page 29, which suggests that pages 29–46 must have occurred somewhere in the 52-year span between 1467 and 1519 (Milbrath 2007). In my more extended discussion of the

Fig. 6.8. Codex Borgia 53 and 54 (Milbrath 2013)

astronomical events in relation to the annual cycle, I tested numerous variables, and found only one year in this 52-year span that helps explain a scene that is completely unique in the lexicon of Mesoamerican visual imagery. Pages 39–40, traditionally interpreted as the sun's journey to the underworld at night, actually shows a solar eclipse linked with an eclipse interval represented along the left side of the Earth Monster's body (Fig. 6.6). Tests of all the eclipses visible in Postclassic Central Mexico resulted in the best candidate being a spectacular eclipse in August of 1496 (year 4 Flint) that was visible throughout Central Mexico (Aveni and Calnek 1999: table 4). This was the year of the most spectacular solar eclipse seen in the entire period running

from 1325 to 1520. The magnitude of the eclipse (96% at 3:36 PM) was so great that the Morning Star, in its last weeks of visibility in the east, was suddenly seen alongside the eclipsed sun in the west. Placing page 40 in the month of August is commensurate with beginning the sequence on page 29 in December, during Atemoztli, and this also places key Venus events and a solar eclipse at appropriate positions, based on the 20-day intervals represented by each page. Clearly, then, the events were recorded observations of real-time events, not predictions. The narrative sequence documents a significant year in the Venus Almanac, when Venus was last seen as the Evening Star on January 2, 1496 (ELast O.S., 1/11 N.S.), shortly after the winter solstice. Venus reappeared as the Morning Star on January 12, 1496 (MFirst), and disappeared again on September 17 (MLast) and reappeared as the Evening Star on November 29 (EFirst), based on dates in Lange and Swerdlow (2006).

The dates for Venus events remain estimates because the observed event can shift 2–3 days for inferior conjunction. Anthony Aveni estimates the MFirst to be January 12, 1496 (O.S 1/21 N.S.), with an inferior conjunction period of 10 days (Milbrath 2007: table 5.2, note 2). More recently, my research incorporating the planetary program developed by Lange and Swerdlow (2006) helps develop the sequence as follows, all given in the Julian calendar (Milbrath 2013):

p. 29: last 17 days of Evening Star, ELast on January 2, 1496 (Julian day 2,267,473)
p. 30: heliacal rise (MFirst) on January 12, 1496 (Julian day 2,267,483)
pp. 30–42: 249 days of Morning Star ends with MLast on September 17 (Julian day 2,267,732)
pp. 42–45: 73 days of Superior Conjunction
p. 46: 17 days of Evening Star begins with EFirst on November 29, 1496 (Julian day 2,267,805).
(17 ES + 9 IC + 249 MS + 73 SC + 17 MS = 365 day year).

Pages 29–46 in the Codex Borgia cover the four main Venus events in a single year with notation of solar event such as the equinox and a solar eclipse. Although this is not technically speaking a true Venus Almanac, it shows a subdivision of that almanac and is clearly focused on integrating the solar cycle with Venus events.

Other Venus Almanacs in the Borgia Codex

Venus is a repeated reference in the Codex Borgia, as is evident from study of other sections of the codex (Aveni 1999; Bricker 2001). Nowhere is this more explicit than in the Venus Almanac on Borgia 53–54 with five Venus warriors representing the heliacal rise of the Morning Star (Fig. 6.8; Aveni 1999: 52–55; Boone 2007: 152–156; Bricker 2001: S36, S25, 40, tables 1, 2).

The first warrior is a skeletal figure with quincunx face painting, and the remainder have similar face painting that is partially covered by masks. One of the Venus warriors wears a mask representing the lunar rabbit, a Precolumbian equivalent of our "man-on-the-moon," best seen on the full moon.[6] Each of the five Venus warriors would coordinate with specific lunar events, because the Venus Almanac also represents an approximate lunar interval ($5 \times 584 = 8 \times 365 = 99 \times 29.49$). Each warrior appears with 13 different heliacal rise dates ($5 \times 13 = 65$) for a total of 104 years ($584 \times 65 = 104 \times 365$). Victoria Bricker notes that this almanac most closely corresponds to heliacal rise dates beginning in AD 1473.[7] Dates for heliacal rise of Venus appear in a series of framed boxes or compartments and also in sets of three unnumbered days signs alongside the image of the Venus god spearing his victim. By 1505, the predicted day of heliacal rise on 9 Flint (represented below the fifth scene) actually occurred after the event, so the table no longer served as a warning device. Presumably this would be when the table was no longer effective. Following the layout suggested by Bricker for pages 53–54, the almanac records one of the last successful "predictions" for heliacal rise on the day 1 Flint (January 19, 1496 N.S.), which is within two days of the heliacal rise (1/21/1496 N.S.) based on Lange and Swerdlow (2006). As discussed in note 5, the modern estimates for specific Venus events vary by up to a week, so a two-day difference is inconsequential in this context. This record may actually be an observation, rather than a prediction, for the same heliacal rise (MFirst) is represented on page 30 in the narrative section of the codex (29–46). A link with the 1 Flint year is also seen in the year bearer sequence on page 52, dated to 1496, the last of the yearbearer dates shown in the codex (Hernández and Bricker 2004).

Dresden Codex Venus Almanac

Like the Codex Borgia 53–54, the Dresden Codex uses dates from the 260-day calendar to mark the heliacal rise of Venus over the course of 104 years, but the Maya codex also shows subdivisions of the Venus cycle with Calendar Round dates keyed to transitional points in the four phases of Venus and seasonal cycles implicit in the Calendar Round dates (Figs 6.10–6.12).[8] The intervals for the superior conjunction phase is set at 90 days, about 40 days longer than the average observational length of that phase. Aveni (1992) has suggested this artificial interval, approximating three lunar months, was used to key the table to lunar eclipses. Indeed, lunar intervals seem to be an integral part of the overall structure of the Dresden Codex Venus table (Šprajc 1996: 64–66). In this regard, it is noteworthy that on the introductory page (24) a Long Count date in the early seventh century (9.9.9.16.0; 2/4/623 O.S.) coincides with the last visible crescent before the new moon in a month following a lunar eclipse (Fig. 6.9; Milbrath 1999: 167).

The alignment of Calendar Round on dates Dresden 46–50 for Venus events in real time developed by Floyd Lounsbury (1983) indicates a span running from the tenth to the thirteenth century. My research suggests that the set of pictures on pages 46–50 documented actual events that were observed on heliacal rise dates in AD 1221–1227 (Milbrath 1999: 170–177). The layout of the pictures and glyphs clearly integrates significant solar events and with heliacal rise, which occurred on June 15, 1227 (O.S. Lange and Swerdlow 2006), the same day as the summer solstice in 1227 (6/15 O.S. or 6/22 N.S. Milbrath 1999: 172). Aveni (1992) places the heliacal rise date two days earlier (6/20/1227, when adjusted for the 584,283 correlation; Milbrath 1999: table 5.2), but in any case there was a significant link between the summer solstice and the 1 Ahau 13 Mac Calendar Round date recorded in dates in the central band of glyphs associated with the last of the Venus gods pictured in the sequence of five. It may be that the Maya selected this particular set of Venus observations for a permanent record associated with pictorial images not only because this run of the 8-year Venus Almanac coordinated the heliacal rise with the summer solstice but also because it overlapped with the eleventh baktun ending, a major milestone in the Long Count calendar.

Sonny Faulseit (2006) studied all the Venus events in the double Calendar Round period starting with 1 Ahau 18 Kayab in November 934 (Lounsbury's first base date) and found that the canonical dates for ELast often occurred before the actual ELast event and the EFirst dates tend to occur after the event, but the MFirst, ELast, and MLast generally reoccur in the same season, dividing the year into four equal periods based on the equinoxes and solstices. He points out that the overly long Superior Conjunction phase cannot be explained as a lunar interval, because the moon phases drifted too far from the canonical intervals to have been a significant factor in the choice of canonical dates, but he did find a significant pattern in the sidereal positioning of Venus, especially in relation to MLast and ELast. He notes that this patterning is not dependent on selecting the 10th century base date for entering the table and would work equally well in the 13th century (Faulseit 2006: 109, n. 1).

Using the 584,283 correlation, the historical base date of 1 Ahau 18 Kayab is related to an entry date associated with the true heliacal rise of Venus on November 21, 934 (O.S. Lange and Swerdlow 2006), a date that Šprajc (pers. comm. 2002) interprets as an historical observation of heliacal rise, rather than a backward calculation, and he notes that subsequent bases may also be historical records. Harvey Bricker and Victoria Bricker (2007, 2011) confirm the tenth century base date (employing the 584,283 correlation), but they propose alternatives to some of Lounsbury's other base dates for the Venus Table. They place the 1 Ahau 13 Mac date on page 50 in July 1123, at the beginning of a 104-year period that was truncated when a new base date was introduced on 1 Ahau 3 Xul in January 1221. They propose that earlier base dates and a Long Count inscription in the table's introduction refer to historical runs of the table, but the 1 Ahau 3 Xul table involved only future predictions because there were no corrections incorporated in the table.

The Brickers note that the current run of

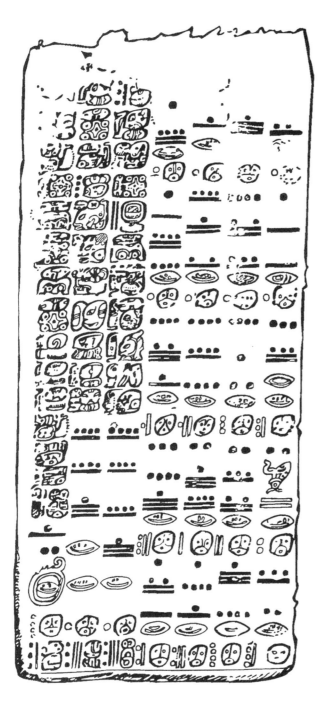

Fig. 6.9. (left) Page 24 Dresden Codex (Milbrath 1999; box 9.9.9.16.0 in third column)

Fig. 6.10. (right) Dresden Codex Venus Almanac 46 (Milbrath 1999: fig. 5.3a)

the table is one that began in AD 1221, and the predictions for future rise dates remained accurate for almost 104 years. Given the new interpretation presented here, I suggest that Maya astronomers adopted the 1 Ahau 3 Xul base by observing the true heliacal rise on 5 Kan 7 Xul in 1221 (1/19/1221 O.S.; Aveni 1992), recording it on page 46 with glyphs and pictures and then counted four days back to 1 Ahau 3 Xul to established a new

base, thereby making the correction needed so that the table could be used to predict future heliacal rises for a span of almost 104 years. The observation made on 5 Kan 7 Xul placed the heliacal rise precisely on the true date of heliacal rise, and marked the beginning of an eight-year Venus Almanac that ended with a precise observation of heliacal rise on 1 Ahau 13 Mac (6/13/1227 O.S., Aveni 1992; Milbrath 1999: table 5.2). At this point the

 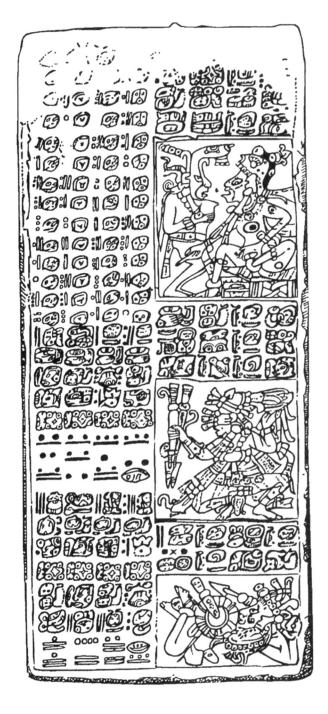

astronomers adopted the new base to make a set of predictions for future Venus events. This is precisely how an ephemeris should work, recording both observed events and predicted events (Aveni, pers. comm. 2006). The actual observations of helical rise over the period spanning 1221–1227 was clearly the departure point for a new set of predictions.

The essence of any eight-year Venus Almanac is a desire to link Venus phases to solar events.

Over the long run, the Venus phases fall out of precise synchronicity with the solar events. The introduction to the Dresden Codex Venus table contains numbers designed to realign the Venus calendar with solar events (Fig. 6.9). Most of the numbers are multiples of Venus Rounds that are associated with different Ahau dates, beginning with the lowest multiple of 8.2.0 or 2920 days representing five Venus Rounds or cycles, the basic period of the eight-

Fig. 6.11. (left) Dresden Codex Venus Almanac 49 (Milbrath 1999: fig. 5.3d)

Fig. 6.12. (right) Dresden Codex Venus Almanac 50 (Milbrath 1999: fig. 5.3e; 1 Ahau 13 Mac in center of column D)

*Fig. 6.13. Dresden
Codex 60 (Villacorta
and Villacorta 1976)*

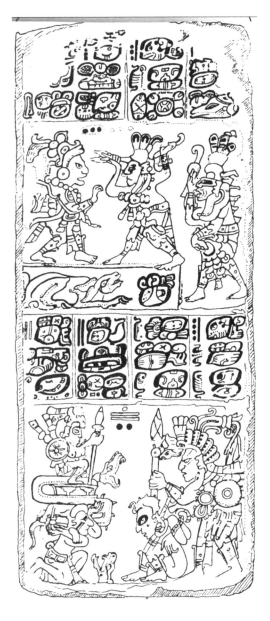

year Venus Almanac. Some multiples are also useful in calculating other planetary cycles.[9] For example, one multiple with an 11 Ahau date represents 55 Venus Rounds (4.9.4.0 or 32,120 days), which is an exact multiple of Mercury's sidereal cycle (88 days × 365) and is also a close approximation of Saturn's synodic cycle (378.1 × 84.951). The numbers associated with 1 Ahau dates on page 24 are recognized as correction factors to realign the Venus calendar while preserving the 1 Ahau Tzolkin date (Lounsbury 1992: 207–208), but they also are apparently intervals useful in calculating the synodic cycles of Jupiter and Saturn.[10]

Returning to the eight-year Venus Almanac

represented by the pictures in the Dresden Codex, the Central Mexican god, Xiuhtecuhtli, armed with an atlatl has speared a turtle god on page 49 (Milbrath 1999: 174; Taube and Base 1991).[11] The same type of scene represented in a different section of the codex on the middle of page 60 (Fig. 6.13). The lower section of page 60 shows close parallels with the Venus warrior on page 49. Both wear an identical plumed headdress with foliation and a bird with spiral wings. Page 49 depicts the Morning Star in the guise of the Central Mexican fire god, coordinating with the dry season when fire ceremonies were performed in Central Mexico to honor Xiuhtecuhtli (Milbrath 1999: 174). A similar seasonal association is apparent for page 60, because a Yaxkin compound on this page refers to the dry season (Thompson 1972: 78–79).

The period represented on page 49 corresponds to the eleventh baktun ending in 1224 (6/8/1224 O.S or 6/15/1224 N.S.[12] Although there is no apparent record of the baktun ending in the Venus Almanac itself, the damaged katun sequence beginning on page 60 may have incorporated such a reference.[13] If this is an historical reference, the katun sequence began on Katun 11 Ahau in January 1047, a katun ending coinciding with the dry season, which is in accord with the representation of Xiuhtecuhtli as a dry season deity (Milbrath 1999: 174) and the glyphic reference to Yaxkin, which fell in the dry season during Katun 11 Ahau in 1047. On the other hand, if Thompson is correct in suggesting that the damaged katun sequence records a series of predictions for future events, the Katun 11 Ahau in April of 1303 would be more likely. This katun end also coincides with the dry season, but also has a number of interesting astronomical events that might be either observed events or predictions.[14]

The Venus Almanac at Chichen Itza

Postclassic Maya records of the Venus Almanac are intriguing because of their calendrical information, but other records of the Venus Almanac may actually provide more detail through complex visual imagery. The sequence of festivals on Codex Borgia 29–46 is one such example. There are other earlier narrative sequences that may be related to the Venus Almanac.

The Upper Temple of the Jaguars at Chichen

Itza features Venus glyphs and feathered serpents in a mural sequence divided into eight parts, representing battles that were apparently timed by the Venus Almanac (Milbrath 1999: 181–183). The eight-year cycle may involve Venus observations made during the dry season, the season of warfare. One scene in the sequence differs because the Sun God and the Venus God, framed by a feathered serpent, face each other in what seems to be a celestial encounter, quite possibly a representation of Venus moving with the sun during the lengthy period of superior conjunction (Fig. 6.14). The

Fig. 6.14. Chichen Itza UTJ murals (Milbrath 1999: Fig. 5.5h)

Fig. 6.15. (below) Carved pillar (Column 40) from the Northwest Colonnade of the Temple of the Warriors (Kowalski 2007: fig. 11)

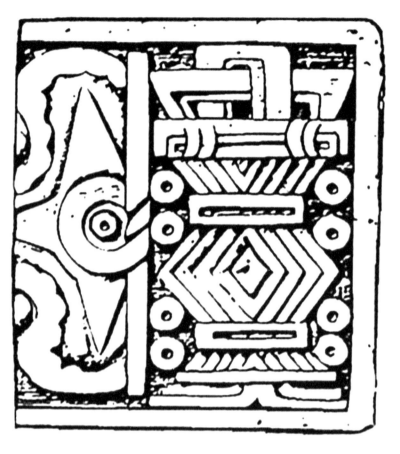

referred to as the man-serpent-bird figure in the literature (Kowalski 2007: 268–269). Generally scholars interpret the scene as a human face in the maws of an earth deity. The feet seem to represent bird talons, and in combination with the serpent tongue, seem to embody the bird-serpent complex associated with Quetzalcoatl. The middle figures also may have Venus attributes, and they certainly are warriors. The one with a star belt and striped body paint seems especially apt for Venus imagery. Although this may be a coincidence, the fact that there are 236 decorated sides to the columns suggests a possible link with the period of 236 days used for the Morning Star phase in the Dresden Codex, which divides the four phases as follows: 236 days Morning Star, 90 days Superior Conjunction, 250 days Evening Star, and 8 days Inferior Conjunction (Milbrath 1999: fig. 5.3, lines 19 and 26).

The Venus platform at Chichen Itza shows a Venus god whose head is enclosed in the jaws of a creature who could be the Earth Monster, but again the feet are represented as bird talons like those seen on the Northwest Colonnade. The same format appears in the Venus platform of the Osario group where the Venus glyph and a bound year bundle crowned by a trapeze-and-ray (Schmidt 2007: fig. 17). This relief is very similar to those on the Venus Platform in the Great Plaza. One of the reliefs on this platform also has the Year Sign and the number eight written in Central Mexican style with a bound year bundle of reeds crowned by a trapeze-and-ray year sign, and a Mexican Venus symbol alongside (Fig. 6.16). Seler (1990, I: 211–212, Fig. 6.15) proposed that this was a symbol for 8 × 52 years (260 Venus cycles of 584 days), which integrates with the Venus Almanac because 104 years brings the solar year, the Venus cycle, and the 260-day calendar into renewed alignment. In his opinion, the bundles represent sets of 52 years, which certainly accords with Aztec traditions of bundling the reeds representing each year into a set of 52 representing the "half-century." More recently, John Carlson (1991: fig. 1.g) identified the Maya symbol for the number five attached to the Venus glyph, proposing that Venus glyph is tied to a bar representing the Maya number five, symbolizing the five Venus cycles in eight solar years of the Venus Almanac, an interpretation that seems plausible (Milbrath 1999: 186, fig. 5.5a).

Fig. 6.16. Chichen Itza Venus Platform (Milbrath 1999: fig. 5.a)

lack of warfare in this scene may be explained by a pattern of dates associated with Classic Maya warfare that indicates warfare was avoided when Venus joined the Sun in superior conjunction (Milbrath 1999: 193).

Representations in the codices suggest that imagery of Venus as a warrior is closely connected to the Morning Star, and a similar pattern may be evident at Chichen Itza. The Northwest Colonnade, located on the east side of the Temple of the Warriors, originally had 236 reliefs on the four sides of each column (59 columns with reliefs), representing a repeated format with three zones per side, and the top zone showing a Venus God throwing darts, interpreted as the Morning Star throwing darts at heliacal rise, and the lower register showing Venus before rebirth, as the feathered serpent still inside the Earth Monster (Fig. 6.15; Roberston and Kurjack 2008: 5–6). The dart-throwing figures, are the counterparts of the Morning Star in the Dresden Codex. The lower figures are all similar, representing a frontal figure with elaborate plumes and a serpent tongue,

Calendar reform revives the Venus Almanac

Venus imagery, so dominant at Terminal Classic Chichen Itza, seems to fade from view by the Early Postclassic, especially during the early occupation of Mayapan, AD 1100–1300 (Milbrath and Peraza 2003). The revival of the katun monuments at Mayapan during the period between AD 1185 and 1263 may be linked with renewed observations of the katun cycle in relation to the retrograde periods of Jupiter and Saturn (Milbrath 2005).

In the Late Postclassic Period, beginning around AD 1300, Mayapan established new calendar paradigms, placing a greater emphasis on the solar cycle, a focus that is encoded in later architectural orientations at the city (Aveni 2004: 161; Aveni *et al.* 2004).[15] This may have involved an increased interest in the Tun, not only because it was an approximation of the solar year, but also because it was useful for measuring long astronomical cycles (Justeson 1989). In tandem with a focus on the solar cycle, Venus imagery became increasingly important in the later art and architecture of the Tases phase, such as effigy censers representing Venus gods (Taube 1992: fig. 63a) and five serpent temples dedicated to Quetzalcoatl (Milbrath and Peraza 2003: table 1). The number of serpent temples certainly evokes the "fiveness" of Venus and suggests a revival of the Venus cult. Five serpent temples are also represented with images of the feathered serpent in the murals of Structures Q80 (Milbrath and Peraza 2003: 26–27, fig. 23). The Venus Almanac is also represented in Mayapan's late murals on Structure Q161, which shows eight solar disks with descending gods that may represent different aspects of Venus, probably symbolizing the eight-year Venus Almanac (Milbrath and Peraza 2003: 28, fig. 29; 2010).

Another mural program in Structure Q95, the Temple of the Fisherman, depicts a god wearing the shell pectoral of Quetzalcoatl who may be holding an atlatl in hand, like the Venus gods in the codices (Milbrath and Peraza 2003: 28, fig. 26; Stuart 2005: 177–179). The mural also merges katun imagery with Venus as a warrior, symbolism that evokes the heliacal rise of Venus. The fish snake in this composition closely resembles the Chicchan Serpent in the Madrid Codex 12b–18b

(Milbrath and Peraza 2003: 28). This suggests we have two different aspects of Venus in the same scene. Quetzalcoatl's dart has killed a bound crocodile very much like the ones in the Paris Codex katun pages. David Stuart notes that texts recorded at Palenque and in the Chilam Balam books help set the Mayapan mural in the context of creation myths that describe how the crocodile was killed to form the earth. It is noteworthy that the Chilam Balam of Tizimin links this primordial event to the cycle of katuns, a significant detail because the bound crocodile is associated with katun imagery in the Paris Codex (Milbrath and Peraza 2003: 28; Edmonson 1982: 41). The Mayapan mural suggests that the sacrifice of the bound crocodile is a symbol of world renewal designed to establish the new world order in the incoming katun.

A Postclassic calendar reform shifted Ahau dates that had traditionally served as katun endings to heliacal rise dates, a shift also evident in the Venus Almanac of the Dresden Codex. The same sort of calendar reform may be evident at Mayapan. Changes in religious imagery occurred at the time of the reform. After AD 1300, Quetzalcoatl's serpent temples and murals related to the Venus almanac replaced images carved on stelae related to the katun cult that had predominated in the first two centuries of Mayapan's occupation (Milbrath and Peraza 2003: table 1). This parallels similar religious changes that took place four centuries earlier, when the feathered serpent cult of the Terminal Classic replaced Classic period deities, associated with the katun monuments (especially Kawil). The spread of Quetzalcoatl's cult in the Terminal Classic could be the result of trade with Central Mexico, as has been proposed, but this religious reformation was surely accompanied by calendar reform, a trend that is documented throughout world history.

The willingness to embrace the Venus cult may reflect a loss of confidence in religious cults and associated calendar ceremonies of the Classic period. My study of Classic Period katun monuments at Tikal, a major center for the katun cult, indicates that stelae marking the katun end were erected only at times that the katun ending corresponded to the retrograde periods of Saturn or Jupiter (Milbrath 2005). The influx of a new religious cult in Yucatan may well be related to calendar reforms that place emphasis on the Venus Almanac. But this cult moved to the background in the Early Postclassic, when there was a revived interest in the katun monuments, which began to be erected at Mayapan precisely at the time that there was a renewed correspondence between the katun ending and the retrograde periods of Jupiter and Saturn (Milbrath 2005). And, later on, by the thirteenth century, when the katun endings no longer synchronized with planetary retrograde, the cult of katun monuments apparently disappeared, and the Venus Almanac was revived or reintroduced from Central Mexico. This calendar remained dominant when Cortez arrived in Mexico and was presented with the regalia of Quetzalcoatl. The Aztecs considered him to be the returning god, arriving in the year 1 Reed, the year ascribed to the birth of the legendary culture hero associated with the planet Venus.

Reviewing the data presented here, it seems that the Venus almanac emphasizing an eight-year period developed in the Classic period in Central Mexico, and some iconographic elements of this calendric complex were transported to the lowland Maya area in the late seventh century and early eighth century in conjunction with warrior iconography. By the ninth century, in the Terminal Classic period, the Venus Almanac had spread to Uxmal, where Tlaloc becomes the fifth Chac in imagery related to the fiveness of Venus (Milbrath 1999: fig. 5.9g). Although warrier imagery of Venus Almanac is not readily apparent, it may be subtly presented in the War owl symbolism evident in the Nunnery (see Kowalski 2007: 258–259). Around the same time, the warrior cult of Venus at Chichen Itza was fully elaborated in tandem with the Venus Almanac. Then still later, the Dresden Codex, with its representations of the warlike Morning star, carried on the warlike context of the Venus Almanac. By around 1300, there seems to be a shift to a more conservative Maya tradition representing the Katun cycles, a major chronological marker of the Classic period that seems to be of little interest at Terminal Classic Chichen Itza. Page 60 of the Dresden Codex expresses this renewed interest in Maya cycles of time, independent of the Venus Almanac with its deep roots in the Teotihuacan culture of Central Mexico.

Notes

1   Study of Tlaloc imagery at Teotihuacan indicates different aspects are linked with warfare and agricultural fertility (Tlaloc A and B; Pasztory 1974). This same sort of the duality evident in Venus imagery in Mesoamerica, for the Evening Star has a clear connection with agricultural fertility, whereas the Morning Star is more often associated with warfare (Šprajc 1993a; 1993b).

2   A connection between Venus and warfare is evident as far back as Protoclassic times. The Venus title was used by warriors on the La Mojarra Stela, which also records battles timed by Venus events (Justeson and Kaufman 1993: 1705, fig. 7c). The Classic Maya apparently avoided warfare during the planet's superior conjunction phase, but "star wars" events are actually are more often linked to significant positions of Jupiter and Saturn, and there is a similar pattern of avoiding warfare during the disappearance intervals of these planets (Aveni and Hotaling 1994; Justeson 1989: 109, table 8.3).

3   This system of counting differs from that proposed by Harvey Bricker *et al.* (1997: S30, table 3). In their opinion, the Madrid Codex Tzolkin was recycled at least twice, over a period of 520 days (2 × 260), which is very close to the interval of the three eclipse half years (519.93 days). They suggest that the presence of four eclipse glyphs indicates that the table was recycled three times. The four eclipse symbols found in the almanac (pp. 12b, 13b, 17b) and their proximity to dates in the Tzolkin allow them "to calculate the length of the intervals between pairs of such iconographically marked *tzolkin* dates and relate them to the interval that separates successive solar eclipses" (Bricker *et al.* 1997: S30). They point out that the date 1 Imix begins the count and see evidence for the numeral one at the beginning of each of the four rows. The remaining glyphs lack numerals but the numbers are implied by positioning in the sequence. Counting forward from the first eclipse symbol on the *bottom* of 13b, assigned to the day 7 Manik (a date that is actually recorded in the *top* row of that page) to the second eclipse on page 12b is calculated at an interval of 177, falling on the date 2 Kan, but no dates or day signs are recorded on this page. They maintain that 2 Kan would fall in the interval of 13 days marked by a black numeral on page 12b, and therefore should be associated with one of the two eclipse signs at the top of that page, presuming that the interval represents the *trecena* of dates missing from the truncated count. This seems reasonable except that the positioning of 2 Kan would actually be on page 18 (marked by the cartouche on row 3), not on page 12b (which

they proposed would cover dates numbered 1–13 to finish the *trecena* in each row). Another problem is posed by the third eclipse, which is presumed to fall on 10 Imix, a date recorded on page 16b, but the actual eclipse sign occurs on page 17b. Perhaps the most controversial aspect of their interpretation is that they link Tzolkin dates to the years AD 924–926, despite the lack of Long Count and Calendar Round inscriptions (Bricker *et al.* 1997: S31–34). Currently, I employ some aspects of their model and find a good fit with paired eclipses in the 15th century (Milbrath n.d.).

4   Similar seasonal patterns can be observed with other important stars along the ecliptic. For example, Venus is seen in proximity to Gemini around the end of the rainy season, and Venus is close to Antares in Scorpius (roughly opposite to the Pleiades in the sky), only in September through December, overlapping with the onset of the season of warfare when the rains tapered off and the maize harvest began (Milbrath 1999: 262, 265).

5   In the Mexican Calendar Round system, there are often two possible solutions to any combination of yearbearer and Tonalpohualli date within a year. Discussing the dates on the lower right of page 28, Anthony Aveni (1999: tables 3–4, fig. 7) reconstructs the date as 5 Movement in the year 1 Reed, corresponding to February 5, 1468, an EFirst date according to Aveni, but it should be noted that this date is a week earlier than those given when setting the Alycone program to a 3° horizon for the mountainous horizon of Tlaxcala (Lange and Swerdlow 2006). Christine Hernández (2004: table 11.6) presents an alternate scenario, choosing an earlier record of the Calendar Round (May 21, 1467) when Venus was the Morning Star. In the cycle of five years shown on page 28, Hernández (2004; 2007) suggests that the second and third dates in each scene bracket periods between May and June associated with the onset of rains. The imagery of rainfall does seem to be more appropriate for this time of year, but her interpretation diminishes the importance of the Venus events in the sequence, whereas Aveni's (1999: tables 3, 4) model coordinates EFirst with dates in both the first (1 Reed 5 Movement) and last scene (5 Reed 1 Water).

6   Another Venus warrior wears a raptor mask, possibly an owl, which would evoke links with imagery of Mercury in Maya art (Milbrath 1999: 214–215). Study of the lunar phases and Mercury events associated with the dates proposed by Bricker (2001: table 2) would be one way of explicating these variations in imagery.

7   In the period beginning in AD 1473, the first set of predicted heliacal rise dates all occur in late August, the second set on page 54 record heliacal rise dates around the end of March (and early April), the third set in early November, the fourth set in mid-June, and the fifth set in early January (Bricker 2001: table 2). The format of equal 584 day intervals proposed by Bricker does not entirely match the dates recorded on pages 53–54. Rather than entering the table with the heliacal rise on 1 Crocodile, she enters with 2 Wind, one of three dates without coefficients in the first five scenes showing Venus warriors. On the next pass through the table the same EFirst scene is associated with the heliacal rise date 9 Crocodile, but this date is found midway through the list of dates in the compartments below the scene. The actual length of the Venus cycle varies with the seasons in a predictable pattern (587, 583, 580, 583, 587 days; Justeson 1989: 79). This variable pattern may be expressed by the dates without coefficients, which would allow some adjustment for the length of the Venus Round.

8   The Almanac on Borgia 53–54 has been regarded as a replica of the Dresden Codex Venus Table (Aveni 1999: S3). With the wealth of information available in the Dresden Codex, it would seem that the Maya manuscript should be the prototype for the more simplified presentation in the Codex Borgia, but a reverse direction in borrowing is indicated by some of the deities represented. Three of the five Venus gods in the Dresden Codex wear Central Mexican costuming and two of them bear glyphic names linking them to the highland deities known as Xiuhtecuhtli and Tlahuizcalpantecuhtli (Milbrath 1999: 173–174; Taube and Bade 1991: 18).

9   Dresden Codex page 24 also records intervals related to the synodic cycles of Jupiter and Saturn among the other multiples of Venus Rounds (Lines 18–22 column E: 2.16.14.0 or 35 VR [20,440 days] = 378.1 × 54.059; Lines 18–22 Column F: 2.8.12.0 or 30 VR [17,520 days] = 398.9 × 43.920; Lines 2326 Column E: 1.4.6.0 or 15 VR [8,760 days] = 398.9 × 21.96). The closest approximation of Mercury's synodic cycle is found in the aberrant number in column A, where the interval 6.2.0 or 2200 days is equivalent to almost 19 synodic cycles of Mercury. Scholars such as Lounsbury (1992) have proposed good solutions for this aberrant number, but it is possible that it was also intended to be the closest whole number approximation of the true length of Mercury's synodic cycle (115.9 × 18.98). Mercury's sidereal cycle also may be encoded in a Long Round inscription of 9.9.16.0.0 in Column B

(lines 14–19), widely recognized as an idealized value of 72 Calendar Rounds that can be divided without remainder by the eight-year Venus Almanac, the shorter eclipse cycle, and the 780-day Mars cycle (Aveni 2001: 190–191; Šprajc 1996: 58, 66; Milbrath 1999: 168). The total number of days (1,366,560) is also a close approximation of both Mercury's 88-day sidereal cycle (88 × 15529.09) and Saturn's sidereal cycle (10760.4 × 127.0002).

10 In column D on page 24, the 1 Ahau inscription with 1.5.14.4.0 (185,120 days) closely approximates Jupiter's synodic cycle (398.9 × 464.076), and the 1 Ahau inscription with 1.5.5.0 (9100 days) is close to Saturn's synodic cycle (378.1 × 24.067). Such intervals are to be expected because the 260-day calendar commensurates the synodic period of the moon and all the visible planets within 4.31 days (Justeson 1989: 82, tables 8.5 and 8.6).

11 A headless figure (T227) is part of the name of the turtle victim on page 49 (T743[281].227) and on page 24 (C11). The same T227 glyph, a homonym for turtle (Milbrath 1999: 172), also appears in the Madrid Codex augural band on page 18b. The turtle is widely recognized as a reference to Orion in the Paris Codex zodiac (Bricker and Bricker 1992; Love 1994). The turtle victim on Dresden 49 may be Orion, which disappeared into the underworld when the Morning Star emerged in November of 1225 (Milbrath 1999: 176). Orion may also be the reference on Madrid 18b, especially since a diving turtle is featured prominently on the preceding page (17b).

12 The baktun ending date given as 5/18/1224 in Milbrath 1999: 172 is in error).

13 Thompson (1972: 78–79) notes that the Katun 11 Ahau record on page 60 is the last on the front side of the codex, and a series of pages recording the rest of the katun cycle are missing. These pages would have given the entire cycle of 13 katuns, a Short Count span totaling some 256-years. The eleventh baktun in 1224 ended on a katun date of 6 Ahau, which was a turning point in the Xiu katun cycle, but page 60 begins the sequence of 13 katuns on Katun 11 Ahau, following the pattern of the Itza katun cycle (Edmonson 1982: xvi). Katun 11 Ahau also begins the katun cycle in Diego de Landa's diagram of the katun cycle, where the starting point is marked with a Maltese Cross (Tozzer 1941: 167).

14 If the 11 Ahau date on page 60 refers to January of 1047 (1/15/1047 N.S. or 1/9/1047 O.S), the eleventh baktun ending in 6 Ahau would be among the missing pages representing the 13 katun sequence. Alternatively, the sequence may be one katun cycle later, in which case

Katun 11 Ahau on page 60 would date to 1303 (4/23/1303 N.S. or 4/15/1303 O.S). The cycle of 13 katuns could have been actual records comparable to the one in the historical texts in the chronicles of the Chilam Balam of Chumayel, or they may be future katun prophecies like those recorded in other sections of that book.

15 According to Munro Edmonson (1988: 70, 136, 202–203), a calendar reform known as the Mayapan calendar was initiated in 1539, but it seems likely that this calendar reform was introduced earlier during the epoch of Mayapan (Vail 2004: 249, n.10).

References

Aveni, Anthony F., 1991. The Real Venus-Kukulcan in the Maya Inscriptions and Alignments. In *Sixth Palenque Round Table, 1986* (M. Greene Robertson and V. M. Fields eds). University of Oklahoma Press, Norman, 309–321.

Aveni, Anthony F., 1992. The Moon and the Venus Table: An Example of the Commensuration in the Maya Calendar. In *The Sky and Mayan Literature,* (A. F. Aveni ed.). Oxford University Press, Oxford, 87–101.

Aveni, Anthony F., 1997. *Stairway to the Stars*. John Wiley & Sons, New York.

Aveni, Anthony F., 1999. Astronomy in the Mexican Codex Borgia. *Archaeoastronomy* (Supplement to the *Journal of the History of Astronomy*) XXX: S1–S20.

Aveni, Anthony F., 2000. *Skywatchers*. University of Texas Press, Austin.

Aveni, Anthony F., 2004. Interallic Structure and Cognate Almancs in the Madrid and Dreden Codices. In *The Madrid Codex: New Approaches to Understanding an Ancient Maya Manuscript* (G. Vail and A. Aveni eds). University Press of Colorado, Boulder, 146–170.

Aveni, Anthony F. and Edward E. Calnek, 1999. Astronomical Considerations in the Aztec Expression of History. *Ancient Mesoamerica* 10(1): 87–98.

Aveni, Anthony F. and Lorren D. Hotaling, 1994. Monumental Inscriptions and the Observational Basis of Maya Planetary Astronomy. *Archaeoastronomy* (Supplement to *Journal for the History of Astronomy* 19): S21–S54.

Aveni, Anthony F., Anne S. Down and Benjamin Vining, 2003. Maya Calendar Reform? Evidence from Orientations of Specialized Architectural Assemblages. *Latin American Antiquity* 14(2): 159–178.

Anders, Ferdinand, Maarten Jansen, and Luis Reyes García, 1993. *Los Templos del cielo y de la oscuridad: Oráculos y literurgia debro explacative del llamado Códice Borgia*. Fondo de Cultura económica, México, D.F.

Bierhorst, Johh, 1992. *History and Mythology of the Aztecs: The Codex Chimalpopoca*. University of Arizona Press, Tuscon.

Berlo, Janet, 1984. *Teotihuacan Art Abroad: A Study of Metropolitan Style and Provincial Transformations in Incensario Workshops*. BAR International Series 199, British Archaeological Reports, Oxford.

Boone, Elizabeth H., 2007. *Cycles of Time and Meaning*

in the Mexican Books of Fate. University of Texas Press, Austin.

Bricker, Harvey and Victoria Bricker, 2007. When Did the Dresden Codex Venus Table Work? In *Culural Astronomy in New World Cosmologies* (C. L. N. Ruggles and G. Urton eds). University of Colorado Press, Boulder, 95–120.

Bricker, Harvey and Victoria Bricker, 2011. *Astronomy in the Maya Codices*. American Philosophical Society.

Bricker, Harvey M., Victoria R. Bricker and Bettina Wulfing. 1997. Determining the Historicity of Three Astronomical Almanacs in the Madrid Codex. *Archaeoastronomy* (Supplement to *Journal for the History of Astronomy* 22): S17–S36.

Bricker, Victoria, 2001. A Method for Dating Venus Almanacs in the Borgia Codex. *Archaeoastronomy.* (Supplement to the *Journal of the History of Astronomy* XXXII): S21–S43.

Carlson, John B., 1993. Venus-regulated Warfare and Ritual Sacrifice in Mesoamerica. In *Astronomies and Cultures* (C.e L. N. Ruggles and N. J. Saunders eds). University of Colorado Press, Boulder, 202–252.

Caso, Alfonso, 1967. *Los Calendarios Prehispánicos.* Universida Nacional Atónoma de México, Mexico, D.F.

Caso, Alfonso, 1971. Calendric Systems of Central Mexico. In *Archaeology of Northern Mesoamerica,* part 1 (G. Ekholm and I. Bernal eds). *Handbook of Middle American Indians* 10 (R. Wauchope, gen. ed.). University of Texas Press, Austin, 333–348.

Cobos, Raphael, 2001. Chichén Itzá. *Oxford Encyclopedia of Mesoamerican Cultures*, Vol. 1 (D. Carrasco ed.). Oxford University Press, New York, 183–187.

Durán, Fray Diego, 1971. *Book of the Gods and Rites and the Ancient Calendar* (F. Horcasitas and D. Heyden trans. and ed.). University of Oklahoma Press, Norman.

Edmonson, Munro S., 1982. *The Ancient Future of the Itza: The Book of Chilam Balam of Tizimin.* University of Texas Press, Austin.

Edmonson, Munro S., 1988 *The Book of the Year: Middle American Calendrical Systems.* University of Utah Press, Salt Lake City.

Faulseit, Sonny, 2006. Periodicityin the Dresden Codex Venus Tables. *Human Mosaic* 36(1): 109–124.

García Quintanilla, Alejandra, 2005. Saak' y el retorno del fin del mundo: La plaga de langota en las profécias del katun 13 Ahau. *Ancient Mesoamerica* 16(2): 327–344.

Hernández, Christine, 2004. "Yearbearer Pages" and their Connection to Planting Almanacs in the Borgia Codex. In *The Madrid Codex: New Approaches to Understanding an Ancient Maya Manuscript* (G. Vail and A. Aveni eds) University Press of Colorado, Boulder, 321–366.

Hernández, Christine, 2005. Using Astronomical Imagery to Cross-Date an Almanac in the Borgia Codex. *Human Mosaic* 36(1): 125–143.

Hernández, Christine, 2006. The Fortunes for Planting Maize in the Borgia Codex. *Ancient America* 8. Boundary End Archaeological Research Center, Barnardsville, N.C., 1–35.

Hernández, Christine and Victoria Bricker, 2004. The Inauguration of Planting in the Borgia and Madrid Codices. In *The Madrid Codex: New Approaches to Understanding an Ancient Maya Manuscript* (G. Vail and A. Aveni eds). University Press of Colorado, Boulder, 277–320.

Just, Byron, 2004. *In Extenso* Almanacs in the Codex Madrid. In *The Madrid Codex: New Approaches to Understanding an Ancient Maya Manuscript* (G. Vail and A. Aveni eds). University Press of Colorado, Boulder, 255–276.

Justeson, John S. 1989. The Ancient Maya Ethnoastronomy: An Overview of Hieroglyphic Sources. In *World Archaeoastronomy: Selected Papers from the Second Oxford International Conference on Archaeoastronomy* (A. F. Aveni, ed.). Cambridge University Press, Cambridge, 76–129.

Justeson, John S. and Terrence Kaufman, 1993. A Decipherment of Epi-Olmec Hieroglyphic Writing. *Science* 259, 1703–1711.

Kowalski, Jeff Karl, 2007. What's "Toltec" at Uxmal and Chichen Itza? Merding Maya and Mesoamerican Worldviews and World Systems in Terminal Classic to Early Postclassic Yucatan. In *Twin Tollans* (J. K. Kowalski and C. Kristan-Graham eds). Dumbarton Oaks, Washington D.C., 251–313.

Lange, Rainer and Noel M. Swerdlow, 2006. *Planetary, Lunar, and Stellar Visibitlity*. Version 3.1.0. Alcyone Software

Lounsbury, Floyd G., 1982. Astronomical Knowledge and Its Uses at Bonampak. In *Archaeoastronomy in the New World* (A. F. Aveni ed.). Cambridge University Press, Cambridge, 143–168.

Lounsbury, Floyd G., 1983. The Base of the Venus Tables of the Dresden Codex, and Its Significance for the Calendar-Correlation Problem. In *Calendars in Mesoamerica and Peru: Native American Computations of Time* (A. F. Aveni and G. Brotherston eds). BAR International Series 174, British Archaeological Reports, Oxford, 1–26.

Lounsbury, Floyd G., 1989. A Palenque King and the Planet Jupiter. In *World Archaeoastronomy: Selected Papers from the Second Oxford International Conference on Archaeoastronomy* (A. F. Aveni ed.). Cambridge University Press, Cambridge, 246–259.

Lounsbury, Floyd G., 1991. Distinguished Lecture: Recent Work in the Decipherment of Palenque's Hieroglyphic Inscriptions. *American Anthropologist* 93: 809–824.

Lounsbury, Floyd G., 1992 A Solution for the Number 1.5.5.0 of the Mayan Venus Table. In *The Sky and Mayan Literature* (A. F. Aveni ed.). Oxford University Press, Oxford, 206–215.

Macri, Martha J. and Laura M. Stark, 1993. *A Sign Catalog of the La Mojarra Script*. Pre-Columbian Art Research Institute Monograph 5, San Francisco.

Love, Bruce, 1994. *The Paris Codex: Handbook for a Maya Priest*. University of Texas Press, Austin.

Milbrath, Susan, 1989. A Seasonal Calendar with Venus Periods in Borgia 29–46. In *The Imagination of Matter: Religion and Ecology in Mesoamerican Traditions,* edited by David Carrasco, pp. 103–127. Oxford: BAR International Series 515.

Milbrath, Susan, 1999. *Star Gods of the Maya: Astronomy in Art, Folklore, and Calendars*. University of Texas Press, Austin.

Milbrath, Susan, 2001. Calendar Wheels. In *Oxford Encyclopedia of Mesoamerican Cultures* Volume 1

(D. Carrasco ed.) Oxford University Press, Oxford, 128–130.

Milbrath, Susan, 2005. The Classic Katun Cycle and the Retrograde Periods of Jupiter and Saturn. *Archaeoastronomy Journal* XVIII: 81–97.

Milbrath, Susan, 2007. Astronomical Cycles in the Imagery of *Codex Borgia* 29–46. In *Cultural Astronomy in New World Cosmologies* (C. L. N. Ruggles and G. Urton eds). University of Colorado Press, Boulder, 157–208.

Milbrath, Susan, 2013. *Heaven and Earth in Ancient Mexico: Astronomy and Seasonal Cycles in the Codex Borgia*. University of Texas Press, Austin.

Milbrath, Susan, n.d. Venus, the Solar Year, and Eclipse Cycles Among the Ancient Maya. Invited lecture presented at the Eighth International Conference on the Inspiration of Astronomical Phenomena. Hayden Planetarium, American Museum of Natural History, New York, July 2013.

Milbrath, Susan and Carlos Lope Peraza, 2003. Revisiting Mayapan: Mexico's Last Maya capital. *Ancient Mesoamerica* 14: 1–46.

Milbrath, Susan and Carlos Lope Peraza, 2010. Religious Imagery in Mayapán's Murals. *PARI Journal*. X(3): 1–10.

Miller, Arthur, 1973. *Mural Painting of Teotihuacán*. Dumbarton Oaks, Washington D.C.

Nagao, Deborah, 1989. Public Proclamation in the Art of Cacaxtla and Xochicalco. In *Mesoamerica after the Decline of Teotihuacan A.D. 700–900* (R. A. Diehl and J. C. Berlo eds.). Dumbarton Oaks, Washington, D.C., 83–104

Pasztory, Esther, 1974. *The Iconography of the Teotihuacan Tlaloc*. Studies in Pre-Columbian Art and Archaeology 15, Dumbarton Oaks, Washington, D.C.

Quiñones Keber, Eloise, 1995. *Codex Telleriano-Remensis: Ritual, Divination, and History in a Pictorial Aztec Manuscript*. University of Texas Press, Austin.

Robertson, Merle Greene and Edward B. Kurjack, 2008. *A School of Sculpture at Chichen Itza, Yucatan, Mexico*. The Pre-Columbian Art Research Institute, San Francisco.

Schele, Linda, and Peter Mathews, 1998. *The Code of Kings: The Language of Seven Sacred Maya Temples and Tombs*. Scribner, New York.

Schmidt, Peter, 2007. Birds, Ceramics, and Cacao: New Excavations at Chichén Itzá, Yucatan. In *Twin Tollans* (J. K. Kowalski and C. Kristan-Graham eds). Dumbarton Oaks, Washington D.C., 151–204.

Seler, Eduard, 1904. Venus Period in the Picture Writings of the Borgian Codex Group. *Bureau of American Ethnology Bulletin* 28, 353–392.

Seler, Eduard, 1990–2000. *Collected Works in Mesoamerican Linguistics and Archaeology* Vols 1–6 (trans. under the supervision of C. P. Bowditch; F. E. Comparato, gen. ed.) Labyrinthos, Lancaster CA.

Šprajc, Ivan, 1993a. The Venus-Rain-Maize Complex in the Mesoamerican World View: Part I. *Journal of the History of Astronomy* 17, 17–70.

Šprajc, Ivan, 1993b. The Venus-Rain-Maize Complex in the Mesoamerican World View: Part II. *Archaeoastronomy* (Supplement to the *Journal of the History of Astronomy* 18), S27–S53.

Šprajc, Ivan, 1996. *La Estrella de Quetzalcoatl: El Planet Venus en Mesoamerica*. Editorial Diana, México.

Šprajc, Ivan, 2000. Astronomical Alignments at Teotihuacan. *Latin American Antiquity* 11(4), 403–415.

Stone, Andrea, 1989. Disconnection, Foreign Insignia, and Political Expansion: Teotihuacan and the Warrior Stelae of Piedras Negras. In *Mesoamerica After the Decline of Teotihuacan A.D. 700–900* (R. A. Diehl and J. C. Berlo eds). Dumbarton Oaks, Washington, D.C., 153–172.

Stuart, David, 2005. *The Inscriptions from Temple XIX at Palenque: A Commentary*. The Pre–Columbian Art Research Institute, San Francisco.

Taube, Karl. A., 1992. T*he Major Gods of Ancient Yucatan*. Studies in Pre-Columbian Art and Archaeology 32. Dumbarton Oaks, Washington, D.C.

Taube, Karl A. and Bonnie L. Bade, 1991. An Appearance of Xiuhtecuhtli in the Dresden Venus Pages. *Research Reports on Ancient Maya Writing* 35. Center for Maya Research, Washington, D.C.

Tedlock, Dennis, 1985. *Popol Vuh*. Simon and Schuster, New York.

Thompson, J. Eric, 1957. Deities Portrayed on Censers at Mayapan. *Current Reports* 40. Carnegie Institution of Washington Department of Archaeology, Washington, D.C.

Thompson, J. Eric, 1960. *Maya Hieroglyphic Writing: An Introduction*. 3rd edn. University of Oklahoma Press, Norman.

Thompson, J. Eric, 1972. *A Commentary on the Dresden Codex: A Maya Hieroglyphic Book*. American Philosophical Society, Philadelphia.

Tozzer, Alfred M., 1941. Landa's "Relación de las Cosas de Yucatán": A Translation. *Papers of the Peabody Museum of Archaeology and Ethnology, Harvard University* 18. Peabody Museum, Cambridge: MA.

Tuckerman, Bryant, 1964. *Planetary, Lunar, and Solar Positions A.D. 2 to A.D. 1649*. Memoirs of the American Philosophical Society 59. American Philosophical Society, Philadelphia.

Vail, Gabrielle, 2004. A Reinterpretation of the *Tzolk'in* Almanacs in the Madrid Codex. In *The Madrid Codex: New Approaches to Understanding an Ancient Maya Manuscript* (G. Vail and A. Aveni eds). University Press of Colorado, Boulder, 215–254.

Vail, Gabrielle and Aveni, Anthony F., eds. 2004. *The Madrid Codex: New Approaches to Understanding an Ancient Maya Manuscript*. University Press of Colorado.

Glyphs G and F: the cycle of nine, the lunar nodes, and the draconic month

Michael J. Grofe

The supplementary series in the Classic period

Several hundred monumental inscriptions and painted texts from the Mayan Classic period demonstrate consistent, codified forms of calendrical and chronological information among the Lowland Maya. The Initial Series of hieroglyphs that introduces many of these texts begins with the distinguishable calendric components known as the Long Count, the Tzolk'in and the Haab'. The latter two cycles, especially on carved monuments, are often separated by what Charles Bowditch (1903; 1910: 244) first described as the Supplementary Series.

After successfully demonstrating the Initial Series of the monuments to be equivalent to the Long Count that Ernst Förstemann identified in the Dresden Codex, Joseph Goodman (1897: 118) next identified the Supplementary Series in the Classic inscriptions, though he was unable to decipher its meaning. Based upon the presence of numerical coefficients with several recurring glyphs thought to be ideographic images of the moon, Sylvanus Morley concluded that the Supplementary Series provided some kind of a lunar count (Morley 1915: 152). He decided that this count was to be read backwards from the position of the last and most regular glyph in the series prior to the Haab' calendar position, and his resulting system of reverse labeling continues to be used for the purposes of analysis. Morley labeled the last glyph in the Supplementary Series Glyph A, and the standard names of the remaining glyphs precede this position as B, C, D, E, F, and G, with a common additional variable glyph between Glyph C and Glyph B designated as Glyph X (Morley 1916). Wyllis Andrews later identified two rare glyphs between Glyphs F and E, labeling them Glyphs Z and Y, in agreement with Morley's reversed lettering system (Andrews 1938: 30). Thus the sequence of the Supplementary Series, when all elements are present, follows from the Initial Series and Tzolk'in as Glyphs G, F, Z, Y, E, D, C, X, B, and A (Fig. 7.1).

The lunar information in the majority of the Supplementary Series has since been demonstrated, and Eric Thompson applied the term Lunar Series to Glyphs E through A, separating Glyphs G and F as non-lunar (Thompson 1935; 1971: 208, 237). As John

*Fig. 7.1. Initial Series
and Supplementary
Series. From Quirigua
Stela J. (after Looper
1995: 305–307, fig.
4.18)*

Initial Series

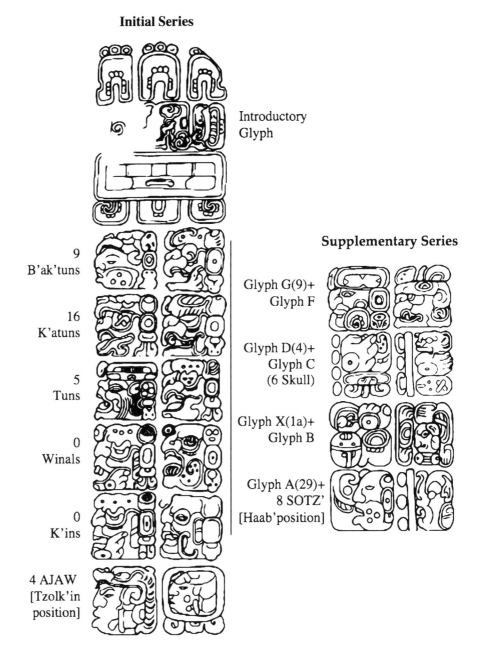

Introductory
Glyph

9
B'ak'tuns

16
K'atuns

5
Tuns

0
Winals

0
K'ins

4 AJAW
[Tzolk'in
position]

Supplementary Series

Glyph G(9)+
Glyph F

Glyph D(4)+
Glyph C
(6 Skull)

Glyph X(1a)+
Glyph B

Glyph A(29)+
8 SOTZ'
[Haab' position]

Teeple (1925; 1931) first demonstrated, Glyph A designates a lunar month of either 29 or 30 days, while Glyphs D and E, whose coefficients range from 1 to 29, record the age of the moon as measured from various points near the new moon.

Upon the suggestion of R. K. Morley, Sylvanus Morley first proposed that Glyph C records a series of six numbered lunations that may correspond to the interval between eclipses, similar to those found in the Dresden Codex (Morley 1920). Teeple (1931) later noticed that the counting of these lunations varied in different times and places, though he identified a "period of uniformity" in the expected coefficients of Glyph C that lasted less than a century among Maya sites during the late Classic period. Linda Schele, Nikolai Grube and Federico Fahsen (1992) and John Linden (1996) independently demonstrated that these six-month lunar semesters generally appear in a repeating sequence of 18 months, in three groups of six months, each identified by one of three head variants.

A New proposal for Glyph C

Morley (1920: 560) first proposed that the infixed heads in Glyph C were numerical coefficients in the form of head variants, as identified by Goodman (1897). He and all subsequent scholars have since abandoned this idea in favor of interpreting these head variants as deities. However, I propose that Morley's first impression was correct, and that the three head variants in Glyph C are indeed numerical. Linden (1996) found that the heads followed the order of "Skull, Human, and Mythical", suggesting that the Long Count Era Base determined that the first in the series was the Skull. However, this is an assumption for which there is little evidence.

The Human head variant, which is typically the profile of a woman or the very similar Maize God, is widely recognizable as the number 'one' (T1000). This would logically represent the first month and the first six-month period, followed by the Mythical head variant, a supernatural with a jaguar ear, recognizable as the number 'seven' (T1018), or simply represented by the eye of this deity (T680). This head variant logically begins the seventh month, which is the first month in the second lunar semester that takes us to the twelfth month. Lastly, a Skull is recognized as the head variant for the number 'ten'. However, typically beginning with the head variant for 'thirteen', a defleshed lower jaw appears with all of the numerical head variants from three to nine to represent the numbers 13 through 19. Therefore, I suggest that the Skull head variant was chosen to represent the last lunar semester, covering the thirteenth through the eighteenth lunar months. While this is a simple numerical solution, additional mythological associations with these three specific head variants and their lunar functions remain a likely possibility. Following the analysis of newly-discovered eclipse tables at Xultun, Guatemala (Saturno et al., 2012:715), the current view (Zender and Skidmore 2012:9) is that these three heads represent the Tonsured Maize God, the Jaguar God of the Underworld, and the Death God (God A).

Glyph C is often followed by Glyph X, a poorly understood series that gives the name of the lunation related to the Glyph C position. Glyph B is simply the phrase 'its name', in reference to Glyph X and Glyph C (Schele *et al.* 1992). Andrews (1934) first demonstrated that the different forms of Glyph X are closely associated with the particular coefficients and forms of Glyph C, and Linden (1986) later proposed that Glyph X and Glyph C together describe a repeating 18-month synodic lunar 'year' that imitates the Maya Haab, the latter of which is divided into 18 periods of 20 days, plus a five-day intercalary period. Following Morley, Linden (1996: 354) also suggested that the Maya could have utilized the cycle of 18 synodic lunar months as "an efficient means to keep track of possible eclipses." While six-month intervals reflect the average period between successive eclipses, Linden demonstrated that an 18-month cycle of three of these lunar semesters approximates the time it takes for an eclipse to return close to the same Tzolk'in day, a fundamental concern for the Maya, as illustrated by the Calendar Round, which commensurates the 365-day Haab with the Tzolk'in (Thompson 1971: 210).

Teeple (1931: 89) first noticed that the sum of two Tzolk'in periods of 260 days each is nearly equivalent to three eclipse half-years of 173.31 days. Therefore, repeating Tzolk'in days could be used to track eclipses by returning the sun to a lunar node. Eclipse events separated by 18 lunar months thus cluster around repeating Tzolk'in days, and Harvey Bricker and Victoria Bricker (1983) have demonstrated the effectiveness of this model for predicting eclipse windows, as found in the Dresden Codex.

Linden (1996: 354) concludes:

> "The utility of an eighteen month lunar synodic calendar is that by arranging the six month semesters in groups of three, the Maya could integrate their lunar calendar with a double Tzolkin period, and thus track the nodal positions needed to warn of possible eclipses."

The sum of 18 lunar synodic cycles extends 11.62 days beyond three eclipse half-years, and 11.55 days beyond a double Tzolk'in cycle. Therefore, eclipses do not regularly repeat every 18 months, nor do they continue to cluster around the same Tzolk'in dates over longer periods of time. However, apart from the variations in uniform counting that Teeple identified, the 18-month cycle of glyph C appears to have run more-or-less continuously, much like most of the other Maya cycles (Schele *et al.* 1993).

If the Maya did use Glyph C as Linden suggests, then it would have been to predict more immediately repeating eclipses that fell on a Tzolk'in day at any point in the cycle, rather than to continue to correlate the entire idealized cycle of Glyph C directly with actual astronomical eclipse cycles. While the 18-month cycle repeats continuously, it may have derived from the way in which eclipses repeat close to the same Tzolk'in day every 18 months. This parallels the Haab cycle of 365 days, which derives from the tropical year while drifting approximately one day from its original position in the tropical year every four years. Similarly, the 360-day Tun was a continuously repeating cycle derived from the tropical year, though it drifted quite independently from it. Such idealized cycles as these likely facilitated the counting of whole days without the need for fractions, while observable corrections could be performed for the purposes of actual astronomical calculations over much longer periods.

Glyph G and the lunar nodes

Given that the remainder of the Supplementary Series deals with the moon, it is reasonable to explore the hypothesis that Glyph G and Glyph F also contain lunar information. In this paper, I propose that the Classic Maya Glyph G and its cycle of nine repeating days commensurated with the 260-day cycle, after which it typically appears in the inscriptions. Together with the Tzolk'in, Glyph G, and its related Glyph F, can be used to track the position of the moon relative to the lunar nodes and the draconic month, the time it takes the moon to reach the same lunar node.

In an analysis of Glyphs G, J. Eric. Thompson (1929) found that Glyph G has nine variations that appear in a continuously repeating cycle. He hypothesized that these correspond, at least in function, to the nine "Lords of the Nights" of central Mexico, a series of deities that sequentially rule over nine separate nights that have been identified in both colonial sources as well as in the surviving Mexican codices. Thompson translates the predominant Glyph G9 (T545) of the Maya series as the "night sun" (Thompson 1971: 210). However, no colonial Maya sources

appear to contain any specific names for deities that are the equivalent of the Mexican series, and Thompson recognized that the nine names from Glyph G "do not correspond closely to the Mexican gods." He conceded, "there is little profit in comparing the two groups at the present time" (Thompson 1971: 208, 210). Thompson concluded that Glyph G, and the more standardized Glyph F that follows it, have nothing to do with the lunar cycle, given that they appear to be an arbitrarily repeating sequence of nine days, and that they occasionally appear without any of the other components of the Lunar Series. As a result, he described Glyph G and Glyph F as a merely ritualistic cycle (Thompson 1935; 1971: 208, 237).

Assuming an astronomical origin, David Kelley (1972: 58) proposed that the Aztec, Zapotec and Maya cycle of nine days represent each of the nine "planets", modeled after the Hindu *Navagraha*, which includes the sun, the moon, all five visible planets, and the ascending and descending lunar nodes, Rahu and Ketu, as invisible planets that cause eclipses. However, Maya sources provide no additional support for this argument.

More recently, Sven Gronemeyer (2006) has proposed that the Maya cycle of nine days represents the growth and development of maize. Gronemeyer's systematic analysis is based on the more recent decipherment of many of the component glyphs found within the names of the nine examples of Glyph G, rather than on Thompson's assumptions about their correspondence with the Mexican Night Lords. Gronemeyer derives much of his argument from the repeated presence of **NAL** (T86), found in several of the names of Glyph G, together with what he identifies as other maize-related terminology. However, while **NAL** can refer to "maize", it can also refer to "place" in many hieroglyphic contexts (Stuart and Houston 1994: 21), and both meanings should be considered. Likewise, while focusing on the thesis that the Glyph G series describes only the development of maize, Gronemeyer interprets the numerical coefficients found on at least four of the nine names of Glyph G as largely symbolic and numerological (Gronemeyer 2006: 6). While the importance of the growth and regeneration of maize certainly permeates Maya symbolism, there are equally relevant components of the names of Glyph G that suggest calendrical and astronomical meanings within the context of the Lunar Series, not the least of which are the specific numerical coefficients mentioned, as well as possible references to eclipses.

While the calendrical significance of the nine variable names of Glyph G has eluded interpretation, Thompson's assumption that this cycle is non-lunar remains the currently accepted convention (Coe 1992: 132–133; Aveni 2001: 156). However, Martha Macri has proposed that these nine originated as the nine days at the end of a month, added to 20 to reach the new moon on the 29th day. Although the Maya reckoned the lunar cycle as alternations of both 29-day and 30-day periods, Macri significantly interprets Glyph G9 as a representation of a possible eclipse, and the time of a new moon (Macri 2005: 284).

An analysis of the specific numerical coefficients in Glyph G suggests additional information regarding the utility of this cycle. These coefficients do not follow a linear progression of one through nine, so we are left to determine what, if anything, they may be counting. Glyph G1 includes the number nine, G4 the number seven, G5 the number five, and G6 the number nine (again). Furthermore, the glyphs depicted alongside these coefficients are distinct, perhaps indicating that different things are being counted. These suggest some other kind of a count that may relate to G9, which in turn may be a reference to an eclipse.

Glyph G9 as an idealized eclipse

The image of Glyph G9 (T545) is a half-darkened sun, **K'IN**, conflated with the **yi** curl (T17), and Barbara MacLeod (1991a), reads this as *yih k'in* "aged sun" (Fig. 7.2a). Based on the appearance of this glyph in the Palenque Tablet of the Foliated Cross, E5, where it describes an event that falls one day after another, several scholars have suggested that T545 relates to "twilight", "dawn", "night" or '24-hour period' (Justeson 1984: 342). However, the half-darkened sun appears to graphically relate to the half-darkened "wing-quincunx" glyph (T326) used in the codices to represent solar and lunar eclipses (Fig. 7.2b). The word *yih* itself means "old" and "ripe", while *yi* means "ear of corn" in Tzotzil (Delgaty 1964). Likewise, *yih* can also be used in Tzotzil to describe the full moon, compared to an old

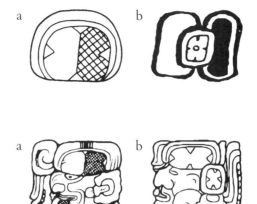

Fig. 7.2. (a) T545 half-darkened K'IN from PNG3O1 (after Looper in Macri and Looper 2003); (b) "wing quincunx" eclipse glyph from Dresden 54bW2

Fig. 7.3. Glyph G9 full personified form: (a) NAR Hieroglyphic Stairway 01 Step 05, J3 (after Graham 1978: 107); (b) QRG Stela D, C15 (after Looper 1995: 351–354, fig. 5.24)

man, or old maize (Laughlin 1975: 74, 385). A similar term for "full moon" is attested in colonial Yucatec as *yiih u*, while *yiih* alone is given as "declining moon" (Barrera Vásquez *et al.* 1980).

In the personified form of Glyph G9, a head variant of a toothless old man appears with an infixed T17 **yi**, and a **NAL** (T86) prefix, which may suggest "old" and "maize", as above. In this case, the **yi** is usually conflated with the half-darkened **K'IN** "sun" glyph (T545) in his headdress (Fig. 7.3a). In several other examples, the **yi** is conflated with the face of the old man (Fig. 7.3b). Taking **yi** as "his grandchild", Gronemeyer (2006: 11) proposes that Glyph G9 reads "grandchild of the sun is the maize" and the last stage in the maize growing cycle. However, given that **NAL** may also refer to "place", another meaning is plausible. Here *nal-yih-k'in*, or *yih-k'in-nal*, may refer to "place of the old sun", indicated by the darkening that suggests the end of some kind of a solar cycle, perhaps the location of a solar or lunar eclipse, namely, the lunar nodes.

We find another example of G9 from Naranjo with a large birthmark on his chin (Fig. 7.3a). David Bolles (1997) notes that contemporary Yucatec refer to birthmarks as *chib'al yuil* "bite of the moon" because lunar eclipses are believed to cause birth defects. In Yucatec, *chí'ib'* means "be bitten" (V. Bricker *et al.* 1998: 70), while in colonial sources, the Yucatec Maya referred to eclipses as *chi'b'il* (Martínez Hernandez 1929: 305). Milbrath (1999: 26) adds that *chi'b'il* specifically refers to partial eclipses that resemble bite marks.

Davoust (1997: 221, 223) suggests that a spelling of **chi-ba** (T671: 501) refers to eclipses in the inscriptions above the Serpent Numbers on pages 61 and 62 of the Dresden Codex. Elsewhere (Grofe 2007: 215–219, 221, 233–234), I have demonstrated a direct correlation between the dates of each of the Serpent Numbers and the eclipse year, where the sun appears at a lunar node on the repeated Tzolk'in day 3 Ix. Indeed, each of the serpents in the Serpent Series displays an upturned, open mouth, above which sits a specific animal or deity. These serpents are essentially identical to two of the serpents on pages 56 and 57 of the Lunar Table in the Dresden Codex, which appear to bite half-darkened solar eclipse glyphs (T326). These biting serpents thus reaffirm the association between eclipses and *chi'ib'* as "bite". Given the presence of the similar half-darkened **K'IN** glyph, and the birthmark, Glyph G9 likewise invokes imagery related to eclipses. These associations support Macri's suggestion that Glyph G9 may relate to eclipse events.

In the inscriptions, Glyph G almost invariably follows the Tzolk'in position, perhaps indicating a relationship between the cycle of nine and the 260-day cycle. In fact, Thompson (1971: 210–211) notes that a specific table on pages 30c–33c in the Dresden records a commensuration of the cycle of nine with the 260-day cycle. Given that 260 is not divisible by nine, the cycles of 260 and nine commensurate only in 9×260=2340 days. Thompson notes that the purpose of this table in the Dresden is to integrate the Tzolk'in with the nine Lords of the Night.

Nine Tzolk'ins as a multiple of the draconic month

Named for the Chinese dragon said to consume the sun or moon during eclipses, the **draconic month** of 27.21222 days marks the time it takes for the moon to reach the same node, regardless of phase (Aveni 2001: 77). Additionally, the **half-draconic month** of 13.60611 days records the time it takes the moon to reach the opposite node, with the effect that the moon reaches a node every 13.60611 days. If we begin with the moon at the node on a solar eclipse, the addition of nine Tzolk'ins (9×260 days), or 2340 days, *returns the moon exactly to the same node*, but at the first

quarter. The interval of 2340 days is also just a quarter of a day short of 86 draconic months:

2340 days = 86 (27.21222 days) − 0.25092 days

Adding twice the interval of 2340 days from a solar eclipse will always reach a lunar eclipse within one day, though these eclipses will not always both be visible from the same geographic location. In the remainder of this paper, I investigate whether the cycle of nine could have been used to track the draconic month and the position of the moon in relationship to the nodes. If so, it would have been a useful tool for eclipse prediction.

Recalling that three cycles of the eclipse half-year of 173.31 days are nearly equivalent to two Tzolk'in cycles of 260 days, Teeple (1931: 90) first demonstrated how the Tzolk'in can be used to track eclipses. Lounsbury (1978: 797) notes that accurate adjustments to the Dresden Lunar Table could be made by tracking the recession of the nodes within the Tzolk'in, though he claims that no evidence exists for such a correction. However, I have demonstrated how the Serpent Series in the Dresden Codex can be used to track the eclipse year, noting the position of the sun when it appears at a lunar node (Grofe 2007: 215–219). Similarly, Glyph G and the cycle of nine may have been used together with the 260-day Tzolk'in to keep track of the draconic month, when the moon appears at a lunar node. An examination of the remaining coefficients of Glyph G provides additional evidence that these cycles may have been used in combination to capture eclipse phenomena.

Every 260 days, the position of Glyph G decreases by one in the cycle of nine. Adding 260 days to G9 reaches G8, and adding another 260 days reaches G7, and so on. In nine Tzolk'in cycles of 260 days, we again reach G9. If Glyph G was used to help predict eclipses, we can use an idealized correlation of Glyph G9 with a solar eclipse and count backwards by cycles of 260 days from this position. This provides a linear progression of the same Tzolk'in day associated with the position of Glyph G increasing by one with each 260-day subtraction. So G1 falls 260 days before reaching G9 as an eclipse.

Because the cycle of nine repeats indefinitely, eclipses would rarely occur on days that coincide with G9. However, all other Maya

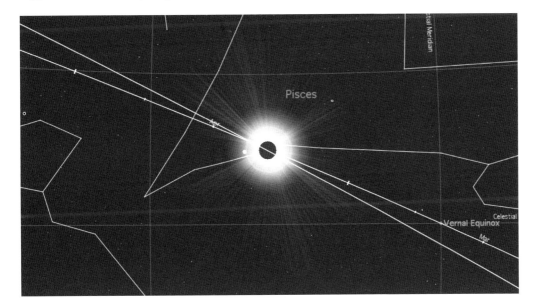

Fig. 7.4. Hypothetical solar eclipse with G9 on April 8, 2005 CE (image made with Starry Night Pro-6 © Imaginova Canada Ltd)

cycles are similarly allowed to continuously repeat, though they may have arisen to keep track of specific astronomical phenomenon, such as the 365-day year. Simply keeping track of the relative position within these cycles, each cycle could still be used to track the astronomical phenomenon for which it was originally intended by performing established corrections. In the case of the cycle of nine, a correction of zero to four days is all that is required to conform to an idealized cycle that places G9 on a predicted eclipse. This is because any eclipse event will be from zero to four days from any actual occurrence of G9. Therefore, eclipse events on specific days of the Tzolk'in can be predicted within a larger cycle of nine Tzolk'ins by associating the predicted eclipse with an idealized position of G9.

Glyph G1

The common form of Glyph G1 includes the coefficient "9", with T1016, Schellhas' God C head **K'UH** (Barthel 1952: 94) and the T670 **CH'AM** hand as "grasp, take, receive" (Schele and Newsome 1991: 4). Together this reads **9-K'UH-CH'AM** "takes nine holy/gods" (Fig. 7.5a). A rare form of Glyph G1 uses the "fish-in-hand" glyph T714 **TZAK** "conjure" (Schele 1991: 86), with an apparent reading **9-TZAK** (TIX: 714), "nine conjurings" (Fig. 7.5b). In the Platform from Temple XIX in Palenque, David Stuart (2005: 63) found in B4 an example of Glyph G1 which he reads as

9-CH'AM-ma-aj-K'UH, with the passive verb *ch'ämaj* "taken", "grasped" or "received". Here, the word "taken" might suggest a subtraction of some kind.

Gronemeyer (2006: 5) suggests that, as the introductory glyph in the series of nine, the coefficient in Glyph G1, together with **K'UH,** describes the specific number of deity names in the series. However, if each of the examples of Glyph G represents a specific deity name, as Thompson also proposed, then why would we find that G1 would not have its own name? This is the only coefficient of Glyph G that Gronemeyer considers to be in reference to an actual counting of items, though we must also consider why Glyph G6 also includes the number "nine", while the Glyph G4 shows "seven", and G5 has "five".

However, if Glyph G was intended to commensurate with the Tzolk'in to predict eclipses, we would expect to find a particular significance for Glyph G1 exactly 260 days prior to an eclipse associated with Glyph G9. Beginning on a hypothetical solar eclipse at the ascending node on April 8, 2005 CE (Fig. 7.4), we can *ideally* associate this date with G9 (though using the 584285 correlation, G9 would not have actually fallen on this date, but a simple adjustment of one day is all that is necessary in this case).

Subtracting 260 days, we reach the proposed idealized position of G1 on July 22, 2004 (Fig. 7.6). Here the coefficient of "nine" may have several possible meanings. On July 22, 2004, the moon is exactly *nine days before the full moon*, but this full moon is not near a node or an eclipse event (Fig. 7.7). However, this lunar cycle is also nine synodic lunar months before the eclipse event 260 days later on April 8, 2005. In this case, there is also a lunar eclipse on April 24, 2005, nine months after the full moon that follows July 22, 2004, also visible from the same location as the solar eclipse, though whether or not both eclipses are always visible is not particularly relevant to this hypothesis.

It is possible that the coefficient of nine refers to either of these intervals of nine. Given that 260 days comprises nine lunar months, it is possible that G1 indicates that an eclipse event will take place on the same Tzolk'in day 260 days later on G9. If we then understand the name of Glyph G1 as a reference to this upcoming eclipse, "Nine Gods/Holy Taken" suggests that it will take nine months for an eclipse to occur on the same Tzolk'in day.

Glyphs G2 and G3

Glyphs G2 and G3 (Fig. 7.8) do not have recognizable numerical coefficients associated with them, but Gronemeyer (2006: 5) notes that they each appear to contain the dotted sign **HUL** (T45) "arrive" (Stuart *et al.* 1999: 37). This is more commonly used in Glyph D to represent the number of days "arrived"

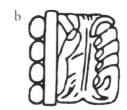

Fig. 7.5. Glyph G1: (a) 9-K'UH-CH'ÄM, from PNG Stela 25 NW, A9; (b) 9-TZAK, from PNG Stela 36 SE, A5 (after Montgomery 1990; 1992)

a   b

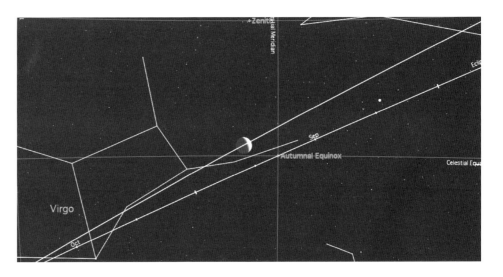

Fig. 7.6. Day of G1, July 22, 2004, 260 days before G9 on April 8, 2005 (image made with Starry Night Pro-6 © Imaginova Canada Ltd)

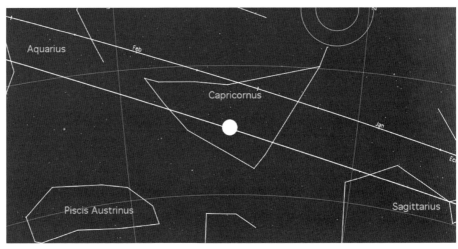

Fig. 7.7. Day of G1+9 days to full moon on July 31, 2004 (image made with Starry Night Pro-6 © Imaginova Canada Ltd)

since the new moon. Glyph G2 has not been successfully translated, though its main sign resembles T709 used in Glyph G4, as **AB'AK**. Coe and Kerr (1997: 150f.) credit Grube with the reading of T709 meaning *ab'ak/yab'ak* "powder, ink, charcoal". G2 would be 2×260 days prior to the idealized eclipse on G9, and this is the double Tzolk'in interval that Teeple (1931) recognized as an eclipse interval. G2 would fall on November 5, 2003, and on this day the moon is very close to the same sidereal position in Pisces as it will be on the G9 eclipse on April 8, 2005. It is also three days prior to a total lunar eclipse on November 8, 2003. Perhaps "charcoal" has something to do with the darkening occurring on a lunar eclipse three days later.

Interestingly, the sidereal position of the moon on this idealized day G2, November 5, 2003, is very close to the same sidereal location of the G9 eclipse, exactly two Tzolk'ins later on April 8, 2005. While they often appear as smoke-like scrolls in Glyph G2, Gronemeyer (2006: 5) identifies substitutions of these with clear examples of **NAL** (T86) in Toniná Monument 30, A2. Rather than a reference to "maize", it is possible that this **NAL** refers to the "place" of darkening, or the sidereal position of the upcoming eclipse exactly two Tzolk'ins in the future.

Glyph G3 appears to contain **JANAB'** (Stuart and Houston 1994: 81), while Gronemeyer (2006: 5) reads this compound as **HUL-JAN-NAL**, meaning "the maize flower arrives", representing an early stage in the growth of maize as depicted in the cycle of Glyph G. It is unclear whether this may have a corresponding numerical or astronomical reading. Barring another reading, Glyph G3 provides the strongest evidence for Gronemeyer's proposal that Glyph G has something to do with the growth cycle of maize. Considering the concurrent evidence in this paper that Glyph G may have been used to calculate eclipses, it is possible to reconcile both of these positions, in part. From ethnographic accounts of the Maya, we find that eclipses are often associated with crop failure and birth defects. Lunar eclipses are specifically regarded as damaging to fertility, and Susan Milbrath (1999: 27) notes:

"The Ch'ortí say that the Moon loses her powers of fecundity during a lunar eclipse [...] Throughout the Maya area, eclipses are believed to cause illness and

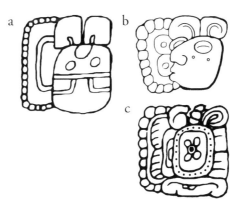

Fig. 7.8. (a) Glyph G2, from DPL Stela 2, B4 (after Graham 1967: 12, fig. 7); (b) Glyph G2, from TNA Mon.69, B1 (after Graham in Graham and Matthews 1997: 103); (c) Glyph G3 (inside Glyph F), from PAL Temple of the Sun, A9 (after Schele 1992).

death and to be particularly dangerous to pregnant women[…]."

Elsewhere, I have identified the term *b'uy* in a reference to an eclipse on page 62 of the Dresden Codex (Grofe 2007: 233). In colonial Yucatec, *b'uy* refers to "the heat or bad vapor that leaves the earth thin, or the roots of trees rotten; that which damages the cotton, jicamas, and such things, and if they sprout, they are lost" (Martínez Hernandez 1929: 158).

Perhaps the "the maize flowers arrive" in Glyph G3 is thus a reference to the *lack* of an eclipse event three Tzolk'ins prior to an eclipse. The Tzolk'in itself parallels the period of human gestation, which itself parallels the growth of maize, and it is possible that, together with the Tzolk'in, Glyph G would have been useful for predicting and avoiding the dangers associated with eclipses during sensitive stages in the development of both crops and gestating children.

Glyph G4

The next Glyph G with a numerical coefficient is G4, with a coefficient of "7" (Fig. 7.9). Similar to Glyph G2, which lacks a coefficient, Glyph G4 appears to read **7-AB'AK** (TVII: 709), as "seven-charcoal". Gronemeyer (2006: 6) reads the personified main sign in Glyph G4 (Fig. 7.9) as partially **WAJ**, meaning "bread, tamale, tortilla". However, while he noted the similarity of Glyph G2 to **AB'AK**, he does not mention that Glyph G4 actually contains the more standard version of the **AB'AK** glyph (T709). Therefore, his reading for glyph G4 does not reference "charcoal". While most examples of G4 are personified (Fig. 7.9b), some examples of Glyph G2 are similarly personified, as on Toniná Monument 69 (Fig.

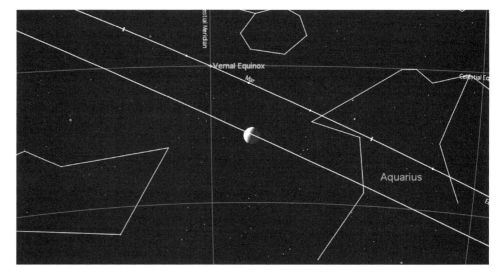

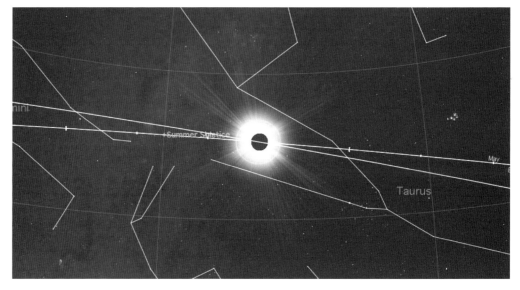

7.8b), whereas other examples of both appear without personification, but with scrolls, which Gronemeyer reads as **NAL** (T86). As a form of the Maize God, I suggest that the personified forms of both of these glyphs likewise substitute for **NAL**, as a suffixed **la** is evident in the example of G4 from Dos Pilas Stela 8, A6 (Fig. 7.9b). As in G2, it is possible

that, in Glyph G4, **NAL** refers to another sidereal location, rather than to "maize".

Subtracting 4×260 days from the G9 solar eclipse on April 8, 2005, we reach the day June 3, 2002 (Fig. 7.10). On this day, the moon is exactly seven days before another solar eclipse event at the ascending node on June 10, 2002 (Fig. 7.11). Also, subtracting seven days from

June 3 brings us close to the opposite node, because seven days is about half of a half-draconic month. Again, as in Glyph G2, it is possible that "charcoal" may have to do with the blackening of an eclipse event in this location. The mathematical relationship between eclipse events associated with G4 and G9 on the same Tzolk'in day 4×260 days later can be expressed in terms of draconic months and lunar synodic months as follows:

$$4 \times 260 \text{ days} = 1040 \text{ days}$$
$$1040 \text{ days} - 7 \text{ days} = 1033 \text{ days}$$
$$= 38 \ (27.21222 \text{ days}) - 1.06 \text{ days}$$
$$= 35 \ (29.53059 \text{ days}) - 0.57 \text{ days}$$

This interval is only one day from a whole multiple of draconic months, and it is very close to a whole multiple of lunar synodic cycles. Both the draconic month and the synodic month are average periodicities, and in this case, the interval of 1033 days closely corresponds to an eclipse cycle. Because of slight fluctuations, the predicted eclipse can be within a day of the estimated Tzolk'in position, but this interval can be used effectively for both solar and lunar eclipses. Another eclipse event occurs 1034 days prior to June 10, 2002 on August 11, 1999.

Glyph G5

Glyph G5 has the numerical coefficient of "5", and the glyph itself may be a phonetic reading of **5-HUL-li** (TV: 45: 24) *5-hul*, meaning "five arrive" (Fig. 7.12a), making it similar to what we find throughout the examples of Glyph G, as well as in Glyph D from the Lunar Series. The T24 "mirror" may appear as a main sign T617, and Nikolai Grube (1991: 224) sees T617 as the full form of T24. Gronemeyer (2006: 7) reads T617 as **TZUK**, due to a rare variant of Glyph G5 from Yaxchilan Lintel 48, C7, which uses a substitution of the personified form of T617, which is actually T1017, facing downward (Fig. 7.13a). Basing this on an earlier reading (Grube and Schele 1991), Gronemeyer derives from this the Yucatacan term *tzukel* "nappy, rags", and he suggests that Glyph G5 has to do with a ritualistic wrapping of the infant maize. However, Carl Callaway (2006: 99–102) has demonstrated that a reading of **TZUK** for T1017 is highly doubtful, and that T1017 is the personified form of the mirror T24, both of which are

found in association with shining objects, such as jades. While Callaway reads T1017 and T24 as "jade signs", he notes that they are found in association with **'UH** (T1049) in the name of the Maya Cross in Palenque, which he reads as "Jade Jewel Tree" (Callaway 2006: 67). While *'uh* is "jewel" in many Maya languages, it is also a common term for "moon", and it is interesting that we find an apparent **wa** (T130) in association with T1017 in Glyph G5 from Yaxchilan Lintel 48. Elsewhere (Grofe 2009), I have noted that the skull **'UH** (T1049) substitutes for the suffixed **wa** in the Classic hieroglyphic names of the Haab' months of Pop, Sek, Mol, and K'ank'in, each of which may reference the moon as *'uh*.

Perhaps most significantly, in the earliest example of Glyph C from the Lunar Series on the Hauberg Stela (Fig. 7.13b), we find T1017 as the head variant patron of the completion of 17 synodic lunar months in what was to be the prototype for the 18-month cycle in later examples of Glyph C (Linden 1996: 351, 355). Therefore, it is equally plausible that T1017 in Glyph G5 references the moon in a collocation that more typically appears to read *5-hul*, "five arrive", much like the same expression we find in Glyph D that describes the number of days since the new moon.

Another interesting variant from the Atkins Museum Lintel has the **CH'AM** (T670) hand holding this mirror (Fig. 7.12b). This is the same glyph commonly seen in G1, and here

a

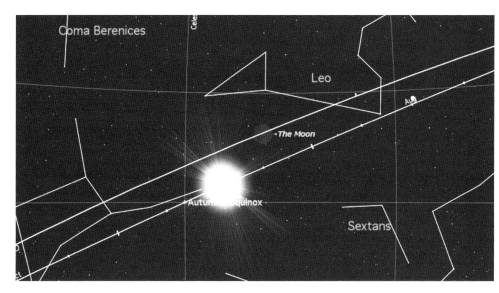

b

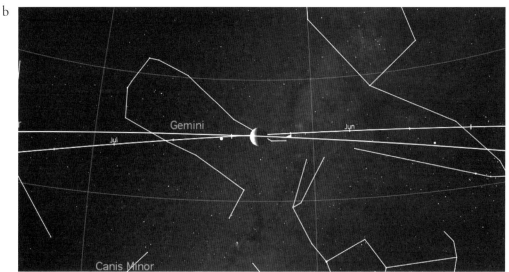

5-CH'AM implies "take five", perhaps as some form of subtraction, as we have proposed for Glyph G1. Glyph G1 employs the God C head **K'UH** (T1016) that resembles the T1017 head found in Glyph G5. However, Callaway (2006: 97–99) notes that these are distinct signs, though one substitution between them does appear in the inscriptions (Stuart 1988: 201). It appears that both signs may have referred to the moon in the Lunar Series.

Subtracting 5×260 days prior to the G9 solar eclipse on April 8, 2005, we reach G5 on September 16, 2001 (Fig. 7.13). The moon is just about new on this date, but it is not near a node. However, *subtracting five days, the moon indeed reaches the ascending node* on September 11 (Fig. 7.14). This may indeed be

the reference of both **5-HUL**, as five days after the node, and **5-CH'AM**, as five days taken away to reach the node. The lunar synodic month and draconic month intervals would be:

5×260 days = 1300 days
   1300 days = 44 (29.53059 days)+0.65 days
   1300 days+5 days = 1305 days = 48 (27.21222 days)–1.17 days

The interval of 1300 days is close to a whole multiple of synodic lunar months, and five additional days is only one day from a whole multiple of draconic months. With slight fluctuations, this interval will produce similar results, and in this case, if the moon is at a node five days before it is new, there will be a solar eclipse 5×260 days later. In the case of a lunar eclipse interval, if the full moon is five days past a node, there will likely be a lunar eclipse in 5×260 days, within a two or three day range.

Because G5 has a coefficient of five, it is also possible that this number represents the five intervals of 260 days before an eclipse event at G9, but this would be the only such coefficient to do so. However, if G1 represents nine lunar months before an eclipse event, G5 may demonstrate a similar pattern.

Glyph G6

Glyph G6 is quite rare, and Thompson (1971: fig. 34, 31) incorrectly confused this glyph with G7, which appears in two common forms. The actual Glyph G6 (Fig. 7.15a) has a coefficient of "9", and the glyph itself appears to be similar to Glyph Y (Fig. 7.15b). Elsewhere (Grofe 2006), I have suggested that Glyph Y is a form of *Unen K'awiil*, GII from the Palenque Triad, whose name implies both "Child" and "Mirror", relating to the mirror on the forehead of this deity. Here, Glyph G6 contains only **UNEN** (T739), without **K'AWIIL** (T1030).

Both Glyph Y and the more standard name of K'awiil are also the subject of the 819-day count. Glyph Y represents a repeating seven-day cycle (Yasugi and Saito 1991), and it is possible that Glyph G6 is also involved in the 819-day cycle. Indeed, because 819 is a multiple of both seven and nine, it is significant that every 819-day station falls on a day with Glyph G6. Whereas Glyph Y may have different coefficients in its cycle of seven days,

Glyph G6 always appears to have the coefficient "9". Nevertheless, the relationship between Glyph G6 and Glyph Y suggests a reference to the 819-day count, and a decipherment of Glyph G6 may help to explain a possible astronomical reference of *Unen K'awiil*.

The superfix in Glyph G6 differs from that in Glyph Y, and it is identifiable as T267, a glyph found more commonly in the codices, where it appears in calendrical contexts with time periods, such as **K'IN** and **TUN** (Fig. 7.16). Following a suggestion by Werner Nahm, Schele and Grube (1997: 82) tentatively propose a Yucatec reading of *xul* "end" for T267, given the bat head **xu** (T756), followed by elements of **lu** (T568). However, in Ch'olan languages, *xul* alternately carries the meanings "cut", "break", and "divide" (Aulie and Aulie

Fig. 7.15. (a) Glyph G6, from Yaxchilan, Stela 6, A6 (after Tate 1992: 193, fig. 88a); (b) Glyph Y, from YAX Lintel 46, C1. (after Graham 1979: 101)

*Fig. 7.16. T267 as a superfix to **K'IN** and **TUN**. Dresden Codex, page 50*

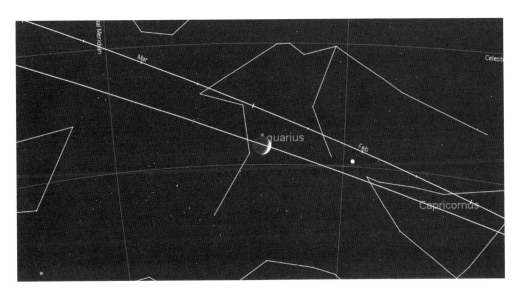

Fig. 7.17. Day of G6 on December 30, 2000, 6×260 days prior to G9 eclipse on April 8, 2005, 9 days before node

Fig. 7.18. (a) Nine days after G6 on January 8, 2001, 6×260 days–9 days prior to G9 eclipse on April 8, 2005. Same sidereal position as in Fig. 7.14b; (b) total lunar eclipse on January 9, 2001, 10 days after G6. 6×260 days–10 days before G9 eclipse on April 8, 2005 (images made with Starry Night Pro-6 © Imaginova Canada Ltd)

a

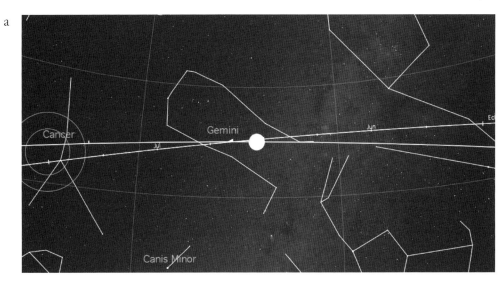

b

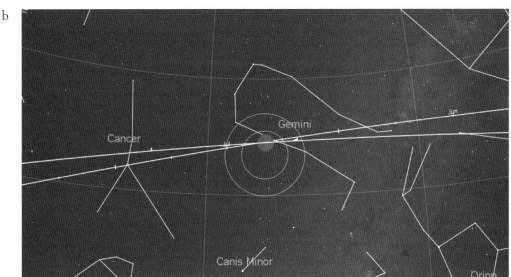

1976: 153; Wisdom 1971: 655). In the context of Glyph G6, **xu-lu-UNEN** as *xul u-nen* may specifically refer to a lunar eclipse either as the "end", or a "cutting of the mirror", accurately comparing the moon to a mirror that reflects the light of the sun. Indeed, for the Yucatec Maya, an ant named *Xulab* causes lunar eclipses, and Milbrath (1999: 26) believes that the name *Xulab* may refer to the cutting of the moon. Thus, it is possible that *Unen K'awiil*, and the 819-day count itself relate to eclipses of the moon. Indeed, the characteristic smoking mirror of this deity suggests the darkening that accompanies lunar eclipses.

Subtracting 6×260 days from the G9 solar eclipse at the ascending node on April 8, 2005, we reach G6 on December 30, 2000 (Fig. 7.17). On this date, the moon will reach

the ascending node nine days later on January 8, 2001 (Fig. 7.18a). This is also close to the same sidereal position of the moon at the node five days before G5 (Fig. 7.14b). A total lunar eclipse on the full moon occurs the next day on January 9 (Fig. 7.18b). The lunar synodic month and the draconic month intervals can be calculated as follows:

6×260 days = 1560 days
1560 days–9 days = 1551 days
In lunar synodic months:
1551 days = 52 (29.53059 days)+15.41 days
In draconic months:
1551 days = 57 (27.21222 days)–0.097 days

This interval is almost exactly a whole multiple of draconic months, and it can be used reliably over long periods of time to determine the position of the moon relative to the node. Because this interval is also one day more than half a synodic lunar cycle, the synodic lunar cycle will differ from the nodal position by about one day in one run of this interval, and this difference will increase over time. However, in some cases, adding nine days will reach both the node and a lunar eclipse. If G9 falls on a lunar eclipse, adding nine days to the previous G6 may reach a solar eclipse.

A commensuration of the 260-day Tzolk'in with the seven-day cycle of Glyph Y could have been used to coordinate the eclipse year with the seasons. Given the correspondence between Glyph G6 and Glyph Y, it is possible that, with corrections like those found so far in the above intervals, the seven-day cycle, the nine-day cycle, and the 260-day cycle were all used together to determine the eclipse year and the draconic month as they move through the tropical year over long periods of time. Indeed, these three cycles commensurate in 20×819 days, and Lounsbury (1978: 807) has noted the importance of this interval of 16,380 days in the Classic period inscriptions from Palenque.

Glyph G7

Glyph G7 does not appear with any certain numerical coefficient. However, Glyph G7 (Fig. 7.19a) always carries a **NAH** (T4) prefix, which can signify the ordinal "first", or "house". In this context, **NAH** appears as a prefix to T1008, with the suffix **la** (T178). Together, these form a common collocation for "north" (Schele 1992: 19–22). The directional association is unclear in Glyph G7, though 7×260 days is an interval of 1820 days, in which the nodes shift their sidereal position from east–west to north–south (Grofe 2007: 154–161). When we subtract 7×260 days from the eclipse at G9 on April 8, 2005, we find that the full moon four days later is at its maximum distance north of the ecliptic, and the use of "north" in Glyph G7 may refer to this shift. Here, the sun is at the exact midpoint between the lunar nodes. But is "north" the actual reference in this case?

Gronemeyer (2006: 9) reads T1008 as **NAL**, due to its resemblance to the Maize God, and the final **la** (T178) suffix in Glyph G7. Given that T4 appears in several other examples of Glyph G7 without T1008, he concludes that the T4 prefix reads "first",

*Fig. 7.19. Glyph G7: (a) From BPK Stela 2 (after Mathews 1980: 62, fig. 2); (b) as **NAH-la**, from YAX Lintel 29, B4 (drawing by author)*

*Fig. 7.20. (a) 'North' as **NAH-hi-li**, from QRG Stela K, B7 (after Looper 1995); (b) Glyph G7 as **NAH-[T1008]-ja**, from CPN Stela 5, A5 (drawing by author)*

rather than serving as a phonetic complement to **NAL**. He thus translates the standard version of G7 as "the first maize ear". However, one example of Glyph G7 from Yaxchilan Lintel 29, B4 includes only T4, **NAH**, followed by a final **la** suffix (Fig. 7.19b). This suggests that T1008 is not essential to the full pronunciation of G7, and Schele has proposed that T4: 1008 is simply the full form of a sign for **na** (Schele *et al.* 1990). Significantly, Glyph G7 only uses T4, **NAH**, found exclusively in the name of structures as "house", or as "first", and we never find a substitution in G7 with the alternate form of the syllabic **na** (T23). This suggests that T4: 1008 actually reads **NAH**.

From a variant of the collocation for "north" in an 819-day count statement from Quirigua Stela K (Fig. 7.20a), we find the alternate spelling **NAH-hi-li**, which further suggests that T1008 is non-essential. No examples of either Glyph G7 or the collocation for "north" are ever found without an initial **NAH** (T4), though T1008 can be absent. Therefore, I propose that T4: 1008 is the full form of a sign for **NAH**, which carries specific logographic meanings as both "first" and "house".

In the collocation for both "north" and Glyph G7, the use of the logographic **NAH** (T4) suggests that the subject is actually "first". In fact, the singular dot on the cheek of T1008 is usually diagnostic of the number "one" for the Hero Twin **1-AJAW**, rather than being an attribute of the Maize God. Here, T1008 may function to clarify the reading of **NAH** as "first". In this case, perhaps "north" was understood to be the first direction, and we do find that the first born of the Palenque Triad

Fig. 7.21. Substitution between **NAH** *(T4) and Maize God (T1000): (a)* **u-tz'i-b'i [T1000]-ja-la yu-k'i-b'i**, *from vase K2914; (b)* **u-tz'i-b'i NAH-ja-la yu-k'i-b'i**, *from vase K2730 (drawings by author)*

a
b

is associated with north in the Temple of the Cross.

If Glyph G07 is the same as the collocation for "north", it is possible that it does not refer to the Maize God at all, with T1008 actually serving with T4 as the full form of **NAH** "first". However, the name of the Maize God may have also originally contained an aspirated or irregular vowel as either **NAHL** or **NA'AL**, the latter of which is given for the name of the Maize God in Chol (Aulie and Aulie 1976: 80). While it is possible that both Glyph G7 and "north" refer to the name of the Maize God, with **NAH** (T4) as acting as a phonetic complement, there are no other examples of T4 operating in this way, and if this were the case, we would expect to find some examples of Glyph G7 or "north" with T1008 alone as a logograph.

The standard head of the Maize God (T1000), with its feminine "IL" markings on the cheek, freely substitutes for the head of a woman in the head variant for the number

"one", conceivably from the homophonous similarity between *na* "mother" and *nah* "first" (Macri 2005: 281). However, it is possible that this homophony additionally relates to the name of the Maize God. While T1008 never substitutes for T1000, on vase K2730 (Fig. 7.21b), we find the logographic **NAH** (T4) in the collocation **NAH-ja-la** (T4: 181: 178), substituting for the more common collocation that includes the head of the Maize God as T1000: 181: 178 on K2914 (Fig. 7.21a). Here, it is possible that T1000 acts phonetically as **na**, rather than as a substitution for **NAH**, since T1000 is always suffixed by **ja** in these examples.

While T1008 never substitutes for T1000, on vase K2730 (Fig. 7.21b), we find the logographic NAH (T4) in the collocation NAH-ja-la (T4: 181: 178), substituting for the more common collocation that includes the head of the Maize God as T1000: 181: 178 on K2914 (Fig. 7.21a). Within the Primary Standard Sequence on ceramic texts, this collocation

a 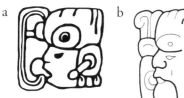 b c  d

Fig. 7.22. (a) Glyph G7 with head variant for 'two', from PNG Stela 3, B4 (after Montgomery 1990); (b) head variant for "two" with **OCH** *and* **SAK** *components, from PNG, Lintel 2, A5a (drawing by author); (c) Glyph G7 with head variant for "two", from CPN Stela 16, D3 (drawing by author); (d) Goddess named on PAL Temple XIV, G9 (after Schele in Schele and Miller 1986: 272–273)*

a  b  c

Fig. 7.23. (a) Glyph G7 from CPN Stela 2, A6 (drawing by author); (b) Glyph G7 from NAR Stela 2, C4 (after Graham 1978: 14); c) **u-SAK-??-NAL?-li**. *(T1:179:503:82), from PAL Palace Tablet (drawing by author)*

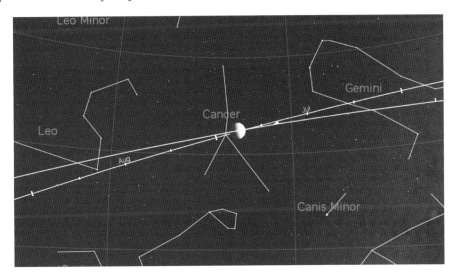

Fig. 7.24. Day of G7 – 2 days on April 12, 2000. 7×260 days+2 days before G9 eclipse on April 8, 2005 (image made with Starry Night Pro-6 © Imaginova Canada Ltd)

appears as both the passive verb u-tz'ib'-naj 'is painted', and as the nominalization u-tz'ib'-najal 'its painting' (MacLeod 1990). In K2914, it is possible that T1000 acts phonetically as **na**, rather than as a substitution for **NAH**, since T1000 is always suffixed by **ja** in these examples. Similarly, we find a **ja** (T181) postfix following T1008 in one example of Glyph G7 from Copán (Fig. 7.20b), and this suggests the lack of differentiation between the final -*j* and -*h* found in some early texts.

Several of the variants of G7 also seem to include an **OCH** (T221) (Fig. 7.22a), and Gronemeyer (2006: 9) sees these as *och* "to enter", and a reference to "the first entering of the maize ear". However, these examples actually appear to be the head variant for the number "two", which is composed of the T1000 head variant for the number "one", together with **OCH** and occasionally **SAK** (T58) components (Fig. 7.22b). A form of **SAK** with a curved "smile" infix is visible above T1000 in another example of Glyph G7 from Copán Stela 16 (Fig. 7.22c). Curiously, these examples of G7 are very similar to the name of a goddess mentioned on Palenque Temple XIV (Fig. 7.22d), suggesting a reference to *na* as "mother", and a possible reading of this collocation as **na**, with the number "two". Several other examples of Glyph G7 appear to include forms of **SAK** with the same "smile" infix (Figs 7.23a and b), though Gronemeyer (2006: 9) reads these as **tz'a[pa]**, with *nah-tz'ap* as "first planting". However, these examples all seem to derive from the head variant for "two", as well as another familiar collocation.

A closer examination of the example of Glyph G7 from Copán Stela 2 (Fig. 7.23a), redrawn from the original, reveals that it is likely to be T179, which Schele (1992: 40) first proposed as *sak-niknal* "white flower" (Fig. 7.23c). Though this reading is somewhat problematic (Kettunen 2005: 2–3), I suggest that the reading of either **NAHL** or **NA'AL** for the usual **IK'** (T503) sign is suggested by the disharmonic substitution **na-li** (T24: 82) on the Copan Hieroglyphic Stairway, as well as the frequent appearance of **na** (T24) with T503: 82 in these collocations (Schele and Looper 1996: 41, 128). In addition, we find that T179 has clear iconographic associations with maize on Copán Stela H, as well as in the Palenque Tablet of the Foliated Cross (Barbara MacLeod, personal communication, 2010). The examples of Glyph G7 from Copán Stela 2 (Fig. 7.23a) and Naranjo Stela 2 (Fig. 7.23b) both show a final **li** (T82), further supporting their identification as a form of T179. I propose that all of these variants of Glyph G7 are not exact substitutions for T1008. Rather, it appears that they may read **na**, **NAHL** or **NA'AL**. As such, they function in the collocation for "first" and "north", usually spelled either **NAH-la** or **NAH-hi-li**, though they may likewise reference the number "two".

If the occasional head variant for the number "two" in Glyph G7 also suggests a coefficient, as well as a reference to "north", it may relate to a count of days for the moon to reach a lunar node, similar to what we find for other examples of Glyph G. In fact, when we subtract 7×260 days from the eclipse at G9

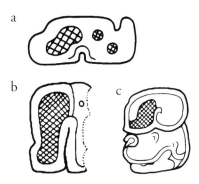

on April 8, 2005, we reach the date of G7 on April 14, 2000, at which time the moon is two days past the ascending node. This is very close to the same time of year as the future G9 eclipse. When the moon is at the node two days earlier on April 12 (Fig. 7.24), it is at the first quarter, while the sun is at the midpoint between the nodes, close to the same position in Pisces where the future eclipse will occur. When a quarter moon is at a node, this is also an important predictor for the 9×260 day cycle, in that there will be eclipse events from this point both 9×260 days in the future, and in the past.

It may also be worth considering that the references to both "first" and "two" within Glyph G7 may derive from a count *following* an ideal eclipse. Given the importance of the double Tzolk'in as a means to keep track of eclipses, it is possible that Glyph G7 represents the "first" time the sun reaches an eclipse node exactly "two" Tzolk'ins *forward* from a G9 eclipse event. If this is the case, we might expect other examples of Glyph G to predict eclipses within a larger pattern of nine double-Tzolk'ins, a precise eclipse interval, but this is unclear.

Glyph G8

Glyph G8 is usually represented by a single glyph, T155 (Fig. 7.25a), which has been read as either **o** or **OL** (MacLeod 1991b). Stuart (2006) suggests that T155 may be read **HUL**, as it appears to substitute for the footprint **HUL** (T331) in the Supplementary Series. However, one rare variant of Glyph G8 from the Lausanne Stela (Fig. 7.25c) contains a **xi** (T48) suffix, which prompted a collaboration between myself, Peter Biro and Barbara MacLeod, in which we resolved the reading

of T155 as **BIX** (Gronemeyer and MacLeod 2010: 49). In addition, I found that *bix* also carries the meaning "octave" and "eighth day" (Martínez Hernandez 1929: 151), which is further supported by its placement as the eighth day in the cycle of Glyph G. As such, Glyph G8 may simply reference its position within a repeating cycle of nine days, while it may also refer to a multiple of eight Tzolk'ins prior to an eclipse event.

We find that an eclipse event occurs very close to eight Tzolk'ins prior to another eclipse. Subtracting 8×260 days prior to the G9 eclipse event on April 8, 2005, we reach the date July 29, 1999. On this day, the moon is just one day past full, and one day past the descending node, with a lunar eclipse on July 28 (Fig. 7.26). Indeed, some of the versions of G8 appear half-darkened (Fig. 7.25b), very similar to the eclipse imagery in G9 and in the eclipse glyph from the codices.

Finally, 9×260 days before the G9 eclipse on April 8, 2005, we reach another day G9 on November 11, 1998, and the moon is at the last quarter and at the node. Given that nine Tzolk'ins is very close to a whole multiple of the draconinc month, Glyph G could easily be used together with the Tzolk'in to track the position of the moon relative to the lunar nodes. Thus, Maya astronomers could have used it to predict both solar and lunar eclipses.

Glyph F

Given the apparent context of possible draconic month calculations and eclipse predictions using the commensuration of the cycle of nine-days and the 260-day Tzolk'in, what might be the function of Glyph F?

Glyph F, which either follows or is combined with Glyph G, consists of standard repeating elements that have proven to be substitutions for the same word. Invariably, T128 is present as a prefix, and David Stuart (2005: 63) reads this glyph as **TI'** "mouth, lips, edge", while several other scholars have previously suggested a phonetic reading of **k'a**, connoting "record" (MacLeod 1995; Macri and Looper 2003: 296–297). The remaining glyphs clearly substitute for the reading *hu'un* or *hun*. This can be spelled variously as **hu** (T740), or **HUUN** (T665), and **na** (T23), with the final **na** usually appearing on all examples as a phonetic suffix (Fig. 7.27a). Several recognizable logographs now known

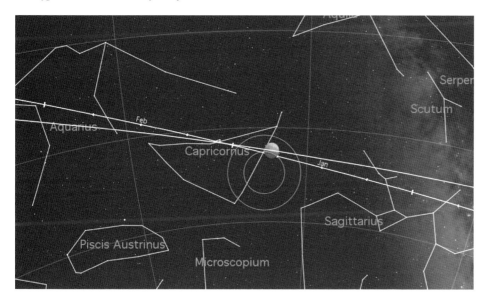

Fig. 7.26. G8 – 1 day to Lunar eclipse on July 28, 1999. 8×260 days+1 day before G9 eclipse on April 8, 2005 (image made with Starry Night Pro–6 © Imaginova Canada Ltd)

*Fig. 7.27. Glyph F: (a) phonetically spelled with **TI'-hu-na** (T128:740:23), from YAX Lintel 56 (after Graham (1979: 121); (b) with Jester God **HUUN** (T128:1030o); from Naranjo Stela 13 (after Graham 1978: 38); (c) with headband **HUUN** (T60abdef) in **TI'-HUUN-na** (T128:60:24), from QRG Stela J. (after Looper 1995: 305- 307, fig. 4.18)*

a  b  c

to represent **HUUN** may also be present, and these have led to various interpretations of Glyph F as references to recorded books (T609b), the Jester God (T1030o) (Fig. 7.27b), or headbands (T60abdef) (Fig. 7.27c). Linda Schele suggests that Glyph F represents a headdress worn by each subsequent Lord of the Night, though its meaning remains unclear (Schele 1991; Schele *et al.* 1992: 2). Stuart (2005: 63) suggests that *ti' huun* refers to the "margin of the page", and he likens this to the recording of the Nine Lords of the Night in the Mixteca-Puebla style codices.

Considering that the various forms of Glyph G that include numerical coefficients may indicate an addition or subtraction of these specific numerals to coordinate the moon with the nodes, and facilitate eclipse prediction, I propose that we may interpret the headband represented in Glyph F as akin to the tied red band used in Ring Numbers in the Dresden Codex (Fig. 7.28). Ring Numbers indicate mathematical operations of addition, "tying" numbers to one another, while they also imply relationships of subtraction, reaching Ring Base dates prior to the Era Base date. I agree with Stuart's reading of T128 as semantically representing "mouth", and in this case, "the mouth of the band" might be equivalent to the placement of numerals within the center of the tied red band in the depiction of Ring Numbers. In fact, many representations of Glyph G appear in the center of the band represented in Glyph F by T60. It is apparent

that the tradition of representing addition and subtraction through the use of Ring Numbers in the Dresden Codex derives from earlier representations in the Classic period, one of which can be seen in the recently excavated inscriptions from Xultun (Saturno *et al.*, 2012:715).

Conclusion

I suggest that the cycle of nine days was commensurated with the 260-day Tzolk'in, next to which it appears at the beginning of the Supplementary Series. Together, these cycles could have been used to track the eclipse year and the position of the moon relative to the nodes in the draconic month. Thus, they would have been useful for the prediction of both solar and lunar eclipses. Table 7.1 summarizes seven of the nine Glyphs G.

From these examples, it appears that Glyphs G and F, like the rest of the Supplementary Series, convey lunar information. Therefore, the entire Supplementary Series, including

Fig. 7.28. Ring Number band from the Dresden Codex, page 63

Table 7.1.

G	Approximate name	translation	possible meaning	to eclipse
G9	Yih K'in Nal	Old Sun Place	Place of the Eclipse	0 × 260
G1	{ 9-K'uh Ch'am	{ 9 Holy Taken	{ +9 mos. to eclipse	1 × 260
	{ 9-Tzak	{ 9 Conjurings	{ +9 days to full moon	
G4	7-Ab'ak	7 Charcoal	+7 days to eclipse	4 × 260
G5	5-Hu-li	5 Arrive	{ − 5 days to node	5 × 260
			{ + 5 x 260 to eclipse?	
G6	9-Xul-u-Nen	9-Cut the Mirror	{ +9 days to node	6 × 260
			{ +9-10 days to lunar eclipse	
G7	Nah-al [2]	North?; First?; Two?	North of ecliptic?	7 × 260
			−2 days to node	
		First double Tzolk'in after eclipse?		+2 × 260
G8	Bix	Eighth	8th day of cycle	9 × 260
			8 Tzolk'ins	

Glyphs G and F, may be described as a Lunar Series. Six examples of Glyph G include possible numerical coefficients. If these were used to determine the draconic month for the purposes of eclipse prediction, as it appears above, then it may be possible in the future to determine the meanings of the remaining glyphs from the series that do not include clear coefficients, namely Glyphs G2 and G3. Likewise, the main element in Glyph G9, the half-darkened **K'IN** (T545), appears elsewhere in the inscriptions, and it will be important to analyze its meanings in these contexts. I propose that, while it clearly represents a darkening sun or an eclipse, G9 may also represent the position of the moon at a lunar node as *Yih K'in Näl* "place of the old sun" and "place of the eclipse".

Lastly, while the standard value for Glyph G is able to be calculated for any given date in the Long Count, with Glyph G9 falling on all multiples of the 360-day Tun, there are several examples of Long Count dates that contain values for Glyph G that do not fit the expected value. Some of these examples can be found in early texts, such as on Tomb 1 in Rio Azul, which apparently uses Glyph G6 instead of the expected G4. Other examples can be found on later texts, as on Copán Stela 5, which gives Glyph G7 rather than the expected G3. It remains a possibility that non-conforming values of Glyph G in these texts are simply due to scribal error, or errors on the part of epigraphers in the calculation of Long Count dates. However, it is also possible that these apparent "errors" represent an astronomically oriented, ideal positioning of Glyph G for the purposes of tracking the lunar nodes and predicting eclipses using multiples of the Tzolk'in, as outlined in this paper. Further research will be necessary to establish whether or not this may be the case.

References

Andrews, Wyllis E., 1934. Glyph X of the Supplementary Series of the Maya Inscriptions. *American Anthropologist* 36, 345–354.

Andrews, Wyllis E., 1938. Glyphs Z and Y of the Supplementary Series. *American Antiquity* 4: 30–35.

Aulie, Wilbur H. and Evelyn W. de Aulie, with Cesar Menéses Díaz, and Cristóbal López Vázquez, 1978. *Diccionario Ch'ol-Espanol, Espanol-Ch'ol.* Serie de vocabularios y diccionarios indegenas 21 (M. Silva y Aceves, ed.). Instituto Lingüístico de Verano, México, D.F.

Aveni, Anthony F., 2001, *Skywatchers*. University of Texas Press, Austin.

Barrera Vásquez, Alfredo, Juan Ramón Bastarrachea Manzano, William Brito Sansores, Refugio Vermont Salas, David Dzul Góngora and Domingo Dzul Poot, 1980. *Diccionario Maya Cordemex. Maya-Español. Español-Maya.* Ediciones Cordemex, Mérida.

Barthel, Thomas, 1952. Der Morgensternkult in den Darstellungen der Dresdener Mayahandschrift. *Ethnos* 17, 73–112.

Bolles, David, 1997. Combined Dictionary–Concordance of the Yucatecan Mayan Language. *Reports Submitted to FAMSI.* 1997 URL: http://www.famsi.org/reports/96072/udic.htm

Bowditch, Charles P., 1903. Notes on the Report of Teobert Maler. *Memoirs of the Peabody Museum* II(II). Peabody Museum of Archaeology and Ethnology, Harvard University, Cambridge MA.

Bowditch, Charles P., 1910 *The Numeration, Calendar Systems and Astronomical Knowledge of the Mayas.* Cambridge University Press, Cambridge

Bricker, Harvey M., and Victoria R. Bricker, 1983 Classic Maya Prediction of Solar Eclipses. *Current Anthropology* 24, 1–23.

Bricker, Victoria R., Eleuterio Po'ot Yah, and Ofelia Dzul de Po'ot, 1998. *A Dictionary of The Maya Language As Spoken in Hocaba, Yucatan.* The University of Utah Press, Salt Lake City.

Callaway, Carl D., 2006. The Maya Cross at Palenque: A Reappraisal. Thesis for the Department of Art History, University of Texas at Austin.

Coe, Michael D., 1992. *Breaking the Maya Code*. Thames & Hudson, New York.

Coe, Michael D. and Justin Kerr, 1997. *The Art of the Maya Scribe*. Harry N. Abrams, New York.

Davoust, Michel, 1995. *L'Ecriture Maya et son dechiffrement*. Centre National de la Recherche Scientifique, Paris.

Davoust, Michel, 1997. *Un Nouveau Commentaire du Codex du Dresde*. Centre National de la Recherche Scientifique, Paris.

Delgaty, Colin, 1964. *Vocabulario tzotzil de San Andrés, Chiapas*. Summer Institute of Linguistics (Serie de vocabularios indígenas 10), México. In Dienhart 1997.

Dienhart, John M. 1997, *The Mayan Languages – A Comparative Vocabulary*, electronic version. Odense University.

Goodman, Joseph T., 1897. The Archaic Maya Inscriptions. Appendix to *Biologia Centrali-americana (Archaeology)* VI (A. P. Maudslay ed.). Porter, London.

Graham, Ian, 1967. Archaeological Explorations in El Peten, Guatemala. *Middle American Research Institute, Tulane University* Publication 33. Middle American Research Institute, Tulane University, New Orleans.

Graham, Ian, 1978. *Corpus of Maya Hieroglyphic Inscriptions, Volume II, Part 2*. Peabody Museum of Archaeology and Ethnology, Harvard University, Cambridge MA.

Graham, Ian, 1979 *Corpus of Maya Hieroglyphic Inscriptions, Volume III, Part 2*. Peabody Museum of Archaeology and Ethnology, Harvard University, Cambridge MA.

Graham, Ian, and Peter Matthews, 1997. *Corpus of Maya Hieroglyphic Inscriptions, Volume VI, Part 2*. Peabody Museum of Archaeology and Ethnology, Harvard University, Cambridge MA.

Grofe, Michael J., 2006. Glyph Y and GII: The Mirror and the Child. *Glyph Dwellers* 21, February 2006. URL: http://cougar.ucdavis.edu/NAS/Maya/R21.pdf

Grofe, Michael J., 2007. The Serpent Series: Precession in the Maya Dresden Codex. Dissertation for the Department of Native American Studies. University of California at Davis.

Grofe, Michael J., 2009. Fruit from the Chocolate Tree II: From the Haab' to Precession. *IMS Explorer*. Institute of Maya Studies 38(2) June, Miami.

Gronemeyer, Sven, 2006. Glyphs G and F identified as aspects of the Maize God. *Wayeb' Notes* 22. URL: http://www.wayeb.org/notes/wayeb_notes0022.pdf

Gronemeyer, Sven and Barbara MacLeod, 2010. What Could Happen in 2012: A Re-Analysis of the 13-Bak'tun Prophecy on Tortuguero Monument 6. *Wayeb' Notes* 34. URL: http://www.wayeb.org/notes/wayeb_notes0034.pdf

Grube, Nikolai, 1991. An Investigation of the Primary Standard Sequence on Classic Maya Ceramics. In *Sixth Palenque Round Table, 1986, Vol. VIII* (V. M. Fields ed.). University of Oklahoma Press, Norman.

Grube, Nikolai and Linda Schele, 1991. *Tzuk* in the Classic Maya Inscriptions. *Texas Notes on Pre-Columbian Art, Writing, and Culture, Number 14,* *September, 1991.* Center of the History and Art of Ancient American Culture, University of Texas at Austin.

Houston, Stephen D., 1993. *Hieroglyphs and History at Dos Pilas: Dynastic Politics of the Classic Maya.* University of Texas Press, Austin.

Imaginova Canada, Ltd. 2006 Starry Night Pro, Version 6.0.0 pcEM. Astronomy Software. URL: http://www.starrynight.com

Justeson, John S., 1984. Appendix B: Interpretations of Mayan Hieroglyphs. In *Phoneticism in Mayan Hieroglyphic Writing* (J. Justeson and L. Campbell, eds). Institute for Mesoamerican Studies, State University of New York Publication 9. Institute for Mesoamerican Studies, State University of New York at Albany, 315–362.

Kelley, David H., 1972. The Nine Lords of the Night. In *Studies in the Archaeology of Mexico and Guatemala* (J. A. Graham ed.). Contributions of the University of California Archaeological Research Facility 16, University of California, Berkeley, 53–68.

Kettunen, Harri, 2005. *An Old Euphemism in New Clothes: Observations on a Possible Death Difrasismo in Maya Hieroglyphic Writing. Wayeb' Notes* 16. URL: http://www.wayeb.org/notes/wayeb_notes0016.pdf

Laughlin, Robert M., 1975. *The Great Tzotzil Dictionary of San Lorenzo Zinacantán.* Smithsonian Contributions to Anthropology 19, Smithsonian Institution Press, Washington, D.C.

Linden, John H., 1986. Glyph X of the Maya Lunar Series: An Eighteen-Month Lunar Synodic Calendar. *American Antiquity* 51(1), 122–136.

Linden, John H., 1996. The Deity Head Variants of Glyph C. In *Eighth Palenque Round Table, 1993* Vol. 10 (M. J. Macri and J. McHargue eds). Pre-Columbian Art Research Center, San Francisco, 369–377.

Looper, Matthew G., 1995. The Sculpture Programs of Butz'-Tiliw, an Eighth-Century Maya King of Quirigua, Guatemala. Ph.D. dissertation, University of Texas at Austin.

Lounsbury, Floyd G., 1978 Maya Numeration, Computation, and Calendrical Astronomy. In *Dictionary of Scientific Biography* XV (C. Couldson Gillespie ed.). Charles Scribner's Sons, New York, 759–818.

MacLeod, Barbara, 1990, *Deciphering the Primary Standard Sequence*. Ph.D. Dissertation, University of Texas at Austin.

MacLeod, Barbara, 1991a, T135 (The G9 Superfix) and T108 (The "Guardian" Superfix). *North Austin Hieroglyphic Hunches* 6 (February 10).

MacLeod, Barbara, 1991b. The Classic Name for Cumku. *North Austin Hieroglyphic Hunches* 8 (February 22).

MacLeod, Barbara, 1995. T128: The Next Generation (and Hopefully, a Resolution)!! *North Austin Hieroglyphic Hunches* 11.

Macri, Martha J., 2005. A Lunar Origin for the Mesoamerican Calendars of 20, 13, 9, and 7 Days. In *Current Studies in Archaeoastronomy: Conversations Across Time and Space. Selected Papers from the Fifth Oxford International Conference at Santa Fe, 1996* (J. W. Fountain and R. M. Sinclair ed.). Carolina Academic Press, Durham.

Macri, Martha J. and Matthew G. Looper, 2003. *The New Catalog of Maya Hieroglyphs, Volume One: The*

Classic Period Inscriptions. University of Oklahoma Press, Norman.

Martínez Hernandez, Juan, 1929. *Diccionario de Motul, Maya Español. Atribuido a Fray Antonio de Cuidad Real y Arte de Lengua Maya por Fray Juan Coronel.* Compañía Tipográfica Yucateca, Mérida.

Mathews, Peter, 1980. Notes on the Dynastic Sequence of Bonampak, Part 1. In *Third Palenque Round Table, 1978 Part 2, Palenque Round Table Series* Vol. 5 (M. Greene Robertson ed.). University of Texas Press, Austin, 60–73.

Mayer, Karl Herbert, 1980. *Maya Monuments of Unknown Provenance in the United States.* Acoma Books. Ramona CA.

Milbrath, Susan, 1999. *Star Gods of the Maya: Astronomy in Art, Folklore, and Calendars.* University of Texas Press, Austin.

Montgomery, John, 1990. A Note on the date of Piedras Negras Lintel 3. In *U Mut Maya III*, (T. Jones and C. Jones eds). Tom Jones & Carolyn Young, Arcata, 139–141.

Morley, Sylvanus Griswold, 1915. *An Introduction to the Study of the Maya Hieroglyphs.* Smithsonian Institution: Bureau of American Ethnology Bulletin 57, Government Printing Office, Washington, D. C.

Morley, Sylvanus Griswold, 1916. The Supplementary Series in the Maya inscriptions. *Holmes Anniversary Volume.* Carnegie Institution of Washington, Washington, D.C., 366–396.

Morley, Sylvanus Griswold, 1920. The Supplementary Series. In *The Inscriptions at Copan.* Carnegie Institution of Washington Publication 219, Washington, D.C.

Saturno, William, David Stuart, Anthony Aveni and Franco Rossi, 2012. Ancient Maya Astronomical Tables from Xultun, Guatemala. *Science* 336.

Schele, Linda, 1985. The Hauberg Stela: Bloodletting and the Mythos of Maya Rulership. In *Fifth Palenque Round Table, 1983,* Vol. VII (V. M. Fields, ed.). The Pre-Columbian Art Research Institute, San Francisco, 135–49.

Schele, Linda, 1991. *Workbook for the XVth Maya Hieroglyphic Workshop at Texas, March 9–10, 1991; Yaxchilan.* Department of Art and Art History and the Institute of Latin American Studies, University of Texas at Austin.

Schele, Linda, 1992. *Notebook for the XVIth Maya Hieroglyphic Workshop at Texas, March 14–15, 1992; Palenque: the Group of the Cross.* Department of Art and Art History and the Institute of Latin American Studies, University of Texas at Austin.

Schele, Linda and Nikolai Grube, 1997. *Notebook for the XXIst Maya Hieroglyphic Forum at Texas, March, 1997.* Department of Art and Art History, the College of Fine Arts and the Institute of Latin American Studies, University of Texas at Austin.

Schele, Linda and Matthew Looper, 1996. *Notebook for the XXth Maya Hieroglyphic Workshop at Texas.* Department of Art and Art History, the College of Fine Arts, and the Institute of the Latin American Studies, University of Texas, Austin.

Schele, Linda, and Mary Ellen Miller, 1986. *The Blood of Kings: Dynasty and Ritual in Maya Art.* Kimball Art Museum, Fort Worth.

Schele, Linda, and Elizabeth Newsome, 1991. Taking the Headband at Copán. *Copán Note* 49. Copán Mosaics Project and Instituto Hondureño de Antropología y Historia, Copán, Honduras.

Schele, Linda, Nikolai Grube and Federico Fahsen, 1992. The Lunar Series in Classic Maya Inscriptions: New Observations and Interpretations. *Texas Notes on Precolumbian Art, Writing, and Cultur* 29. Center of the History and Art of Ancient American Culture, Art Department, University of Texas at Austin.

Schele, Linda, Peter Matthews and Floyd Lounsbury, 1990. *The Nal Suffix at Palenque and Elsewhere.* Texas Notes on Precolumbian Art, Writing, and Culture 6. Center of the History and Art of Ancient American Culture, Art Department, University of Texas at Austin.

Stuart, David, 1988. Blood Symbolism in Maya Iconography. In *Maya Iconography* (E. P. Benson and G. G. Griffin eds). Princeton University Press, Princeton, New Jersey, 173–221.

Stuart, David, 2005 *The Inscriptions from Temple XIX at Palenque.* The Pre-Columbian Art Research Institute, San Francisco.

Stuart, David and Stephen Houston, 1994. Classic Maya Place Names. *Studies in Pre-Columbian Art and Archaeology 33.* Washington, D. C.: Dumbarton Oaks Research Library and Collection.

Stuart, David and Stephen Houston, 2005. *The Inscriptions from Temple XIX at Palenque.* The Pre-Columbian Art Research Institute, San Francisco.

Stuart, David, Stephen D. Houston and John Robertson, 1999. Recovering the Past: Classic Maya Language and Classic Maya Gods. *Notebook for the XXIIIrd Maya Hieroglyphic Forum at Texas.* Department of Art and Art History, the College of Fine Arts, and the Institute of Latin American Studies, University of Texas at Austin.

Tate, Carolyn E., 1992 *Yaxchilan: The Design of a Maya Ceremonial City.* University of Texas Press, Austin.

Tedlock, Barbara, 1982. *Time and the Highland Maya.* University of New Mexico Press, Albuquerque.

Teeple, John E., 1925 Maya Inscriptions: Glyphs C, D, and E of the Supplementary Series. *American Anthropologist* 27, 108–115.

Teeple, John E., 1931. *Maya Astronomy.* Contributions to American Archaeology I(2). Carnegie Publication 403, Carnegie Institution of Washington, Washington, D. C., 29–116.

Thompson, J. Eric S., 1929. Maya Chronology: Glyph G of the Lunar Series. *American Anthropologist,* 31, 223–31.

Thompson, J. Eric S., 1935 *Maya Chronology: the Correlation Question.* Carnegie Publication 403, Contribution 14, Carnegie Institution of Washington, Washington, D. C.

Thompson, J. Eric S., 1971. *Maya Hieroglyphic Writing: An Introduction.* University of Oklahoma Press, Norman.

Yasugi, Yoshiho and Kenji Saito, 1991. Glyph Y of the Maya Supplementary Series. *Research Reports on Ancient Maya Writing* 34–35, April, Center for Maya Research, Washington, D.C., 1–12.

Zender, Marc and Joel Skidmore, 2012. Unearthing the Heavens: Classic Maya Murals and Astronomical Tables at Xultun, Guatemala. *Mesoweb*: www.mesoweb.com/reports/Xultun.pdf.

8

Epilogue: Mayan astronomers at work

Gerardo Aldana y Villalobos

Stephen McCluskey, historian of Medieval science, has recently noted that while we often refer to 'skywatching' as the practice of ancient astronomers across cultures, we very rarely refer to the skywatchers themselves (2011). In part, of course, this is a very natural response to the nature of the data available – from the Precontact Western Hemisphere we have very little opportunity to identify individuals. It is only within Classic Mayan hieroglyphic inscriptions and a few late Postclassic Central Mexican codices that we have historical records with even the potential for naming individual astronomers. We have been left therefore with scholarly attempts at recovering the practices of groups of skywatchers, which are then categorized very broadly as "Mayan astronomy," "Aztecan astronomy," or even "Mesoamerican astronomy." Such an approach undoubtedly has been productive revealing many interesting patterns over large scales; unfortunately, such approaches reveal none of the historical subtlety that may have influenced the courtly astronomers from early Classic Piedras Negras, for instance, yet been completely ignored by those at late Classic Quirigua.[1] That is, the scientists are hidden behind the science.

While not originating with an interest in addressing the astronomer's absence, this book can be thought of as facilitating the incorporation of a framework that becomes productive when applied to archaeoastronomical concerns – one that would re-insert the skywatcher into the academic reconstruction of the practice of skywatching (*cf.* McCluskey 2011). Such a move, of course, is not outside a broader intellectual context, and here, that context serves to illuminate the emerging project of examining Mesoamerican astronomers at work. In this epilogue, I explore the notion alluded to elsewhere (Aldana 2007; 2011) that Bruno Latour's consideration of *Science In Action* may be very productive for building an intellectual infrastructure for the investigation of ancient Mesoamerican astronomies.

This volume does not constitute a methodological integration of Latour's work into the recovery of ancient skywatching; it is not a culmination of such a process, but it certainly facilitates such a transition. The chapters – which were originally organized by the celestial body they addressed – are here categorized into three parts, each speaking to a methodological consideration of Mayan astronomy that fits within a larger Science Studies framework. The first – what we might call Part 1, comprising Chapters 1 and 2 – considers the form of what Bruno Latour calls the "inscription" of scientific endeavors. The theme addressed here is the translation of a modern-journal-article-representation of science into something analogous within ancient Mesoamerican intellectual communities. In particular, Part 1 can be seen to examine architectural orientations to observable horizon phenomena as "inscriptional devices." Part 2 goes into the labor of the skywatcher. The two chapters included therein investigate the specific kinds of technical knowledges behind inscriptional devices. Next, having explored inscriptions and the science behind them, Part 3 comprises three chapters considering the uses to which astronomical inscriptions may have been put. All three chapters herein explore the nesting of astronomical inscriptions within other intellectual constructs.

Inscriptions

Within the relatively young field of Science Studies, Bruno Latour (1987) offers a constructivist approach to investigating the production of scientific knowledge. Responding to prior work in the field that took science as progressing outside of sociological constraints, Latour develops a framework that includes the agency of individual initiative, while recognizing various forms of community inertia, constraining any given scientific "development." While this framework does provide some of the utility of recognizing normalized practices and assumptions within a given "paradigm," it does not carry along the necessity that paradigms shift because prior paradigms were wrong or at least less correct in some objective sense (Latour 1987: 35). Rather, changes in paradigms, or paradigm shifts (to the extent that they still occur) may be generated by various different types of pressures coming from social-constructivist recognized influences. These various characteristics, I have claimed, make Latour's a useful framework for studying Mesoamerican astronomy (Aldana 2007; 2011). The following makes this explicit by stepping through some of the basic components of Latour's framework.

One of the building blocks to Latour's project is the identification of 'inscriptions' (1987: 64–70).[2] The inscription for Latour – as he studies Early Modern and more recent sciences – is that final record of the scientific argument that makes it into publication (1987: 68). A chromatograph, for instance, would be

an inscriptional device producing the graphic output – the inscription – quantifying the relative amounts of differentiable substances in a gas or liquid sample. A bubble chamber could serve as another inscriptional device, providing a graphic depiction of radioactive decay – the inscription. Inscriptional devices, then, are any combination of human and electromechanical labor – the instrumentation – that produce an inscription.

But we should not stop at readily recognizable instrumentation. In Latour's definition (1987: 69), the ethnographer taking field notes becomes an inscriptional device to the extent that the quotes that s/he writes down get incorporated into the final document. Social scientists with surveys in hand, too, become inscriptional devices. Latour transforms the production of the inscription into a combination of human and non-human interactions, without prior epistemological privilege. Each inscriptional device, whatever its human or non-human constitution, need only be appropriate for the given application to which it is put. In this sense, a sociologist has no epistemological place in the knowledge production of particle physics experiments. And by the same token, a bubble chamber does not become an inscriptional device at all in the ethnographic study of youth culture in downtown Los Angeles.

When we transport this framework across time and space for archaeoastronomical research, we may postulate that much of the effort in the field thus far has gone into determining what constitutes an inscription for Mesoamerican astronomy. That is, if we leave the modern (and Early Modern) venues of scholarly publication with its well-defined inscriptions, what are we to count as cross-cultural equivalences? What are the "inscriptions" from ancient Mesoamerica? Certainly the Dresden Codex Eclipse Table or Venus Table would qualify and would appear directly analogous to modern publications. Indeed, both appear to be copies of tables drawn from earlier manuscripts (Thompson 1972: 15), so each was a product of concerted investigation using at the least the instrumentation of human observation coupled with Mayan calendrics. Furthermore, the fact that the specific tables of the Dresden Codex appear to be copies of an earlier version, which were then found to be applicable in different contexts, is an important factor. As products of a scientific community, the inscription and the inscriptional device find legitimation by their appropriation and re-use (Latour 1987: 25).

But as Ethnic Studies and Cultural Studies, and Postmodern, Postprocessual, (and post-fill-in-the-blank-ism) approaches have shown for decades now, alphanumerically composed documents are not all that we may consider to be 'text.' The chapters by Hal Green and Ivan Sprajc – making up Part 1 – reveal a Latourian conceptualization of inscriptions while following a well-established tradition within archaeoastronomy. In each of these chapters, the position and orientation of ceremonial center architecture is 'read' relative to its geographic horizon. In fact, the cultural phenomenon these chapters consider is precisely that which created archaeoastronomy as a field with the investigation of Stonehenge during the 1960s and 1970s (Aveni 1980: 4). As we saw in the Introduction, Anthony Aveni and Horst Hartung adapted the interest to Mesoamerican architectural alignments to celestial phenomena, and there even found support in documented events.

For example, Toribio de Benavente, one of the first twelve Franciscans to reach the Western Hemisphere, explicitly noted the reconstruction of the Aztec Templo Mayor at Tenochtitlan by Motecuhzoma Xocoyotzin to accommodate the sighting of the equinox sunrise (Aveni 1980: 246). Aveni and Sharon Gibbs argued that this type of adjustment would have been required since structures were often built to encompass previous important structures (Aveni 1980: 248–249). As it increased in height, the resulting change relative to the horizon would throw the alignment out of line, necessitating the kind of re-build Benavente suggested. This corroboration between architectural alignment and historical attestation bolstered the confidence in the recovery of other forms of archaeoastronomy in Mesoamerican and South America. Indeed, whether or not Stonehenge or Newgrange ever are borne out as astronomically inspired, it is clear that a tradition of astronomically oriented architecture did exist in ancient Mesoamerica and was significantly robust, suggesting a significant history of such practices.

Through Latour, then, we may suggest that within this tradition, the architecture and its relationship to the visible horizon constitute an inscriptional device. Accordingly, the inscription is the celestial object's visibility aligned with the architecture read through the calendar. The 'output' in this case becomes a text that is re-inscribed on an annual (or other periodic) basis.

In Chapter 1 Harold Green turns to an inscriptional device in southern, coastal Guatemala at Chocolá. As we have seen, Green goes beyond Malmström's investigation to observe the horizon phenomena from Chocolá itself. In a Latourian sense, we find that in witnessing sunrise events at Chocolá, Green physically re-constitutes the inscriptional device, generating a new text to be read.

As with Green's work at Chocolá, Sprajc recognizes an inscriptional device showing up at multiple locations. In his chapter, Sprajc shows that the same alignment is present at several sites in the area, but in each case, it is built to inscribe sunrise phenomena, and in each case it involves two of the largest structures at the site – two structures that are intervisible above the floral canopy (*cf.* Aldana 2005). The two buildings and the sunrise position along the horizon construct an inscriptional device. Here, then, we encounter the notion of the integrity of an inscriptional device. In utilizing the same mechanism for similar observations at different sites, the instrumentation is transported such that each new construction becomes a "citation" of a previous "publication" (Latour 1987: 38).

Both chapters in Part 1 show that it is possible to adapt a key element of Latour's framework to Mesoamerican science. But it goes further than that. Taken together, and focusing on the inscriptional devices therein, Green's and Sprajc's chapters dovetail to present a new hypothesis: the architectural commemoration of a 260-day interval may have originated in the southern Mayan region, and slowly moved north through the Preclassic period. While Green's work may speak to the origins of the Long Count as well, it may be that Sprajc's work is providing a degree of texture to the data that may corroborate Malmström's argument for the diffusion of the inscriptional device.

If Part 1 speaks to the utility of Latour's inscription when accommodated to Meso-american astronomy, the recognition of inscriptional devices brings along with it a methodological constraint. Researchers into ancient or modern science should restrict their interpretations to those matching the capabilities of the recognized inscriptional devices generating them. There is no use, for instance, arguing for an astronomical precision that is unattainable given the instrumentation available.

For example, if one were to come across an interval between two Long Count dates of tropical years accurate to five decimal places, then without taking into consideration how this accuracy was achieved, s/he would be 'right' to put forward the hypothesis that it was intended. But if there is no recognized instrumentation that would allow for this type of accuracy, then we are forced to consider the possibility that the interval was generated out of coincidence, and not intent. Now, this does not preclude yet another scholar from seeking other instrumentation that would make possible a substantially greater accuracy. If that were to transpire, then we would be justified in entertaining the increased accuracy based on the new method. The important point is that the response is simply conservative; it defers the possibility, it does not negate it.

What this suggests is that we must explicitly consider the work behind the inscriptional device. In this aspect, we find resemblance to Peter Novick's differentiation between "internalist" versus "externalist" history. Novick treats American historiography by distinguishing between internalists producing histories of the fields in which they work – often for teaching or self-congratulatory purposes – and externalists who write histories about a field in which they do not work (1994: 5). Focusing on inscriptions resembles externalist history, whereas a focus on the operation of inscriptional devices resembles an internalist approach – one that necessitates a substantive understanding of the field from an insider's perspective. This is not unlike Owen Gingerich's work on Johannes Kepler's *Astronomia Nova* (1993). Gingerich worked through the observations and computations that Kepler made, at some level endeavoring to become a colleague of Kepler's astronomical community – to understand Kepler's work as a peer and colleague.

In application to the sciences of ancient Mesoamerica, such an approach does seem a natural next step for the field. Anthony Aveni defined much of the work of the modern scholar interested in ancient astronomy in 1980 and again in 2001. Both volumes, however, follow more or less an externalist

approach. They provide the researcher with a method for extracting an astronomical artifact and then displaying it in a museum. It is cleaned and polished and wondrous to contemplate, but it gives us little sense of the cultural and/ or social messiness from which it was excavated (*cf.* Kintigh 1992).

Within a Latourian framework, the identification of inscriptions is important, but more important is that the repository of inscriptions makes the atemporal project of an internalist history possible. By working backward from the inscription, through the inscriptional device, to the labor of the practitioner, one comes to approximate the understanding of an insider to the field. For the celestially aligned architecture of Green's and Sprajc's chapters, this may seem relatively straightforward. Modern investigators have only to place themselves in the specified physical locations, and then reflect on the relationship of their observations to the functioning of the various components of Mesoamerican calendars.

Constructing Inscriptional Devices

A critical step in moving toward this type of contextualization can be found in the second part of this anthology. Both chapters in Part 2 unpack the human and non-human interactions that constitute the inscriptional devices, and which in turn generate inscriptions. This requires the recovery of the astronomer's labor – the work of the practitioner – in constructing an inscriptional device. In Chapter 3, Mendez, Barnhart, Powell, and Karasik, study an inscriptional device that is a distant descendent of the devices investigated by Green and Sprajc. Mendez *et al.* explore the relationships between astronomical events and their observable effects in the Cross Group at Palenque – a set of three structures patronized by the eleventh ruler of the dynasty, Kan B'ahlam during the Late Classic – some 6–700 years after the horizon calendars of Chocolá and Yaxnohcah.

The astronomical inscription taken up by Mendez *et al.* is generated by a complex interaction of architectural walls, rays of the sun, and human observation. Mendez *et al.* reflect on the symmetry, for one, within the floor plan of the Temple of the Sun, and its similarity in design to the other two temples of the Cross Group – the Temple of the Cross, and the Temple of the Foliated Cross. But they go on to demonstrate that the walls of the Temple of the Sun were modified to break symmetry – and that this violation of symmetry is precisely what creates the astronomical inscription. Namely, on the summer solstice, a ray of light enters the building at sunrise. With the movement of the Sun over the course of the morning, this ray of light reaches toward the back of the temple, shaped by the walls to form a thin dagger.[3] Mendez *et al.* interpret this as a hierophany resonating with the recognized importance of astronomy in the construction of the Cross Group (Aldana 2007; Anderson *et al.* 1981; Aveni and Hartung 1978; Carlson 1976).

From a Latourian perspective, this level of accessing the astronomer's work allows for the investigation of different kinds of sociological, political, religious, or scientific reasons behind the variation in floor plan of the three temples forming the Cross Group. Mendez *et al.* engage this work by considering the relationship between the iconography and text of the temple and the astronomy it is meant to commemorate.

In a similar spirit of attempting to access the astronomer's daily work, Chapter 4 on the Dresden Codex Venus Table moves upstream from the inscription – the table of dates itself – to contextualize it within other known Mayan calendric practices, i.e. other inscriptional devices.

Chapter 4 finds a new coherence to the work of the ancient astronomer/daykeeper by placing the operation of the Venus Table within a context of the intellectual labor [omens] reflected in the rest of the manuscript. That is, in the case of the Dresden Codex, we can take oracular statements as the inscriptions. Then we find that the inscriptional devices are the combinations of human observation of astronomical events and computations using the calendar. In so doing, it turns to the need to culturally translate intellectual labor, and so constructs the conception of an oracle within modern culture. This allows us to reconsider the oracular context of the astronomer's work, and so place it in dialogue with the ontology of the indigenous Mayan cosmos. By finally focusing on the linguistic analysis of the titles taken by astronomers and rulers, an intellectual context is developed for the arena in which omens, economics, and politics (for example) would be mediated by the ruler of a given city. In other words, this reconstruction of the astronomer's labor makes possible a recognition of the interactions astronomy may have had with other realms of knowledge without implicitly invoking a romanticized image of Galileo confronting the Church, or an antithesis.

In Part 2 of this book, then, the focus is on the 'tools of the trade,' which in turn make possible the nesting of astronomical inscriptions within larger sociological and/or cultural contexts. In fact, this is not unlike the treatments of Green and Sprajc in Part 1, in their considerations of context. That is, they both take into account the local (temporal and geographic) non-scientific pressures that may have influenced the specific interpretations they make of the inscriptional devices they have recovered. Sprajc, for example, considers that the maize agricultural cycle may have influenced the selection of the specific alignment of the temples to February/August. The interplay between astronomy and agriculture, then, would have motivated urban planning as much, if not moreso, than other factors. Likewise, Green considers that there were other factors important to consider in the origin of the 260-Day Count. Here, he is opening up the perspective of the astronomer at work. By not coming down firmly with an argument that the 260-Day Count was strictly derived by astronomical means, Green opens up the scientific controversy that may have existed at the origins of Mayan calendrics.

With Latour's first methodological move, then, we confront the ramifications of placing any given inscription within the labor of the scientist. Beyond the recognition and comprehension of inscriptions and the devices that generated them, Latour then moves to distance the project from the study of scientific facts in themselves. Here we find a clear resonance with the published discussion between Kintigh and Aveni reviewed in the Introduction. Rather than focus on just the generation or consideration of "scientific facts," Latour 'travels upstream' to the point when any given established fact is still a tentative – and potentially contentious – scientific claim. By itself, this move actually would present a challenge to most of what we currently consider to constitute the scholarship on Mesoamerican astronomy. As soon as we are asked to push this astronomical evidence back into a scientific claim, the ground will have shifted. For example, rather than focus on a statistical demonstration that the windows in the Caracol at Chich'en Itza were aligned to observable Venus phenomena, we now must ask who proposed that the Caracol at Chich'en Itza be constructed with windows aligned to observable Venus phenomena in the first place. Was that proposal contested on a technical level? Was there precedent for such a construct? Did anyone protest that a monument to Mercury would have been more appropriate? As we generate answers – general and/or specific – to these questions, we begin to reveal the work of Mesoamerican astronomers and the pressures that shaped it.

Notice, though, that posing these questions – i.e. exploring the competing interests within and external to scientific activity – does nothing to unseat the necessity of understanding any given astronomical claim on a technical level. It is still requisite for modern researchers to comprehend the variegated composition of inscriptional devices underlying the resulting claim – planetary periodicities, calendric renderings, and architectural alignments. The point is that these "external" factors – at the time of the scientific claim – enter into a field of pressures, motives, and constraints. In short, they enter an historical context in which 'good science' must compete with budgetary constraints, or with political ideology, even with idiosyncratic personalities. To get at this level of the study of science, one must introduce the "sociologics" of the scientific community (Latour 1987: 195–205).

And it is at this point that a caveat becomes useful. We should not presume that this methodological move invalidates science, or demotes it to the status of a political tool. Olga Amersterdamska, for example, protests that Latour's methodological suggestions would make actual science irrelevant – the loudest voice (be it political, ideological, economic) would win in any given scientific controversy, not the "right" one (1990). Science would not progress in an objective sense; it would be set adrift, tossed about on waves of the ephemeral interests of those in power. But Amsterdamska goes too far.

Certainly non-scientific factors do become relevant to the development of science when we examine the point of controversy, but they do not subvert the practice of science within the community of scientists. A scientist must be accountable to her peers at the moment of controversy, but she must also find non-scientific rationales to complement her scientific pursuits. These non-scientific rationales enable her to recruit allies in support of her further research, which then allow her to engage or possibly settle the controversy in question. We recognize these constraints on science on a daily basis in modern society: stem cell research, nuclear power generation, alternative fuel sources. Latour suggests that looking into these aspects of the work of scientists is more productive than restricting our view to internalist histories (1987: 59).

Science in context

With Part 2, we have actually engaged Latour's second methodological intervention, allowing for the examination of the various forces impinging on the scientific claim before it becomes established fact. The scientist never relies on a scientific result alone, as it must also demonstrate relevance to larger societal concerns. As such, *before it becomes an accepted scientific fact*, other societal pressures can be just as important as the "correctness" of the science itself. So we must understand the practice of utilizing inscriptional devices so that we can also access the types of pressures to which they may have been susceptible.

For Latour, then, it is important to not stop at the questioning of the technical integrity of any given scientific claim. Latour demonstrates that while it is still in contention, any number of non-scientific factors can contribute to settling (or de-bunking) the claim in question (1987: 99–100). This is where the issues become more complicated and less formulaic. The tendency, though, is to cast this as "external" to the science being recovered, as we have done here. Latour's provocation is to show that this externality is only a rhetorical device constructed after the controversy is settled.

In this context, we may see the chapters of Part 3 as attempts to unpack astronomical inscriptions from their embedding within broader iconographic or textual records and so within broader sociological contexts. In each case, the chapter looks at the life of the astronomical inscription after it has been consumed/after it has been put to use in a more elaborate context. Not only are astronomical events recorded directly, but the artistic context provides layers of further information on the nesting of astronomical knowledge into other elite intellectual activities. This might provide one form of access into types of sociological, political, and/or religious pressures impinging on astronomical investigation and inscription.

Mendez and Karasik use this method to explore zenith and nadir passages of the Sun within the artistic and architectural patronage of Kan B'ahlam at Palenque. They begin with the mythistory detailed in the Temple of the Cross at Palenque, reading the events transpiring in the narrative relative to events observable in the night sky. As the Palenque patron deity dedicates a house in the North, Mendez and Karasik find that the event occurs on a nadir passage of the Sun at Palenque. Through a metaphoric link between the north and nadir passage, they argue that the mythology becomes a record of astronomical events.

The authors move on to the orientations of the temples to argue that zenith and nadir passages of the Sun are attested: zenith passage (May 7 and August 5 at Palenque) is marked by sunrise out of the center of the Temple of the Cross roof comb from the central doorway of the Temple of the Sun, and by sunset behind the Temple of Inscriptions from the Temple of the Cross. Nadir passage (January 29 and November 9 at Palenque) is marked by sunset behind the Temple of the Sun viewed from the Temple of the Cross and sunrise behind the Temple of the Cross, viewed from the Temple of Inscriptions. Mendez and Karasik turn to dynastic history records along with the geometry of Janaab' Pakal's sarcophagus lid to argue for a coherent message constructed out of mythology, history, geometry, artistic imagery, and astronomy – the dense articulation of an astronomical inscription within the products of other intellectual communities in the "service of the religion" (King 1993).

The recognition of a Venus inscription within the Madrid Codex inspires Milbrath to look for similar constructs in other Mayan as well as Central Mexican venues. Here we find a resonance with Latour's emphasis on the reiteration of the inscription – its appropriation into other, later works. The inscription of the Venus Almanac for Milbrath becomes cited within various other cosmological narratives as a whole concept – in a Latourian sense, it is "blackboxed." Chapter 6 goes on to unpack Venus inscriptions throughout Mesoamerica, essentially arguing for a widespread convention for constituting inscriptional devices. That is, this work implies an astronomical community whose inscriptions would be recognized across geographic artistic conventions through the use of a common inscriptional device.

Finally, in Chapter 7, Michael Grofe reconsiders Glyphs F and G of the Supplementary Series. Specifically, Grofe builds from Teeple's recognition that each subsequent repetition of a 260-Day Count date corresponds to a backwards sequence through the Glyphs G1 through G9. He suggests that a skywatcher keeping track of this pattern would be able to correlate it with the fact that three draconic periods are (very nearly) equivalent to two 260-Day rounds ($3 \times 173.31 = 519.93 \sim 2 \times 260 = 520$). Here again, we confront an intriguing argument for an astronomical inscription (eclipse records) within a ubiquitous calendric device (the "cycle of 9"). In the end, Grofe is suggesting that the immediate hieroglyphic context of what has been considered a rather opaque calendric component may illuminate the astronomical origins buried within the utility of the 9-day cycle.

Part 3, then, asks us to reconsider the limits of what "external" factors must be considered in the utilization of an inscription. It seeks to illuminate these larger projects motivating inscriptions of astronomical events and the forms of representation they might take.

* * *

In sum, aside from their individual contributions, the chapters in this book serve to illustrate a scaffolding for the advancement of the scholarship on Mayan astronomy. Through an appropriately adapted Latourian lens, we can place any given hypothesis of a Mayan astronomical artifact within a methodological context for analysis.

But if we are willing to move in the direction implied by this book, we might also wonder what new studies and interpretations await us. How might this framework be productive, rather than simply act as an a posteriori organizational model? For one – in line with McCluskey's call – we may begin focusing on the question of "who". Especially when Diego de Landa's sixteenth century recording of the *ah k'in* ('person of the day/time') "title" is not explicitly attested in Classic period hieroglyphic texts, we have to question what the job description was for ancient skywatchers. Marc Zender's dissertation provides a much more refined look at the titled members of the royal court, along with many more options, but none can straightforwardly be designated 'astronomer' (2004).

Not just the 'who' becomes interesting, but also the 'how.' What happens when we place any given E-Group in its architectural history? Were the motivations the same for builders during the middle Preclassic as those of the middle Classic? Were they both building "E-Groups"? Also, akin to the example of the Caracol at Chich'en Itza above: can we get at the possibility of competing architectural agendae in the archaeological record?

One example might show up in the fact that scholars have argued for a Venus window at Copan in Structure 10L-22 (Closs *et al.* 1984), but the horizon's visibility from that window was blocked by a later ruler's construction of an adjacent temple, 10L-22a (Fash *et al.* 1992). The former was built by Waxaklajun Ub'aah K'awiil at the height of Copan's regional influence; the latter after Waxaklajun Ub'aah K'awiil was defeated by his neighbor at Quirigua who seems to have betrayed his former allegiance through a new relationship with Calakmul (Aldana 2002; 2006; Martin and Grube 2000). What may have been the role of astronomy in the debates surrounding the construction of 10L-22a, labeled by Barbara Fash and her colleagues as a "Council House" (Fash *et al.* 1992)? Did the nobility of Copan explicitly dismiss the luxury of Waxaklajun Ub'aah K'awiil's Venus viewing window for the political needs coalescing in the form of a building dedicated to the collective?

When we reflect on the individual components of the arguments presented in each of these chapters, and then categorized according to distinct themes or 'parts' of the book, we find that Latour's framework does not necessarily constitute a radically new approach. He does not have to be seen as providing us with specific interventions that have not already been attempted in the field. Rather, Latour – when adapted for ancient civilizations and the appropriate forms of evidence – provides a structure by which investigations in archaeoastronomy or the history of Mesoamerican astronomies might be made more productive in anthropological or historical contexts.

In this sense, all of the chapters in this volume help us to picture the specific work of skywatchers – in plazas, performing as part of an inscriptional device; in their studies, puzzling over the applications of their inscriptions – all help us to see Mayan astronomers at work. This becomes productive whether we bring Latour along or not.

Notes

1   This may sound like anathema to some, but should we not entertain the possibility that some Classic Mayan royal courts did not even maintain an active astronomer within them? Certainly, no city could be without its calendric specialists, but given the range of populations and locally available resources, did all require a specialist with a concerted interest in tracking the inhabitants of the night sky?

2   At some level, this is an unfortunate choice of term for the study of Mayan astronomy since much of the archaeological record is made up of hieroglyphic texts referred to as "inscriptions." While some ambiguity may result, I will continue using the same term for both signifiers, expecting that the context will make the meaning clear for any given usage.

3   The resulting effect is strongly reminiscent of the solar calendars found within rock formations in Baja California, and the much later solar ray effects within (currently United States Southwest) Pueblo cultures. At some level, this pattern begs for historical study to address the role that Mayan astronomy may have played in the diffusion of culture throughout the western hemisphere.

References

Aldana, Gerardo, 2007. *The Apotheosis of Janaab' Pakal: Science, History, and Religion at Classic Maya Palenque.* University Press of Colorado, Boulder.

Aldana, Gerardo, 2011. The Maya Calendar Correlation Problem. In *Calendars and Years II* (J. Steele, ed.). Oxbow Books, Oxford.

Aldana, Gerardo, 2002. Solar Stelae and a Venus Window: Science and Royal Personality in Late Classic Copán. *Archaeoastronomy* 27 (Supplement to the *Journal for the History of Astronomy* XXXIII), S30–S50.

Aldana, Gerardo, 2003. K'uk'ulkan at Mayapan: Venus and Postclassic Maya Statecraft. *Journal for the History of Astronomy* XXXIV, 33–51.

Anderson, Neal, Alfonso Morales and Moises Morales, 1981. A Solar Alignment of the Palace Tower at Palenque. *Archaeoastronomy: the Bulletin of the Center for Archaeoastronomy*, IV(3), 34–36.

Amsterdamska, Olga, 1990. Surely You Are Joking, Monsieur Latour! Review of *Science In Action* by Bruno Latour. *Science, Technology, and Human Values* 15(4) Autumn, 495–504.

Aveni, Anthony, 1980. *Skywatchers of Ancient Mexico*. University of Texas Press, Austin.

Aveni, Anthony F. and Horst Hartung, 1978. Some Suggestions about the Arrangement of Buildings at Palenque. In *Proceedings of the Third Palenque Round Table* (M. Greene Robertson ed.). Pre-Columbian Research Institute, San Francisco, 173–177.

Bricker, H. and Bricker, V., 2007. When was the Dresden Codex Efficaceous? In *Skywatching in the Ancient World: New Perspectives in Cultural Astronomy Studies in Honor of Anthony F. Aveni* (C. Ruggles and G. Urton eds). University of Texas Press, Austin, 95–120.

Carlson, John, 1976. Astronomical Investigations and Site Orientation Influences at Palenque. *Art, Iconography and Dynastic History of Palenque Part 3*. Pre-Columbian Art Research Institute, Pebble Beach, CA, 107–122.

Closs, Michael, Anthony Aveni and Bruce Crowley, 1984. The Planet Venus and Temple 22 at Copán. *Indiana* 9, 221–247.

Fash, Barbara, Sheree Lane, Rudy Larios, Linda Schele, Jeffrey Stomper, David Stuart and William Fash, 1992. Investigations of a Classic Maya council house at Copán, Honduras. *Journal of Field Archaeology*, 19(4), 419–442.

Freidel, David, Linda Schele and Joy Parker, 1993. *Maya Cosmos: Three Thousand Years on the Shaman's Path*. William Morrow and Co., New York.

Gingerich, Owen, 1993. *The Eye of Heaven: Ptolemy, Copernicus, Kepler*. The American Institute of Physics, New York.

King, David A., 1993. Sience in the Service of Religion: The Case of Islam. In *Astronomy in the Service of Islam*. Variorum Collected Studies, Cs 416, Ashgate, Aldershot.

Latour, Bruno, 1987. *Science In Action*. Harvard University Press, Cambridge.

Lounsbury, Floyd, 1983. The Base of the Venus Table of the Dresden Codex, and its Significance for the Calendar- Correlation Problem. In *Calendars in Mesoamerica and Peru: Native American Computations of Time* (A. F. Aveni and G. Brotherston eds). BAR International Series 174, Archaeopress, Oxford, 1–26.

Lounsbury, Floyd, 1992a. Derivation of the Mayan-to-Julian Calendar Correlation from the Dresden Codex Venus Chronology. In *The Sky in Mayan Literature* (A. Aveni). Oxford University Press, New York, 184–206.

Lounsbury, Floyd, 1992b. A Solution for the Number 1.5.5.0 of the Mayan Venus Table. In *The Sky in Mayan Literature* (A. F. Aveni ed.). Oxford University Press, New York, 207–215.

Malmström, Vincent, 1997. *Cycles of the Sun, Mysteries of the Moon: the Calendar in Mesoamerican Civilization*. University of Texas Press, Austin.

Martin, Simon and Nikolai Grube, 2000. *Chronicles of Maya Kings and Queens*. Thames & Hudson, New York.

McCluskey, Stephen, 2011. The cultures of archaeo-astronomy and the history of science. *Oxford IX International Symposium on Archaeoastronomy, Proceedings IAU Symposium No. 278*.

Novick, Peter, 1994. *That Noble Dream: The Objectivity Question in the American Historical Profession*. Cambridge University Press, Cambridge.

Stuart, David, 2005. *The Inscriptions from Temple XIX at Palenque*. Pre-Columbian Art Research Institute, San Francisco.

Thompson, J. Eric S., 1972. *A Commentary on the Dresden Codex*. American Philosophical Society, Philadelphia.

Zender, Marc, 2004. A Study of Classic Maya Priesthood. University of Calgary Ph.D. Dissertation. Department of Archaeology.